T0300274

# ROUTLEDGE LIBRARY EDITIONS: INDUSTRIAL RELATIONS

Volume 1

# AGENDA FOR CHANGE

# AGENDA FOR CHANGE

## An International Analysis of Industrial Relations in Transition

Edited by
**OLIVER CLARKE**
**AND**
**JOHN NILAND**

**Routledge**
Taylor & Francis Group

LONDON AND NEW YORK

First published in 1991 by Allen & Unwin

This edition first published in 2025
by Routledge
4 Park Square, Milton Park, Abingdon, Oxon OX14 4RN

and by Routledge
605 Third Avenue, New York, NY 10158

*Routledge is an imprint of the Taylor & Francis Group, an informa business*

*British Library Cataloguing in Publication Data*
A catalogue record for this book is available from the British Library

ISBN: 978-1-032-81770-5 (Set)
ISBN: 978-1-032-83526-6 (Volume 1) (hbk)
ISBN: 978-1-032-83530-3 (Volume 1) (pbk)
ISBN: 978-1-003-50974-5 (Volume 1) (ebk)

DOI: 10.4324/9781003509745

**Publisher's Note**
The publisher has gone to great lengths to ensure the quality of this reprint but points out that some imperfections in the original copies may be apparent.

**Disclaimer**
The publisher has made every effort to trace copyright holders and would welcome correspondence from those they have been unable to trace.

# AGENDA FOR CHANGE: AN INTERNATIONAL ANALYSIS OF INDUSTRIAL RELATIONS IN TRANSITION

Edited by
OLIVER CLARKE and JOHN NILAND

ALLEN & UNWIN

First published in 1991
Allen & Unwin Pty Ltd
8 Napier Street, North Sydney NSW 2059 Australia

National Library of Australia
Cataloguing-in-Publication entry:
Agenda for change: an international analysis of industrial relations in transition.
 Bibliography.
 Includes index.
 ISBN 0 04 442270 9.
 1. Industrial relations. I. Clarke, Oliver
 II. Niland, John, 1940–
331

Set in 10/11 pt Plantin by Times Graphics, Singapore
Printed by SRM Production Services, Malaysia

# Contents

List of tables    vii
Contributors    ix

1    Can industrial relations change? An international perspective
*Oliver Clarke and John Niland*    1

2    United States of America
*Thomas A. Kochan and Kirsten R. Wever*    19

3    The Federal Republic of Germany
*Wolfgang Streeck*    53

4    France
*Yves Delamotte*    90

5    Britain
*Laurie Hunter*    115

6    Australia
*John Niland and Keri Spooner*    147

7    The dynamics and dimensions of change
*Oliver Clarke and John Niland*    164

Bibliography    183

Index    192

# List of Tables

| | | |
|---|---|---|
| 1.1 | Industrial employment and production (manufacturing) | 5 |
| 1.2 | Unionisation | 7 |
| 1.3 | Industrial disputes: number of working days lost | 10 |
| 2.1 | Union membership and income in the ten largest United States unions, 1984 | 22 |
| 2.2 | Annual average output per hour, United States | 28 |
| 2.3 | Comparative civilian unemployment | 29 |
| 2.4 | Comparative female labour force participation | 30 |
| 2.5 | Total employees and production workers on durable goods and manufacturing payrolls by industry, United States | 31 |
| 2.6 | Average hourly earnings of production and non-supervisory workers on private non-agricultural payrolls, United States | 32 |
| 2.7 | Employment cost index civilian workforce, 1981–88, United States | 34 |
| 2.8 | Changes in contract settlements (1970–87), United States | 35 |
| 2.9 | Comparative unit labour costs | 36 |
| 2.10 | Hourly compensation costs for production workers in manufacturing | 38 |
| 2.11 | Comparative hourly compensation costs for manufacturing production workers | 38 |
| 2.12 | Work stoppages involving over 1000 workers, United States | 41 |
| 3.1 | Economic conditions, Federal Republic of Germany | 57 |
| 3.2 | Yearly changes in nominal and real wages and productivity, 1975–85, Federal Republic of Germany | 58 |
| 3.3 | Distribution of economically active population over sectors, Federal Republic of Germany | 66 |
| 3.4 | Foreign nationals and employment of foreign workers in Federal Republic of Germany 1975–85 | 68 |
| 3.5 | Trade union membership (in thousands) and density, 1973–85, Federal Republic of Germany | 71 |

4.1   Works council elections, France                          112
4.2   Number of workdays lost owing to labour disputes
      (agriculture and government services excepted), France   113
4.3   National Consumer Price Index, France                    114
5.1   Changes in industrial composition of employees in
      employment, United Kingdom, 1977–88                      116
5.2   Employed labour force and unemployment rate in
      United Kingdom, 1977–88                                  118
5.3   Year-on-year changes in retail prices and average
      earnings, 1977–88                                        119
5.4   Male, female and part-time employment,
      United Kingdom, 1977–88                                  122
5.5   Stoppage of work and working days lost in stoppages,
      United Kingdom, 1977–88                                  130

# Contributors

OLIVER CLARKE is an industrial relations consultant based in London. He has been secretary of a major British employers' association; a Research Fellow at the London School of Economics; responsible for industrial relations work for 18 years at the Organisation for Economic Co-operation and Development in Paris; and has held visiting appointments at the Universities of Western Australia, New South Wales, Leuven, Curtin and, most recently, Michigan State University. He has written widely on comparative industrial relations, industrial democracy, and industrial conflict.

YVES DELAMOTTE is Professor of Labour Law and Social Security at the Conservatoire National des Arts et Metiers, Paris, France. He was for many years with the French Department of Labour, and was the first director of the Agence Nationale pour l'Amelioration des Conditions deTravail (ANACT), a public institution whose mission is to promote the quality of working life. He is currently the President of the French Association of Industrial Relations.

THOMAS A. KOCHAN is a professor of industrial relations and Head of the Behaviour and Policy Sciences Area at the MIT Sloan School of Management. He has written widely in various facets of industrial relations and human resource management. He is President-Elect of the International Industrial Relations Association.

LAURIE HUNTER is a Professor of Applied Economics in the Department of Social and Economic Research, University of Glasgow. His published work includes books and articles on labour economics and industrial relations and he is a Past President of the British Universities Industrial Relations Association (1979-81). He was Visiting Professor at Cornell University in 1973.

JOHN NILAND is the Professor of Industrial Relations and Dean of the Faculty of Commerce and Economics at the University of New South Wales. He has been editor of the *Journal of Industrial Relations* since 1974, and is currently President of the International Industrial Relaitons Association.

**WOLFGANG STREECK** is Professor of Sociology and Industrial Relations at the University of Wisconsin-Madison. He has been Senior Research Fellow, Wissenschaftszentrum Berlin (1988); Visiting Professor, European University Institute, Florence (1983–4); Leverhulme Visiting Professor in European Industrial Relations, University of Warwick (1985); and Visiting Professor, Centre for Advanced Studies in the Social Sciences, Madrid (1988).

**KIRSTEN R. WEVER** is an assistant professor of Labor and Human Resource Management at the Northeastern University School of Management. Formerly, she was special assistant to the Secretary-Treasurer of the AFL-CIO.

# 1

# Can industrial relations change?
# An international perspective

OLIVER CLARKE and JOHN NILAND

It is well nigh impossible to quantify the contribution that a 'good' industrial relations system can make to the economic and social advance of a nation, but few would deny that there is such a contribution. What, then, are the characteristics of a 'good' system? Four particular features come to mind. First, the system must satisfy the employers and trade unions, managers and workers who are the principal actors in it. Second, it should operate without undue industrial conflict. Third, it must determine wages, working conditions and working practices that are consistent with national economic and social needs. And fourth, closely linked with the third, it should facilitate the organisational and technological change that is essential to a successful economy, while at the same time ensuring that the costs of adjustment are equitably shared.

The obvious qualitative variations between existing industrial relations systems in different countries are such that there is certainly room for efforts to improve the less effective systems. But this raises at least four basic questions. Are the characteristics of industrial relations so bound up with the history and culture of a country that fundamental change is impossible? What are the obstacles to change and where are the levers that could effect it? What are the respective roles of employers, unions and governments in bringing about improvement? And is there any single model of an industrial relations system to which a country can or should aspire?

This book, while not pretending to answer all these questions, seeks to throw some light on them, at least for the advanced industrialised market economies that are its concern. To provide an initial perspective, the present chapter continues with a review of how industrial relations have developed in these countries since the war and summarises the noteworthy changes during the 1980s. The five subsequent chapters deal respectively with the recent industrial relations experience of five countries with differing experience, namely the United States, Germany, France, the United Kingdom and Australia, these chapters being prepared by citizens of the countries concerned. The guidelines given for preparing the country chapters were that they should address the significant changes taking place in industrial relations, indicating which seemed to be permanent and which transient, and noting such new trends as seemed to be appearing. While discussion in other parts of the book goes beyond the five countries and draws on the experience of Japan and Sweden as well, and to a lesser extent of other industrialised market economies, these five chapters provide the primary base for the analysis. The final chapter, on a cross-country basis, returns to the basic questions of the nature and dynamics of change in industrial relations. The editors are jointly responsible for this introduction and for the concluding chapter.

## The postwar development of industrial relations

The advanced industrialised market economy countries can be taken as the 24 member countries of the OECD. Of these only Spain, Sweden, Portugal, Ireland, Switzerland and Turkey were spared direct involvement in the Second World War. Apart from those six countries, and the victorious allies, nearly all of the present OECD countries were faced, at the end of the war, with establishing new industrial relations systems. It is ironic that the systems this created in the defeated countries of Germany, Japan and Austria have been among the most successful over the postwar years. For Germany, the victors' supported a nucleus of trade union militants who had passed the war in exile or underground (Cullingford, 1976) in ensuring an industrial relations system in which —for obvious historical reasons—the state distanced itself from the industrial relations arena, while unions and employer associations interacted in a well-articulated framework. Austria, too, developed a highly sophisticated structure, leaving a great deal of responsibility to worker and employer organisations. In Japan, the (mainly American) occupying authorities saw to it that trade unions and collective bargaining were encouraged in a new system that owed much to the American 'New Deal' model. An implication of the experience of the defeated countries is that change in industrial relations systems comes about easily in a cataclysmic situation.

In France and Italy, trade union leaders had been particularly active in Resistance movements, and they had a big say in the reconstruction of industrial relations, though political differences within the countries lessened the chances of really effective systems being introduced. Norway, Denmark, the Netherlands and Belgium all had governments in exile that developed close relations with trade union leaders in the cause of national unity for postwar reconstruction. The outcome was that the industrial relations policies followed in those countries were, on the whole, consensual, with institutions reflecting that tendency.

As to the victorious countries, little need was seen in most to make changes in industrial relations, though in the United States opinion had moved on from the New Deal of the 1930s to the criticism of trade union action that led to the Labor–Management Relations Act (the Taft–Hartley Act) 1947 and the Labor–Management Reporting and Disclosures Act (the Landrum–Griffin Act) 1959. In Britain, public opinion across the whole political spectrum was that British industrial relations were the best in the world. The system was not, until around 1960, deemed to require any significant improvement. In Australia and New Zealand, on the other hand, the war had little lasting effect on the way the parties approached industrial relations.

An interesting aspect of reconstruction in continental Europe was that nearly all of the new systems featured national or regional industry-wide collective bargaining and mandatory worker participation through workplace committees. Thus, in essence, conflictual matters in the employment relationship came to be dealt with *outside* the enterprise; matters on which management and workers were deemed to have common interests were dealt with at the workplace; and worker representation in the enterprise was, at least in some measure, independent of the trade unions. The works councils or committees owed something to the successful British wartime consultative committees—though differing from them in important respects—and something to the works councils set up in pre-war Germany by the Weimar Republic. They also embodied the stress on consensus building that sprang from realisation of the immense task of economic reconstruction.

The essentials of the present systems of industrial relations in the industrialised market economies were in place by 1952, except in Spain, Portugal and Turkey, where political factors were such that they were established much later.

It would be tedious indeed to trace the detailed development of industrial relations in all of the countries since 1952. The general course of events is, however, of some interest. Broadly, the 25 years of unprecedented and sustained economic growth and, to a large extent, full employment, that started in the late 1940s, enabled workers to receive regular improvements in their living standards and working conditions. Before the war, the determination of wages and working conditions reflected the state of trade: improvement when business was good and no improvement or even cuts when business was bad. Now, however, workers acquired an expectation of constant improvement. At least up to the time that economic growth faltered, near the end of the 1960s, such improvement helped ensure a high degree of industrial peace in most of the countries. Meanwhile a new and more assertive generation of workers was growing up, better—and differently—educated from earlier generations and with confidence born of the assurance of full employment. The new assertiveness found expression in the demands for more industrial democracy that came to the fore in the late

1960s and in the 1970s, and was also at the root of the increased interest in new forms of work organisation and the quality of working life generally. It was also evident in the pressure for improved wages even when the economy turned sour, this leading in some countries to the adoption of incomes policies of one kind or another. Finally, as economic growth faltered it led to a surge of industrial conflict, of which the French student revolt of May 1968 and the wildcat strikes in peaceful Belgium, Germany and Sweden of 1969/70 were manifestations.

There is no knowing now what might have come from the increased tension of the early seventies, but in the event, the massive increase in oil prices—OPEC 1—at the end of 1973, accompanied by other adverse economic factors, administered a serious economic shock to the non-oil-producing countries. These reacted in different ways. In some, such as Germany, Austria and Switzerland, the oil price increase was seen for what it was: a tax on the non-producers that could only be recompensed in wages at the cost of raising productivity or accepting inflation. In Japan, the reality became apparent only after a steep rise in prices followed quickly upon massive wage increases in 1974, whereafter there was no difficulty in avoiding inflationary effects. The countries that had built-in indexation of wages on prices, such as Italy, Belgium and Denmark, found themselves automatically saddled with inflationary wage increases, while in some other countries, like Britain, Australia and Ireland, collective bargainers—and the industrial tribunals in the case of Australia—had become so used to recompensing increases in living costs by wage increases that they too suffered heavily from wage-led inflation.

Many industrial relations systems had not really adjusted to the changed economic environment when, in 1979, the second major rise in oil prices hit the non-oil-producing countries. The difference this time was that most governments had learned from their earlier experience and, increasingly, where they feared pressure from wages, they adopted non-accommodating monetary and fiscal policies such that it became increasingly difficult for employers to give inflationary wage increases.

By now, however, the countries were already sliding into what was to become the worst recession since the 1930s. If, to this point, industrial relations systems had weathered a deteriorating economic environment with little structural change, now they were to meet their most serious challenge of the postwar era. What this challenge has amounted to and how the countries have responded to it is the central concern of this book. An overview is provided in the next section.

### The challenge of the 1980s

In the 1980s the industrialised market economies found that their economic advantages over the rest of the world had seriously declined.

Not only were they discomfited by the competition afforded by the newly industrialised countries, notably South Korea, Taiwan, Hong Kong and Singapore, but also global rationalisation of production had led to multinational enterprises carrying out an increasing proportion of work in low-cost countries.

The new economic, industrial and political disposition is so familiar as to need no argument here. In summary, the key factors involved are as follows, although, of course, we note that their effects are unevenly distributed across countries.

First, there has been a massive decline in several basic industries, notably steel, shipbuilding, textiles and coal, involving an economic decline of the old industrial regions where these industries were located. There has been a (usually lesser) decline in many manufacturing industries (in the United States and Britain it became common to speak of a 'deindustrialisation' of the economy). The service sector, on the other hand, has increased in size. Table 1.1 shows how employment in manufacturing has fallen while production has actually increased.

**Table 1.1 Industrial employment and production (manufacturing)**

| Country | Industrial employment 1986 (1980 = 100) | Industrial production 1986 (1980 = 100) |
|---|---|---|
| Austria | 89 | 110 |
| Belgium | — | 105 |
| Canada | 110 | 123 |
| Denmark | 100 | 126 |
| Finland | 91 | 122 |
| France | 84 | 106 |
| Germany | 89 | 103 |
| Greece | — | 98 |
| Italy | — | 102 |
| Japan | 102 | 127 |
| Luxembourg | 92 | 126 |
| Netherlands | 86 | 111 |
| Norway | 91 | 110 |
| Portugal | 90 (1985) | 125 |
| Spain | — | 111 |
| Sweden | 88 | 116 |
| Switzerland | 95 | 105 |
| United States | 92 | 124 |

Source: OECD Indicators of Industrial Activity

Second, the wave of new technology that started in the late seventies, and has spread widely across the countries, has greatly facilitated communications and made possible both greater centralised control in enterprises and at the same time more autonomy at individual sites. It has made short production runs more economical and thus facilitated rapid changes in production. It has contributed, directly or indirectly, to a small decline in the average size of workplaces.

Third, in some countries, though by no means all, there has been a shift to the right politically. In some other countries, nominally left-of-centre governments have adopted several of the policies commonly associated with the political right. Assumptions in vogue in the early postwar years, such as the value of public ownership, the superiority of planning over *laissez-faire*, and the desirability of government intervention in industry, have come increasingly to be questioned.

Fourth, unemployment in a substantial number of countries has become heavy and persistent. Yet even if countries were willing to accept a relative decline in their competitiveness, the existence of unemployment at such levels is a social ill they would find difficult to tolerate over the longer term.

## Impacts on industrial relations in the 1980s

### The trade unions

The most obvious change in industrial relations across the decade has been in the trade unions—or at least a majority of them.

As table 1.2 shows, in the United States, the United Kingdom, Italy and the Netherlands, union membership density has declined substantially. In France, as Delamotte shows in chapter 4, and in Italy, there have been signs of increased rank and file action carried on, or at least commenced, outside the official trade unions. There has been a modest decline in unionisation rates in Japan, Germany, Australia and Switzerland. On the other hand, union strength remains unimpaired, or at times during the decade has increased, in Canada (at least until recently), the Scandinavian countries, Belgium and Austria.

Given the factors mentioned in the last section, this decline is not surprising: decline in the basic industries and old industrial regions where unions have traditionally been strong, and growth of the hard-to-organise service sector, have been bad news for trade unions. Another factor has been the growing number of women workers and part-time, temporary, and fixed-term workers. It is arguable that women seem a little less likely than men to join unions and certainly workers in the less regular categories are not so likely to unionise as those on full-time work with indefinite employment. Then, too, it is more difficult to organise the small enterprises that are becoming increasingly common than the

**Table 1.2 Unionisation**

| Country | Rate of unionisation % | |
|---|---|---|
| | 1980 | 1986 |
| Sweden | 83 | 86 |
| Denmark | 74 | 84 (1985) |
| Finland | 81 | 80 |
| Belgium | 75 | 74 |
| Norway | 58 | 58 |
| Austria | 58 | 57 |
| Great Britain | 54 | 43 (1985) |
| Canada | 38 | 40 (1982) |
| Italy | 44 | 36 (1985) |
| Switzerland | 37 | 34 (1985) |
| Germany | 33 | 31 |
| Japan | 31 | 28 |
| Netherlands | 38 | 28 |
| United States | 23 | 18 |
| France | 17 | 15 (1985) |

Source: A Kjellberg in *L.O. Tidningen*, Stockholm, 20 May 1988. Here cited from UIMM, 'Social International', August–September 1988. Unless otherwise stated, measures are as at 31 December 1980 and 31 December 1986.

large plants characteristic of earlier times. And the workers in small 'hi-tech' firms are often people who see little value in union membership.

This said, one might ask why union membership has held up so well in, for instance, Scandinavia, Belgium, Canada and Austria. In most of these cases the characteristics for success seem to be that the unions concerned were numerically strong to start with, and also well integrated in the life of the nation. In some of them, the unions concerned play a part in the handling of social security benefits. Most of these countries either did not have substantial declining industries (Canada) or were particularly successful in running them down (Sweden). And in all of them government policy was more or less supportive of unions: certainly, though Belgian and Danish unions were often critical of their governments, those governments did not embark on policies to weaken the unions.

A shrinking membership base usually means a shrinking income, which in turn leads to decreased staffing and perhaps ultimately less influence on governments. Reduced bargaining power is also likely to mean that unions have less to offer potential members; thus decline has the potential to become a vicious circle.

## Employers and their associations

In the United States, as Kochan and Wever demonstrate (chapter 2), numerous employers have gone to considerable lengths to get rid of unions, or to avoid having to deal with them, as well as seeking concessions from unions in collective bargaining, including two-tier agreements (that is, providing for new starters to be employed on less favourable arrangements than existing employees), though these were more common earlier in the decade. Nowhere else have more than a small minority of employers gone so far, though the force of competition, the struggle for survival, has been such that employers in most countries have found it necessary to take a tougher line in bargaining and to be more insistent on efficient working practices than in the past. It has, further, been feasible for them to do so because of the shift of bargaining power in their favour.

Parallel with a tougher approach to eliminating impediments to efficient production, many managements have adopted human resource management techniques, including sophisticated staff planning, human resource formation and performance appraisal, assurance of good pay and working conditions, effective grievance procedures, and involvement of workers in lower-level decision making (quality control circles, 'just in time' programmes and more classic forms of joint consultation). In some cases, notably in the United States, such techniques have been used to demonstrate to employees that there is little to be gained from joining a trade union, but this is by no means the only reason for their adoption. They are used because management considers that, of themselves, they enhance the efficient operation of the enterprise.

Such 'bonding' techniques and staff planning, in the increasingly common situation where the workload of the enterprise varies both as to the product and the amount produced, have been associated with a tendency towards segmentation in the labour market, leading to an advantaged core labour force, to meet normal requirements, and a much less favourably treated group drawn from the external labour market to meet peaks in work load. A similar effect is seen in working conditions of the subcontractor commonly being less favourable than in the contracting firm.

Associations of employers, politically influential though they may be, have never played a very great role in industrial relations in the United States. In Europe it has been a different story. There the associations usually face unions, and commonly negotiate with them, on an industry-by-industry basis, as well as playing a prominent part in numerous tripartite bodies, nationally and locally. Australian employer bodies are more in the European tradition, although more riven by inter-group competition and rivalries. Employer bodies have been somewhat affected by the decline of industries in which they too have traditionally been strong and by the shift away from industry-wide bargaining. But neither their influence on government nor their bargaining power could be said to have declined.

## Collective bargaining, the workplace, and conflict

Clearly, in no country is collective bargaining wholly centralised or wholly at enterprise level. In the most centralised systems enterprise bargaining also occurs—and wage drift as well—and where enterprise bargaining is the norm, there are examples of industry-wide bargaining. This said, the trend in recent years in most of the countries considered here has been towards more negotiation at the enterprise or workplace.

In the United States not only has industry-wide bargaining never been dominant but the recent trend has been to less collective bargaining. Even so, there are American examples of movement from industry to enterprise bargaining, as in the steel industry. In Germany, more and more negotiation is carried out at the workplace, as exemplified by the decentralisation introduced in the metal industry by the collective agreements of 1984. In Britain, bargaining moved towards the enterprise or workplace level long ago. The government's intention to abolish the remaining wages councils further underlines the decentralisation of wage determination. The French law of 13 November 1982 required each enterprise where there was a union presence to negotiate at least once a year on wages and working time, thus embodying a shift of emphasis from the customary industry-wide bargaining. In Sweden, apparently strongly established central–national bargaining has given way to lower-level bargaining in most bargaining rounds in the 1980s. And, as Niland and Spooner emphasise (chapter 6), recent awards of the Australian Conciliation and Arbitration Commission (now the Industrial Relations Commission) have called for a substantial element of pay increases to be earned by negotiated improvements in operational efficiency. Finally, the New Zealand Labour Relations Act 1987 envisaged a strengthening of enterprise bargaining. Nevertheless, some counter forces are at work. Ireland, where the series of national wage rounds appeared to have petered out, succeeded in making a new central-national agreement late in 1987. In Spain and Portugal, efforts—in some years successful, in others unsuccessful—have been made to arrive at such agreements. And in Australia, the various phases of the national Accord, which first came into force in 1983, have kept a large measure of overall control over wage movements.

The nature of collective bargaining has shifted too. In the United

States, as Kochan and Wever explain (chapter 2), there has been a considerable amount of concession bargaining and some two-tier bargaining in the 1980s. Though little such bargaining appears to have taken place in other countries, as already noted, employers have tended to take a harder line in bargaining under the pressure of competition. In Britain (see chapter 5), a few companies have 'de-recognised' trade unions with which they have dealt in the past. Union claims for higher wages now often put less emphasis on cost of living and comparability than in the past, and more emphasis on productivity and profitability.

In most of the countries, the outcome of collective bargaining no longer poses serious threats to price stability, but in others there are still difficulties in reconciling union bargaining objectives with the needs of the economy, notably in the Scandinavian countries, Spain, Portugal and Greece. In Britain, despite high unemployment, wage increases persistently surpass what might be expected to flow from improvements in productivity, and in Australia the government's periodic discussions with the Australian Council of Trade Unions on updating the Accord made in 1983 often have difficulty in arriving at an outcome that, when given effect, is not to some extent inflationary.

Not surprisingly, given the high levels of unemployment in most countries and the difficult economic position of many firms, and indeed industries, the volume of industrial conflict has declined over the decade. Of the eleven countries listed in table 1.3 only Austria shows an

**Table 1.3 Industrial disputes: number of working days lost (thousands)**

| Country | 1979 | 1986 |
| --- | --- | --- |
| Australia | 3 964.40 | 1 390.70 |
| Austria | 0.76 | 3.25 |
| Canada | 7 834.23 | 7 133.80 |
| France | 3 656.60 | 473.80 |
| Germany (Federal Republic) | 483.08 | 34.40 (1985) |
| Italy | 27 530.43 | 5 643.70 |
| Japan | 930.30 | 253.42 |
| Spain | 18 917.00 | 3 223.50 (1985) |
| Switzerland | 2.33 | 0.97 |
| United Kingdom | 29 474.00 | 1 920.00 |
| United States | 34 754.00 | 11 861.00 |
| *Total* | 97 547.13 | 31 927.64 |

*Source:* ILO Yearbook of Labour Statistics, 1987

*Note:* Owing to a change in the compilation of statistics, the figures for the United States are not comparable, but there is no doubt that the figure for 1986, on the same base, would have been very much less than the figure for 1979.

increase in 1986 compared with 1979, and that is only noticeable because such low levels are involved in both years.

*Change at the workplace*

Among the issues involving change at the workplace in recent years, three have been particularly significant. The first concerns the very life of the enterprise. The economic vicissitudes and broad structural adjustments already described appear to have entailed substantially greater mortality of firms, or at least sections of firms, than was usual in the fifties and sixties. Clearly this was of great concern to workers. Over the years of growth more and more job protection had been introduced in most countries. Works councils were often required to be consulted before dismissals could be effected on economic grounds and in some cases an agreed 'social plan' had to be drawn up to ensure protection for workers adversely affected. In France, Spain and the Netherlands administrative approval had to be secured before workers could be dismissed. Extended periods of notice were increasingly required and payment of substantial lump sums to displaced workers were also common. In Italy the Cassa Integrazione Guadagni was a means of supporting workers temporarily laid off at public expense.

With plenty of jobs to go round, dismissal, though always serious to those whose jobs were lost, had not usually been a disaster, and the cost of assistance to workers needed from employers and the state had not been crippling. But with the recession of 1980–82, and after, redundancy became widespread. In the case of some of the industries that suffered worst it was not unusual for large establishments around which whole towns had grown up to be closed down. This was notably the case with the steel industry. Certainly, most of this retrenchment was carried out much more humanely than would have been the case before the war: public employment services were geared up to help those displaced, and public training and retraining facilities were made available; sometimes the state provided financial assistance that made early retirement possible. Firms only partially affected delayed recruiting and reduced subcontracting and overtime working. But all this help did not disguise the disadvantages to workers.

As an indication of the severity of the cutbacks, it may be noted that, in the steel industry alone, employment decreased in the EEC countries by 44 per cent between 1974 and 1984. Between 1979 and 1984, employment in the Dutch textile industry decreased by 33.8 per cent and in German textiles by 21.5 per cent. (For manufacturing industry in general see table 1.3.)

By and large, European industrial relations systems have coped well with the cutbacks of recent years. There have been disputes, certainly, and considerable pressure has been put on governments; thus redundant steelworkers from the north of France marched on Paris, and redundant shipyard workers in the south blocked railway lines: both groups ended up by getting help from the state. But no radical change in industrial relations arrangements and no political upheavals have resulted.

A second cause of change in the 1980s has been new technology. Here again industrial relations systems have coped well. Certainly there have been a few cases here and there of resistance to the introduction of new technology, but on the whole workers have seen it as essential to the viability of their enterprises and potentially a means towards better wages and conditions. Change has been facilitated, in several countries, by a requirement that the advent of new technology must be discussed in advance between managements and works councils. In the Scandinavian countries, laws and central agreements set out how new technology should be introduced. Sometimes the law goes further. Thus the Norwegian Worker Protection and Working Environment Act 1977 stresses the importance of utilising technological development to create a fully satisfactory working environment in physical, mental and social terms.

A third form of change concerns working time, which has been a prominent issue in Europe throughout the decade. Trade union pressure to reduce hours grew at the end of the 1970s. Wage increases were hard to get; order books were low and unemployment high; and the unions therefore thought that hours reduction would be a means of securing a permanent gain for workers at a time when employers might be more amenable, rather than when they were fully stretched and public opinion would favour a means of creating more jobs. The Munich Congress of the European Trade Union Confederation (ETUC) in 1979 therefore decided that a campaign should be launched for a 35-hour week, 6 weeks, holiday with pay, and retirement at sixty.

A few governments also declared themselves sympathetic towards at least some reductions in working time, notably the French socialist government elected in 1981. The French decided on a modest reduction to start with but the government offered financial inducements to firms willing to make more substantial cuts. Effectively, however, further general reduction in France stopped in 1982 when the government was forced to adopt an economic austerity programme. The Belgian government, coping with particularly high unemployment, sought to couple hours reductions with job creation in what was called the 5:3:3 formula, under which a 5 per cent reduction in normal weekly working hours would be partly compensated by a 3 per cent saving on the wage increase that would otherwise be given under the national practice of wage indexation. In addition, the employer would be expected to engage 3 per cent new labour or, if unable to do so, to pay over the savings in wages into a national fund to be used for promoting employment. Belgium has also experimented with weekend shift arrangements. In Germany reduction was influenced by a massive strike in the metals industry in 1984, the biggest strike that the Federal Republic had ever known. A particularly interesting characteristic of the ensuing metal agreements was that the working week in firms should be permitted to vary, both over time and between departments, within specified periods of settlement, the modalities to be determined within the plant. (Hitherto, all working hours had had to conform to the fixed standard prescribed by the relevant regional–industrial agreement.)

Agreed working time fell appreciably in nearly all European countries in the eighties, but the evidence suggested that the number of jobs created as a result was relatively small and, of course, a straight reduction without loss of pay, as many reductions were in the early 1980s, did nothing for competitiveness. But in recent years there has been a greater trade union readiness to concede a measure of flexibility of working hours at the plant and sometimes to make a deal on pay compensation.

## Industrial democracy and labour–management co-operation

The Europe of the 1970s was remarkable for its innovation in worker participation in management, or industrial democracy. In that decade the Scandinavian countries, the Netherlands, Austria and Luxembourg all joined Germany in requiring worker representation on boards of directors (albeit, in some of these countries, on a supervisory rather than a management board). In the same period compulsory works councils were also strengthened and in Sweden the Codetermination at Work Act 1976, gave unions a powerful voice in managerial decisions—though less powerful in practice than appeared at the time. The Swedish Act did, however, lead to a considerable increase in workplace consultation, and the termination of the central agreement on Works Committees in 1977 was more than compensated in this way.

Though no extravagant claims could be made for the success of worker representation on company boards, it seems clear that the arrangements have been modestly successful. The works councils, too, have been quite successful and there is no suggestion that their responsibilities, or those of worker–directors, should be scaled down. Indeed, arrangements for worker–directors in Scandinavia have been strengthened in recent years. But in the eighties, as other aspects of work relations have come to seem more important, the pressure for strengthening industrial democracy has fallen off almost everywhere.

No major advanced industrialised market economy country outside Europe has set up works councils of the continental European kind, that is to say, mandatory agencies that have specified rights vis-à-vis management—and sometimes responsibilities—but that are not intended to be collective bargaining institutions. In Japan their functions are subsumed by participative ways of management; in North America the practice of contract administration and the hierarchy of grievance and arbitration procedures leave little ground for such a body; and in Britain the strongly developed shop steward system could not support a parallel form of labour–management relations with decision-making powers.

It should be noted that the works councils' assumption of a negotiating role, at least in some cases, has weakened the postwar principle of conflictual matters being dealt with at industry level and only consensual matters within the enterprise.

Interest in human aspects of the organisation of work sprang from the same social and economic currents, and arose at the same time as interest in industrial democracy—indeed new forms of work organisation are often in themselves highly participative. Several European countries have been leaders in this field and several have established public agencies, usually with union and employer involvement, to encourage adoption of the new forms, which tend to build on the sociotechnical system concept pioneered by the British Tavistock Institute. The most advanced countries are certainly, though in different ways, Sweden and Norway. In Sweden the movement has been led by the central employer organisation (though with the support of the unions), with considerable energy and appreciable success. In Norway, on the other hand, the objective has been a more fundamental change in thinking about the nature of the enterprise, which has been more difficult to obtain, so that progress seems to have been slower (Dundelach & Mortensen 1979:39).

As has already been noted, in striving to be competitive some managements have sought to strengthen co-operation with their workforce. As to institutionalised co-operation, in the United States labour representation committees set up by employers in the early 1920s acquired a bad reputation as an anti-union tool. Not surprisingly, given that context, the framework of industrial relations initiated by the Wagner Act of 1935 made no provision for formalised co-operation—indeed a representative worker body might, in certain circumstances, fall foul of the legal ban on company unions. Only a few labour–management bodies were formed in the postwar years up to the 1980s: since then, however, as Kochan and Wever point out (see chapter 2), much progress has been made, with the administration making considerable efforts (Stepp, 1986, Labor–Management Cooperation Act 1978) to promote co-operation as a means of increasing competitiveness. In addition a number of labour–management bodies have been formed in connection with concession bargaining, particularly where extensive redundancy was involved. There has also been quite a vogue for quality control circles.

It is well known that in Japan participative decision making and labour–management co-operation are part of the way of life, and the challenges of the eighties have done no more than confirm the pattern. In Britain, the joint consultative committees set up during and shortly after the war fell into disuse in the ensuing years, but this form of co-operation has enjoyed something of a revival in the 1980s.

For continental Europe there has been little change, in the 1980s, in the established forms of worker representation in the enterprise; such change as did occur was in the direction of strengthening it. Thus one of the French Auroux laws, that of 4 August 1982, sought to enhance the expression of workers' views, and Germany enacted a strengthening of the rights of works councils relevant to technological change at the end of 1988.

## The role of the state

The role of the state in industrial relations may be taken as being to:

- set the ground rules concerning employers, workers, and their organisations, and the relations between them,
- provide basic protection for people at work,
- be a major employer in its own right, and
- (in some countries) provide assistance to the parties in cases of industrial conflict.

Additionally, the responsibilities normally shouldered by governments in relation to the national economy require them to have regard to such increases in labour costs as the parties might decide, with the aim of intervening if those increases seem likely to have adverse effects on the national economy.

There were no fundamental changes in the ground rules during the 1980s. The more important changes were the four Auroux laws in France in 1982, seeking to strengthen workers' position at the enterprise and strengthening collective bargaining there (see chapter 4); and the succession of laws in the United Kingdom (1980, 1982, 1984, 1986, 1988 and 1989) gradually narrowing the right to strike, increasing union internal democracy, tightening the rules governing the closed shop, and effecting changes concerning the payment of wages and the powers of wages councils (see chapter 5). A New Zealand Act of 1987 and an Australian Act of 1988 (see chapter 6) revised and consolidated earlier legislation and encouraged improvement in union structure.

Up to the early 1980s, the picture was one of continuous extension of legislated protection for workers, notably in respect of health and safety but also concerning such things as minimum wages and employment security. As the 1980s continued, however, new protective measures were reduced to a trickle, and governments appeared both to consider that a plateau had been reached and to have increasing regard to the cost of such measures to production and employment. Then, as the stress on competitiveness developed, and attention came to concentrate on how to make labour markets more flexible, cases of cutting back protection, albeit usually at the margins, occurred. In the United States it was clear, under the Reagan administration, that the Occupational Safety and Health Act 1970 was being less strictly policed.

The debate on flexible working time led, in some countries, to re-laxation of earlier rigid rules and notably to a reconsideration of restrictions on the employment of part-time and temporary workers and the employment of women and youth on nightwork, in this last case, for example, Iceland and the Netherlands renounced their adherence to the International Labour Organisation's Convention number 89 of 1948, and Belgium, Britain, France and Switzerland also recently considered the easing of these restrictions. As regards wages, the real level of the national minimum wage in France, the Netherlands and the United States—where the wage was unchanged from 1981 to 1989—was allowed to decline over much of the decade. The British government, in 1989, announced plans to wind up the wages councils, which for 80 years had put a floor under wages in occupations that, in the main, had a low level of union organisation.

Over the postwar years it became both increasingly difficult and increasingly expensive to dismiss workers who were no longer required. As already mentioned, in France, Spain and the Netherlands administrative authorisation was required before dismissals could be effected. Redundancy payments, longer notice of dismissal and facilities for challenging dismissals were extended or introduced in many countries. In some countries works councils were given specific rights to negotiate the conditions of impending collective dismissals (which were also covered, in member countries, by an EEC Directive). Again, changes, albeit relatively minor, occurred in the late 1980s. Thus France abolished the need for administrative authorisation, and Britain raised the threshold at which workers became eligible to dispute dismissal.

But it was perhaps in the role of the state as employer that the most pronounced shift took place. In the postwar years governments took on more and more responsibilities, requiring a considerable expansion of their own labour force. The expansion, in some countries, of public ownership of industries brought more workers into a situation where the state was the ultimate guarantor of wages if not the immediate paymaster. Both the extent of the increase in public employment and the response to it varied between countries. Some governments, as in Germany, retained the old tradition of civil servants as agents of the sovereign power, others, as the United States, starting with President Kennedy's Executive Order number 10988 of 1962, extended a greater degree of recognition to public service unionism, and some went further, as in the case of Canada, in authorising a practice of collective bargaining for public employees.

In assessing civil service pay adjustment in the absence of a profit criterion, governments sometimes established special, independent machinery to advise them. One method, used, with variation, in the United

States and Japan, is for an impartial proposal to be formulated by an independent agency. In Britain a Civil Service Pay Research Unit for a long time, until abolished by the Thatcher administration, established data about private sector analogues of civil service jobs with the purpose of guiding government in its consideration of pay.

With the expansion of their numbers, the postwar era up to 1980 was generally good for public employees. In the early 1980s, however, conditions became more difficult for them. In the recession, governments found it increasingly difficult to raise revenue while their costs, notably spiralling health care costs, were rising rapidly. Many governments found it necessary to economise on their own payrolls, both by holding down the number employed and by adopting a tougher line on pay adjustment. Later, the growing tendency to privatise elements of the public sector, evident in several countries, also spelled a change in the treatment of public employees. That is not to say that there was any long-term cutback in the public service. According to figures provided by the OECD's Labour Force Statistics for the percentage of the total labour force employed by governments, between 1979 and 1986 the percentage fell from 16.2 per cent to 15.8 per cent in the United States and from 6.6 per cent to 6.4 per cent (1985) in Japan. But over the same period the proportion increased in Germany from 14.8 per cent to 16.1 per cent; in France from 15.4 per cent to 18.1 per cent; in the United Kingdom from 21.2 per cent to 21.8 per cent; and in Sweden from 29.9 per cent to 33 per cent.

*International aspects of industrial relations*

The quiet postwar growth of the international element of industrial relations continued, slowly, in the 1980s, though without breaking much new ground. After the introduction of international guidelines for multinational enterprises in 1976/77 there was little change on that count; indeed, governments seemed reluctant to make any significant effort beyond keeping the guidelines in being. In the European Community most of the significant initiatives of the Commission concerning industrial relations continued to meet with resistance from the Council of Ministers. However, with the decision of 1986 to proceed to a genuinely common market by the end of 1992, the adoption of qualified majority voting in place of the unanimity rule for certain decisions, and Social Action Program put forward in the context of the (contested) Social Charter, more development of industrial relations initiatives seems likely. One proposal (which had originally been put forward in 1970, but had long been in abeyance) concerning the statute for a European Company, to be established under European law, was revived in 1988, with new ideas to overcome the stumbling block of the role of workers in the management structure. The 'Single Europe' legislation also enjoined the Commission to develop dialogue with and between employer and worker organisations, thereby strengthening the so-called Val Duchesse talks, which had been developing since 1985. The Commission is intent on ensuring that the Europe that comes into being at the end of 1992 will have a social as well as an economic dimension.

The 1980s, then, have not been a time of radical reconstruction of the bases of industrial relations, but they have nevertheless witnessed change in the power relationships between unions and employers and a strengthening of emphasis on operational efficiency—in particular through enhancing flexibility at the workplace. Industrial relations systems continue to vary considerably between countries, both in their form and in their efficacy. The significance of the differences between them, and the prospects for change, will be addressed in chapter 7.

# 2

# United States of America

THOMAS A. KOCHAN
and
KIRSTEN R. WEVER

Over the past several decades all of the advanced industrial societies have experienced growing pressures on the institutions governing their industrial relations systems. These pressures, which can be traced to long-term changes in the nature of the international economy, have manifested themselves in different ways in each country. The cases of the OECD member countries are strikingly similar, however, insofar as general macroeconomic problems (in the United States, sluggish productivity growth and large trade deficits) have generated the pressing need for thoroughgoing changes in the ways in which the government, organised labour and businesses deal with one another.

It has become increasingly obvious that widespread economic problems require solutions that depend critically on the active participation and co-operation of all three parties to the employment relationship. The tasks of revitalising our industrial base and international competitiveness, while simultaneously avoiding a decline in the general standard of living, demand new forms of industrial relations. Although the shape of this imminent transition has not yet become clear, a variety of experiments and changes have taken place in industrial relations in the United States during the first half of the 1980s, which the parties can now begin to evaluate and learn from. The nature of the system that ultimately emerges from this transition process will be determined in large measure by the environmental conditions within which labour, business and government operate, and by the strategies they adopt as they continue to pursue the variety of organisational and industrial relations adjustment processes initiated in recent years.

The main purpose of this chapter is to lay out the historical and environmental contexts in which the current changes are taking place in the United States. We will describe and document contemporary trends in employment and industrial relations, suggest some areas in which we believe problems are likely to emerge or intensify over the coming decade, and point to some avenues and opportunities for constructive change. Underlying our discussion is the central premise that sustaining and diffusing changes in industrial relations will be necessary to achieving a solution to the broader macroeconomic pressures of the day.

## Historical and structural background: the New Deal system

To understand the nature and significance of contemporary developments we first need to characterise the essential functions of the industrial relations systems, which were shaped in the 1930s by the government policies of the New Deal. The primary feature of the New Deal industrial relations system was that it relied on collective bargaining as the preferred means for setting the terms and conditions of employment in the largest companies in the United States. The principles and policies established in collective bargaining were in many ways then replicated in non-union firms and sectors of the economy. The collective bargaining process itself was considered to be the best method of accommodating a 'mixed' adversarial/co-operative relationship between workers and business enterprises.

One of the primary attractions of this method of regulating industrial relations was that it was consistent with a non-interventionist policy on the part of the federal government. The National Labor Relations Act, passed in 1935, essentially established rules governing the processes of union organising and the negotiation of contracts, but it did not specify the content of these contracts. Management was required to bargain in good faith, but what was agreed to was left up to the private parties. This approach was consistent with the 'pragmatic' and 'business unionist' philosophy of American labour, and it did not challenge the fundamental principles of free enterprise that the American business community staunchly defended.

In return for their role in negotiating wages, hours and working conditions, unions implicitly accepted managerial control over strategic decision making and the organisation of shopfloor production process. Labour pursued a sort of 'job control unionism', which narrowly delineated tasks and work jurisdictions within those managerially defined processes. An equally formalised grievance and arbitration procedure ensured that disputes over the interpretation of agreements were settled impartially, and when necessary by a third party. Within the limits thus defined in highly complex and formalised contracts, management maintained its rights to make basic investment, technology, production and related strategic decisions.

The institutional structure for industrial relations operated within, and over time came to support, a Keynesian macroeconomic policy that encouraged economic growth through the maintenance of high levels of purchasing power. These policies were accompanied by an expanding domestic market fuelled first by wartime production demands and later by a mixture of consumer and government demand for manufactured goods, as well as growing economies of scale. In combination, these circumstances provided steady productivity growth, which could support rising incomes and standards of living. Collective bargaining adapted to this environment over time, establishing wage-setting principles and structures to 'take wages out of competition' by standardising wages across United States firms competing in the same product and labour markets. More generally, the collective bargaining process adjusted wages upward in ways consistent with long-run increases in productivity and the cost of living. Yet because collective bargaining remained highly decentralised, there was sufficient variation in bargaining outcomes for contracts to be responsive to the specific economic circumstances of individual industries and firms.

Thus, the complex, decentralised, collective-bargaining-oriented, job-control unionism of the New Deal system contained features that were attractive to leaders in government, businesses and labour. For the government the system established rules to regulate labour–management relations without requiring substantive (as opposed to formal or procedural) state intervention. For the business community, it stabilised a potentially volatile workforce and limited union influence in management to the areas of wages, hours and working conditions. For union leaders, New Deal industrial relations provided the foundation for what would be a rapidly growing union base, and a rapid growth in the level of wages for unionised workers.

### The American Federation of Labor and Congress of Industrial Organizations

The umbrella association for the vast majority of American unions is the American Federation of Labor and Congress of Industrial Organizations (AFL–CIO). The AFL was founded in 1886 to represent the combined interests of the nation's craft unions. Craft unions represent skilled workers in a variety of plants, firms and industries, and generally focus on the definition, status and defence of relatively narrow occupational jurisdictions. Industrial unions channel their efforts toward representing all the workers—regardless of skill or job definition—in a given plant, firm or industry. The Congress of Industrial Organizations (CIO) was created in 1938 to co-ordinate the activities of several emergent industrial unions that broke away from the AFL in 1935. The AFL and the CIO merged in 1955 with the intention of forming a unified national labour federation. Both before and since the merger the primary function of the federation has been to represent workers' interests in political affairs through lobbying, political endorsements, research, education, and communications and public relations. The memberships and the revenues of the ten largest unions in the United States in 1984 are shown in table 2.1.

**Table 2.1 Union membership and income in the ten largest United States unions, 1984**

|  | Membership ('000) | Income ('000) | Net income after expenses ('000) |
|---|---|---|---|
| Teamsters (IBT) | 1523 | 90 389 | 9 631 |
| National Education Association (NEA) | 1444 | 77 293 | 3 764 |
| Food and Commercial Workers (UFCW) | 1068 | 79 094 | 7 026 |
| Auto Workers (UAW) | 904 | 105 257 | 36 223 |
| State, County and Municipal Employees (AFSCME) | 955 | 39 982 | 1 480 |
| Electrical Workers (IBEW) | 998 | 118 825 | 29 706 |
| Steel Workers (USW) | 474 | 153 171 | 31 121 |
| Carpenters | 589 | 58 858 | 20 067 |
| Service Employees (SEA) | 579 | 18 027 | 2 469 |
| Communication Workers (CWA) | 578 | 58 086 | 3 671 |

*Source:* Union Sourcebook, Industrial Relations Data Information Services, West Orange, NJ, 1985.

While labour generally aligns with candidates from the Democratic Party in national elections, exceptions to this pattern are fairly common at the state and local levels. At these levels, candidates from the Republican Party who are responsive to union interests sometimes receive organised labour's support. Moreover, the largest union (which only recently reaffiliated with the AFL-CIO), the International Brotherhood of Teamsters, has generally supported Republican candidates in recent presidential elections.

The political influence of labour in the United States should not be entirely discounted simply because of the lack of a labour party, or because of the very loose affiliation between labour and the Democratic Party. Labour's influence over broad areas of social and economic policy has varied considerably over the years. Most would agree that its influence at the national level has been limited in the 1980s by the conservative philosophies and policies of the Reagan administration and the ascendancy of a more conservative political climate in the country. Still, over the years the labour movement has been one of the most influential forces behind the passage of and improvements in major bodies of civil rights, occupational safety and health, minimum wage, pension reform and social security legislation (Goldberg et al., 1976). Compared with the more socially and politically active labour movements of most other OECD countries, however, the United States labour movement stands out as being:

- less committed to any sort of socialist ideology or political agenda;
- less formally integrated into and aligned with the agenda of a single political party; and
- more interested in policies that foster decentralised collective bargaining (rather than comprehensive legislation governing the workplace).

Later in this chapter we argue, as others have done, that the political role of the American labour movement will become increasingly important in the years to come.

## Unionisation levels

Between the mid-1930s and the 1950s private sector unionism grew at a rapid rate. In 1932 only 10 per cent of the non-agricultural workforce was unionised; in 1955 that figure had increased to an all-time peak of 35 per cent, and it stayed more or less stable for the next decade. But while private sector unionism slid into a steady decline in the 1960s, from the mid-1960s onward there was a burst of public sector unionisation, which grew from 12 per cent to 40 per cent of all public sector workers between 1960 and 1980 (Burton, 1979). Public sector workers now account for more than a third of all union members in the United States. The net effect of these developments is that the overall percentage of the labour force unionised has continued to fall since the late 1950s, and at present is almost the lowest among the OECD countries, at just under 17 per cent of the labour force in 1988.

## Employer associations

Paralleling labour's focus on collective bargaining and the decentralised nature of industrial relations in the United States, peak employer associations have played limited roles in the United States. The three major peak employer associations are the National Association of Manufacturers, the Chamber of Commerce, and the Business Roundtable (Windmuller & Gladstone, 1984). All of these have generally opposed legislation designed to expand or strengthen worker rights and union power. From time to time, however, these organisations have engaged in legislative activity that has weakened the protections and rights extended to unions under United States labour law. The most notable example is the 1947 Taft–Hartley Act, which imposed restrictions on union use of secondary boycotts and closed shops, and gave states the right to outlaw union shop clauses in collective bargaining agreements. But beyond lobbying to counter union influence, these associations have never been major forces in shaping employer approaches to United States industrial relations. Rather, the centre of power on the management side of industrial relations lies at the level of the individual corporation. It is true that patterns of collective bargaining and the shapes of contracts were set by certain industry models, perhaps most importantly that of the automobile manufacturing sector. But labour–management relations remained determined primarily on a firm-by-firm (or plant-by-plant) basis.

The major exceptions to plant-centred or firm-centred industrial relations were found in those industries where the structure of bargaining was co-ordinated on an industry-wide or regional basis, as in the steel, coal, trucking and construction industries. As bargaining in these industries centralised, employer associations organised to co-ordinate management strategy, and to represent member firms at the bargaining table (Windmuller & Gladstone, 1984). In recent years, however, the power and influence of these industry associations have declined considerably, paralleling the decline (or, as in steel, the demise) of industry-wide bargaining (Freedman & Fulmer, 1982).

## Labor law

The two primary pieces of labour legislation of the New Deal system are the Railway Labor Act 1926, which initially applied only to railroads but was later extended to airlines, and the National Labor Relations Act 1935, which covers most industries in the economy. The Railway Labor Act entails elaborate dispute resolution mechanisms administered for the most part by the National Mediation Board. Provisions for extensive mandatory mediation and voluntary arbitration procedures under the Railway Labor Act were effected in the interest of minimising work stoppages in the transportation sector, which was believed to be vital to the national interest. The dispute resolution procedures of the National Labor Relations Act are less encompassing. Over the postwar period, the tendency of this Act's National Labor Relations Board has been to defer dispute resolution to arbitration procedures voluntarily agreed to by the parties to the employment relationship. To date, grievance arbitration remains the most common form of dispute resolution for issues pertaining to day-to-day interpretations of labour contracts. But since 1960, with the growth of legislation and regulations governing worker rights, federal and state courts have come to play an increasingly important part in adjudicating worker–employer disputes over discrimination, safety and health, and a range of other workplace issues.

Formal arrangements for labour–management co-operation in the United States have historically been quite limited. War Labor Boards were established during both world wars to ensure price stability and low levels of labour strife during wartime. Since the second War Labor Board, only a small number of labour–management forums have been initiated by the government. Most of these were short-lived, such as President Kennedy's Labor–Management Advisory Panel. Most were also focused on specific issues, such as the wage–price guidelines and controls of the Nixon, Ford and Carter Administrations in the 1970s (Moye, 1980). A small number of private labour–management groups have met to discuss issues of national importance. Most of these bodies, however, have tended to avoid labour policy issues, since it has seldom been possible to reach any consensus in this area.

*Tripartite consultation*

In recent years, however, in the face of increasing international competitive pressures on the United States economy, a number of public and private groups of management, labour and government leaders have begun to meet in order to search for ways to improve the performance of the United States economy. If history is any guide, it will be very difficult for these groups to come to agreement on matters affecting labour and human resource policy, and even harder to generate the political influence and discipline needed to implement any recommendations reached. However, the emergence of such groups may have an important subtle and indirect influence on the nature of the policy agenda. For instance, they may illuminate some areas of shared understanding about how labour and employment policies should fit into broader national economic policies, or establish informal communication networks among labour and management leaders.

It is consistent with the decentralised nature of United States industrial relations that labour–management co-operation has been most visible at the community level, and within individual collective bargaining relationships. At present, there are over a hundred community level labour–management committees in the United States. Most of these are concerned with improving the climate of labour–management relations, in the hopes of attracting greater economic development resources. The more active among them also provide training and technical assistance to firm-level co-operative efforts. A few of these committees have sometimes provided mediators during strikes (Cutcher-Gershenfeld, 1986).

We return to the role of co-operative labour–management efforts in specific bargaining relationships below. For the time being, suffice it to say that while the number and scope of co-operative activities have increased in recent years, such efforts have not been widely diffused across industries. Indeed, one of the central strategic questions for the future of United States industrial relations is whether and how such experiments should be encouraged, diffused and institutionalised.

*The role of the federal government*

Also in keeping with the decentralisation of labour–management relations in the United States, the role of the federal government has historically been quite limited compared with most major industrialised countries. As noted above, the main pieces of labour legislation were promulgated for railways in the 1920s and for general industry in the 1930s. Since that time, however, the role of government in shaping industrial relations has not changed significantly. Indeed, mounting evidence suggests that the law has become less effective in the 1970s and 1980s in achieving its intent, particularly with respect to protecting the rights of workers to organise. In part, the lack of state intervention can be attributed to rapid postwar economic growth, when steadily rising profits were accompanied by steady enhancements of labour contracts and, until the 1960s, steady increases in the level of unionisation.

The reluctance of the government to intervene in the industrial relations arena was clearly signalled by the failure of comparatively mild labour law reform legislation in 1978. The reforms were designed to stiffen penalties imposed on labour law violators, and to reduce delays in representation elections. The defeat of this legislation can be attributed in large measure to the opposition of individual large corporations, the Business Roundtable, and the National Association of Manufacturers.

On the other hand, the 1960s and 1970s did see a rapid increase in the amount and scope of legislation directly affecting employment. Such legislation created the Occupational Safety and Health Administration, and Affirmative Action and Equal Opportunity Employment programmes, and the Employee Retirement and Income Security Act. However, the period since 1978 has again been marked by a shift toward more *laissez-faire* federal economic and labour policies. This is signalled, for example, by recent deregulation affecting the airline, trucking, railroad and communications industries.

While extensive decentralisation continues to characterise contemporary United States industrial relations, the foundations of the New Deal system that supported such decentralisation have begun to erode. Case-by-case experiments with new forms for labour–management relations—both including and excluding unions—are of increasing scope and importance. We will now consider the environmental pressures that have produced these changes, and the measures taken by labour and management organisations to cope with them.

## The changing environment

### The economy

The underlying stimulus to the changes occurring in collective bargaining and industrial relations in the 1980s can be traced in large measure to the continued weak performance of the economy. Output per hour in the United States has lagged since the late 1970s. Productivity growth remains sluggish, both by the historical standard of 3 per cent established in the two decades following the Second World War and as compared with major trading partners and the newly industrialising nations. For instance, between 1979 and 1983, the average annual percentage growth in United States productivity was only 0.2 per cent, as against 2.6 per cent for Japan, and 1.3 per cent for western Europe in the aggregate (OECD, 1986). In the fourteen quarters of recovery since the recession of 1982–83, productivity gains in the business sector have been the lowest of any similar recovery period since 1949, although in manufacturing the recovery has been stronger (table 2.2) (Fulco, 1986).

Another important development affecting the United States economy in general, and collective bargaining in particular, has been the growing trade interdependence of the world economy and the declining performance of American firms in world markets. In the 1970s the percentage of United States gross national product (GNP) attributable to exports and imports grew steadily: by 1986 exports accounted for approximately 9 per cent of the GNP, and imports for another 11.4 per cent. Moreover, the United States trade deficit grew immensely in the first half of the 1980s, from US$9 thousand million in 1982 to US$170 thousand million in 1986. Deficits in bilateral trade balances further suggest that the problem of American competitiveness is not limited to one or two countries. Rather, between 1982 and 1985, deficits increased with Canada (US$4.6 thousand million), Japan (US$29.8 thousand million), western Europe (US$21.1 thousand million), Latin America (US$10.4 thousand million), and the newly industrialising countries of East Asia (US$16.4 thousand million). The size of the United States' trade deficit with Japan (US$55 thousand million in 1986) has engendered a heated political debate around increased Japanese penetration of United States manufacturing markets. The deficit with Japan amounts to about one-third of the total trade deficit. Still, the magnitude and scope of the problem is clearly much more significant than the focus on Japan would suggest.

The declining competitiveness of United States firms in world and domestic markets reflects a number of cyclical factors as well as various aspects of long-term decline. Economists will continue to debate how much of the decline is due to the 25 per cent increase in the value of the American dollar relative to the Japanese yen that occured between 1981 and 1985. They will argue about how much the subsequent decline of the dollar (by a nearly equivalent amount) will do to reverse the trend. Resolving this debate is beyond the scope of this chapter. Yet, given the fact that union membership in the United States is disproportionately concentrated in import and export-sensitive industries, the increased exposure to international competition has taken a significant

## 2 Annual average output per hour (1977 = 100)

|  | 1970 | 1973 | 1976 | 1979 | 1981 | 1983 | 1985 | 1986* | 1987 |
|---|---|---|---|---|---|---|---|---|---|
|  | 88.4 | 95.9 | 98.3 | 99.6 | 100.7 | 103.0 | 106.4 | 109.5 | 110.5 |
| business | 89.3 | 96.4 | 98.5 | 99.3 | 99.3 | 102.4 | 104.8 | 107.5 | 108.4 |
| cial corporations | 91.1 | 97.5 | 98.4 | 99.8 | 99.6 | 103.5 | 108.0 | 109.9 | 110.2 |
| uring | 80.8 | 93.4 | 97.1 | 101.4 | 103.6 | 112.0 | 121.7 | 128.8 | 133.1 |

ures from third quarter.

onthly Labor Review, Bureau of Labor Statistics, Washington DC, January 1970 to May 1989.

toll on union member's jobs and on real (and nominal) wages. For example, one recent study links import penetration to lower wage settlements in the transportation equipment and other manufacturing sectors, and to lower levels of unionised employment in the clothing, rubber and plastics, and fabricated metals sectors (Abowd, 1987).

## *Unemployment*

Unemployment rates have also remained persistently high, but have nonetheless been lower than in many other OECD countries. The rate is currently 6.7 per cent, a full percentage point higher than in 1979. Still, French, British and German unemployment levels have now risen above United States levels (see table 2.3).

### Table 2.3 Comparative civilian unemployment

|                | 1970 | 1974 | 1977 | 1980 | 1983 | 1984 | 1985 | 1986  | 1987 |
|----------------|------|------|------|------|------|------|------|-------|------|
| United States  | 5.9  | 5.6  | 7.1  | 7.1  | 9.6  | 7.5  | 7.2  | 6.9   | 6.2  |
| France         | 2.7  | 2.9  | 4.9  | 6.5  | 8.8  | 9.9  | 10.4 | 10.7  | 11.1 |
| Germany        | 0.6  | 1.6  | 3.5  | 2.9  | 7.3  | 7.8  | 7.9  | 7.5   | 6.9  |
| United Kingdom | 3.9  | 3.1  | 6.3  | 7.0  | 13.4 | 12.9 | 13.1 | 11.7* | 10.3 |
| Sweden         | 2.6  | 2.0  | 1.8  | 2.0  | 3.5  | 3.1  | 2.8  | 2.6   | 1.9  |

*Note:* *Figure from second quarter.

*Source: Monthly Labor Review*, Bureau of Labor Statistics, Washington DC, various issues.

Much of the long-term component of current unemployment can be traced to employment declines, plant closing, and structural adjustments in high-wage manufacturing industries, such as steel, meatpacking, and rubber. (Unfortunately, nationwide data on plant closings are only available for the year 1982, so it is hard to make longitudinal comparisons.) Between January 1981 and January 1986, 10.8 million jobs were 'permanently' lost—almost half of them by 'experienced' workers (now considered officially 'displaced'). A presidential task force consisting of academics, labour leaders and businessmen concluded that 'responses to worker dislocation from both government and the private sector have been spotty and narrowly focused, and the United States lacks a comprehensive, coordinated strategy to deal with the problem' (Lovell, 1986:4). In 1988 Congress took a step in this direction by enacting a law requiring 60 days advance notice of a plant shutdown or mass lay-off, and providing funding for workers' retraining and adjustment.

*Worker dislocation, demographic changes and employment shifts*

Worker dislocation appears to persist over long periods for a substantial minority of the workforce. One analyst estimates, for example, that about 8 per cent of both men and women in their prime earning years, and active in the labour market, were unable for a period of five or more years (in a ten-year measurement period) to earn more than 50 per cent of the wage that would place an average family of four at the poverty level. Beyond these discouraging trends among low-earning workers, there are trends to suggest that it is becoming increasingly difficult for those who lose their jobs to find new ones. For example, 25 per cent of men and women between 26 and 55 years old who lost their jobs before 1983 had been unable to find new jobs in 1984, over a year later (Osterman, 1988).

Meanwhile, as the problem of worker dislocation seems to have worsened in the past decade, a higher percentage of women are entering the workforce. The labour force participation of women has increased sharply during the postwar period, and the female percentage of the total labour force in the United States is surpassed only by that of Sweden, among the countries in our study (see table 2.4). By the same

**Table 2.4 Comparative female labour force participation**

|  | 1971 | 1974 | 1977 | 1980 | 1983 |
|---|---|---|---|---|---|
| United States | 43.4 | 45.7 | 48.4 | 51.5 | 52.9 |
| France | 39.8 | 41.6 | 44.2 | 42.7 | n.a. |
| Germany | 38.5 | 38.8 | 37.8 | 38.2 | n.a. |
| United Kingdom | 42.5 | 46.2 | 47.5 | 48.5 | n.a. |
| Sweden | 50.9 | 53.3 | 56.7 | 59.3 | 61.2 |

*Source: Handbook of Labor Statistics*, Washington DC, Bureau of Labor Statistics, June 1985.

token, employment has declined in the traditionally unionised sectors of the economy, such as manufacturing, and has increased in traditionally non-union (and apparently hard-to-organise) sectors, such as retailing and services. Within the durable goods manufacturing industries, employment trends are more varied, dropping in subsectors such as primary and fabricated metals, and motor vehicles and equipment, but rising in machinery, and in electrical and electronic equipment (table 2.5).

It is clear, however, that more jobs are being created in the service sector than anywhere else. The Bureau of Labor Statistics estimates that 90 per cent of current and future job growth will come from services. Some of these jobs command fairly high salaries and allow for oppor-

**Table 2.5 Total employees and production workers on durable goods and manufacturing payrolls by industry ('000)**

|                                     | 1971   | 1974   | 1977   | 1980   | 1983   | 1986   |
|-------------------------------------|--------|--------|--------|--------|--------|--------|
| Total                               | 10 636 | 11 925 | 11 597 | 12 187 | 10 774 | 11 244 |
| Stone, clay, glass                  | 664    | 707    | 668    | 662    | 512    | 586    |
| Primary metals                      | 1 171  | 1 288  | 1 181  | 1 142  | 838    | 753    |
| Fabricated metals                   | 1 480  | 1 638  | 1 582  | 1 613  | 1 373  | 1 431  |
| Nonelectrical machinery             | 1 815  | 2 208  | 2 174  | 2 494  | 2 038  | 2 060  |
| Electrical and electronic equipment | 1 744  | 1 987  | 1 878  | 2 090  | 2 023  | 2 123  |
| Motor vehicle and equipment         | 848    | 907    | 947    | 788    | 757    | 865    |

Source: *Handbook of Labor Statistics*, Washington DC, Bureau of Labor Statistics, 1988.

tunities for advancement and a good measure of job security. At the same time, however, many of these jobs are low-paying and unstable, and between 20 and 30 per cent are part-time positions. In any case, service sector jobs on average are lower paying than jobs in the manufacturing sector, and since 1978 income inequality has increased more rapidly in services than in manufacturing. This rise in income inequality in services can be accounted for in substantial measure by two factors: the increase in the number of part-time workers, and the drop in the annual wages of such workers. The overall level of income inequality increased so sharply in the seven years after 1978 that by 1985 it had returned to 1965 levels (Tilly et al., 1986). (Interestingly, the entrance of large numbers of women, youth and minorities into the workforce is not significantly linked to the increasing variation in service income distribution.) Finally, wage increases have been considerably lower in services (sectors such as retailing, and finance, insurance, and real estate) than in the more heavily unionised mining, construction, transportation and public utilities sectors (see table 2.6).

*The decline in unionisation*

No single factor explains the magnitude of the decline in unionisation in the private sector of the United States economy since 1960. Instead, most researchers now agree that a complete explanation must take into account changes in the structure of the economy, increased management resistance to unionisation, increased management innovation in personnel and human resource policies, and the failure of the labour movement to develop new organising and representational strategies that appeal to workers in the growth occupations and sectors (Farber,

**Table 2.6 Average hourly earnings of production and non-supervisory workers on private non-agricultural payrolls**

|                                   | 1971 | 1974 | 1977 | 1980 | 1983  | 1987  |
|-----------------------------------|------|------|------|------|-------|-------|
| Total private                     | 3.45 | 4.24 | 5.25 | 6.66 | 8.02  | 8.98  |
| Mining                            | 4.06 | 5.23 | 6.94 | 9.17 | 11.27 | 12.45 |
| Construction                      | 5.69 | 6.81 | 8.10 | 9.94 | 11.92 | 12.66 |
| Manufacturing                     | 3.57 | 4.42 | 5.68 | 7.27 | 8.83  | 9.91  |
| Public utilities and transportation | 4.21 | 5.41 | 6.99 | 8.87 | 10.80 | 12.01 |
| Retail                            | 2.60 | 3.14 | 3.85 | 4.88 | 5.74  | 6.12  |
| Finance, insurance and real estate | 3.22 | 3.77 | 4.54 | 5.79 | 7.29  | 8.76  |
| Services                          | 3.04 | 3.75 | 4.65 | 5.85 | 7.30  | 8.47  |

*Source: Handbook of Labor Statistics*, Washington DC, Bureau of Labor Statistics, 1988.

1985; Dickens, 1983; Weiler, 1983; Dickens & Leonard, 1985; Freeman & Medoff, 1984; Kochan, McKersie & Chalykoff, 1986; Kochan, Katz & McKersie, 1986). There is a vast and growing literature on this subject, which we need not review here. For our purposes, it is sufficient to note that all of the causal forces listed above have played important roles in the decline in union membership from 35 per cent of the labour force in the mid-1950s to approximately 17 per cent in 1986.

The decline of the more heavily unionised industries is paralleled by a number of other developments that are also detrimental to the union movement. Many plants have cut costs by increasing their reliance on subcontracting and part-time and temporary employment. For example, 30 per cent of General Motors components are now produced by subcontractors; for Ford, this figure is 50 per cent; and for the Chrysler Corporation—the third largest auto maker in the United States—that number is about 66 per cent. Each of these firms would prefer to increase outsourcing in the future. However, contractual provisions negotiated with the United Auto Workers in 1982 and 1984 impose significant costs on these auto makers if workers are displaced by outsourcing. Similar trends are visible in other industries. In the clothing industry some employers have been able to shift the burden of insecurity onto part-time and temporary workers, which has been made easier by recent government legislation lifting long-standing restrictions on 'home work'. Taken together, these trends tend to lower unionisation by creating a new workforce with interests that differ from those of the existing union membership, or which may be considerably more difficult to organise.

The difficulty of organising new workers is enhanced also by employers' unfair labour practices, which have increased sharply since the early 1970s (Freeman & Medoff, 1984). While the number of National Labor Relations Board union representation elections remained relatively constant between 1960 and 1980 (around 9000 per year), the number of unfair labour practice charges against employers increased fourfold in that period. Furthermore, in 1980 one in twenty workers who favoured bringing in a union were fired from their jobs. In 1981 and 1983 (the last year for which the figures are available) the number of charges of unfair labour practices dropped slightly to about 40 000, but the number of elections conducted has dropped to about 4500—about half of 1980 levels (*Labor Law Report*, 1987).

As noted by Freeman and Medoff (1984), the increase in the measure of employer resistance to unionisation is not difficult to explain. Both the incentives and the ability to resist unionisation increased over the course of the 1970s. The motivation increased because the union/non-union wage and fringe benefit differentials increased from the 10 to 15 per cent range of the 1960s to a range of 20 to 30 per cent in the 1970s. Moreover, the penalties for employer violations of the recognition principles of the Wagner Act are quite mild, and their imposition is often delayed for years after the violation occurred. More importantly, illegal management opposition to unionisation campaigns has been shown to increase significantly the probability that the union will be defeated in the legally prescribed procedure for election as the workers' bargaining agent, or that it will fail to achieve an initial contract (collective agreement) with the employer (Cooke, 1985). Thus, over the past decade employers learned that the costs of unionisation were increasing at the same time as the cost of avoiding unionisation through both legal and illegal means was declining.

The combination of the decline of the (highly unionised) mature manufacturing sectors, the continued increase in both 'low quality' and 'high quality' service jobs, growing income inequality, persistently high unemployment, the increasing resort to 'secondary' (subcontracted, part-time and temporary) employment and, importantly, the continued decline of unionisation, have now come to place tremendous pressures on the decentralised and collective bargaining-oriented nature of the New Deal industrial relations system. Private experimentation and innovation in labour–management relations—developments that deviate from the traditional pattern—have grown quickly in the 1980s, but it is not clear how successful or permanent such efforts will be. We will now consider the effects of all these environmental changes on employers, unions, and labour–management relations.

## The collapse of the New Deal model

### The effects on collective bargaining

The globalisation of markets and structural adjustments within the American economy have combined to make it more and more difficult for unions to 'take wages out of competition' through collective bargaining by standardising costs among United States producers. Table 2.8 shows the sharp decline in the average annual wage adjustment in major collective bargaining agreements (including over 1000 workers) since 1970. The increases conceded in the first year of long-term contracts dropped sharply from 9.8 per cent to 3.8 per cent in 1982, to 2.6 per cent in 1983, and down to 2.3 per cent in 1985 (see table 2.8). (At the same time, the employment cost index has increased by about a third since 1981; see table 2.7.) The drop in wage increases in 1982 and 1983 was connected with the severe recession in those years. In 1983, of 3.1 million workers covered by major union–employer contracts, 0.8 million received either a wage cut or no wage increase at all (Current Wage Developments, April 1984). (United States unit labour costs are still quite high, by OECD standards; see table 2.9.)

**Table 2.7 Employment cost index civilian workforce, 1981–88**

| June 1981 | 100.0 |
|---|---|
| December 1981 | 104.5 |
| December 1982 | 111.3 |
| December 1983 | 117.8 |
| December 1984 | 123.9 |
| December 1985 | 129.2 |
| December 1986 | 133.8 |
| December 1987 | 139.0 |
| December 1988 | 145.5 |

Source: Department of Labor, Bureau of Labor Statistics, News, Washington DC, January 1982 to May 1988.

Our analysis of the trends in wage determination in major collective bargaining units indicates that wage settlements averaged 1 to 3 per cent below the settlements that would have resulted had collective bargaining continued to follow the wage patterns of the 1970s. The largest deviations from earlier patterns were observed in the most centralised bargaining structures, and in those that relied most heavily on pattern bargaining (Kochan, Katz & McKersie, 1986). This again illustrates the fact that increased product market competition, combined with declining

**8 Changes in contract settlements 1970–87 (contracts affecting over 1000 workers)**

| | 1970 | 1972 | 1974 | 1976 | 1978 | 1980 | 1981 | 1982 | 1983 | 1984 | 1985 | 1986 |
|---|---|---|---|---|---|---|---|---|---|---|---|---|
| increase | 10.9 | 7.3 | 9.8 | 8.4 | 7.6 | 9.5 | 9.8 | 3.8 | 2.6 | 2.4 | 2.3 | 1.1 |
| over life of contract | 8.9 | 6.4 | 7.3 | 6.4 | 6.4 | 7.1 | 7.9 | 3.6 | 2.8 | 2.4 | 2.7 | 1.6 |

ırrent Wage Developments, Washington DC, Bureau of Labor Statistics, 1970–87.

**9 Comparative unit labor costs (1977 constant US dollars)**

| | 1960 | 1970 | 1974 | 1979 | 1981 | 1983 | 1985 |
|---|---|---|---|---|---|---|---|
| ates | 58.7 | 70.9 | 84.1 | 117.0 | 140.1 | 144.5 | 145.0 |
| | 41.7 | 46.8 | 74.5 | 135.5 | 132.2 | 112.9 | 102.6 |
| | 25.9 | 42.9 | 79.1 | 135.9 | 124.9 | 113.4 | 98.6 |
| | 30.1 | 41.1 | 65.1 | 112.9 | 115.4 | 80.4 | 79.1 |
| ngdom | 44.4 | 54.4 | 80.1 | 163.9 | 203.1 | 159.4 | 147.3 |

onthly Labor Review, Washington DC, Bureau of Labor Statistics, February, 1988.

levels of unionisation, produced a fundamental shift in wage setting institutions and in collective bargaining outcomes in the early 1980s.

Some part of the decline in the amount of wage increase in new collective bargaining contracts can be attributed to a spate of labour 'concessions', beginning in 1979 with the highly publicised bailout of Chrysler Corporation by government loan guarantees and employee wage concessions. Labour concessions, including wage and benefit cuts and freezes and productivity-enhancing work rule changes, can be found in fully 44 per cent of all major collective bargaining contracts negoti-ated in 1982 and 1983 (Cullen, 1985). While those two years were marked by unusually deep recession (some say depression), concessions have been made since then, in more stable years, and in plants and firms that are still earning substantial profits. In airlines, for example, unions were forced to grant concessions even with the financially strongest carriers in the industry (such as American and United Airlines), and even after the end of the recession (Cappelli, 1986). More recently, firms have begun to give lump sum bonuses rather than increases that are permanently built into the wage and benefit base. Although the data on these bonuses are still quite limited, the Bureau of Labor Statistics estimates that in 1986 as many as 40 per cent of major contract settle-ments provided lump sum or other kinds of bonuses in lieu of increases in base wages.

Wages are, however, still relatively high in the United States. For instance, table 2.10 shows that production workers in manufacturing still earn about as much as or more than similar workers in all the other countries in this study. Moreover, the downward pressure on American wages is likely to continue, given the comparatively low wages of the newly industrialising countries in the Pacific Basin, Mexico, and Latin America. Table 2.11 presents data on average hourly compensation costs as a percentage of United States wages for selected countries that are often attractive to American firms making product sourcing and plant location decisions. Given the wide disparities in labour costs, it is clear that United States workers and unions will continue to find it difficult, if not impossible, to 'take wages out of competition' by tradi-tional means. New strategies for encouraging American employers to compete on some basis other than labour cost will be required if the erosion of American manufacturing jobs and workers' incomes is to be stemmed.

Because the United States Department of Labor does not collect contract settlement data for units of less than 1000 workers, it is difficult to state precisely the extent and nature of concessions over the past half dozen years. However, another indication of the relative prevalence of labour concessions was the widespread emergence of so-called 'two-tier wage scales' in the early and middle years of the decade. These wage structures create a 'B Scale' (as opposed to 'A Scale') or 'lower-tier' wage

| | 6.35 | 7.59 | 9.07 | 10.95 | 12.26 | 12.40 | 12.82 | 13.09 | 13.46 |
| | 4.58 | 5.31 | 7.85 | 8.16 | 7.66 | 7.48 | 7.71 | 10.45 | 12.42 |
| | 6.19 | 7.80 | 11.29 | 10.54 | 10.41 | 9.44 | 9.60 | 13.44 | 16.87 |
| gdom | 3.26 | 3.36 | 5.50 | 7.13 | 6.48 | 5.88 | 6.14 | 7.46 | 8.97 |
| | 7.18 | 8.88 | 11.33 | 11.80 | 8.97 | 9.17 | 9.66 | 12.23 | 15.17 |

onthly Labor Review, Bureau of Labor Statistics, Washington DC, February 1988.

**11 Comparative hourly compensation costs for manufacturing production workers (US = 100)**

| | 1975 | 1977 | 1979 | 1981 | 1983 | 1985 | 1986 | 1987 |
|---|---|---|---|---|---|---|---|---|
| ates | 92 | 95 | 86 | 87 | 92 | 85 | 84 | 89 |
| | 14 | 15 | 16 | 15 | 11 | 10 | 12 | 11 |
| | 31 | 23 | 27 | 34 | 15 | 16 | 11 | 12 |
| | 12 | 14 | 15 | 14 | 13 | 16 | 14 | 16 |
| | 48 | 53 | 61 | 57 | 41 | 40 | 73 | 83 |
| ng | 13 | 12 | 14 | 17 | 18 | 19 | n.a. | 17 |
| e | 6 | 7 | 9 | 11 | 11 | 11 | 13 | 10 |

s Bureau of Labor Statistics, Washington DC, February 1989

rate for new hires, thereby cutting future labour costs while avoiding cutting into the wages of workers who must ratify the contract. In 1984 only 4 per cent of all non-construction contracts included two-tier provisions, but by 1985 that figure had doubled, and in 1986 10 per cent of non-construction contracts included them. In certain industries, the two-tier provisions became widespread. In airlines, for example, 70 per cent of all 1986 contracts included a two-tier scale, up from 62 per cent in the previous year and 35 per cent in 1984 (*Daily Labor Report*, February 1987). Two-tier wage scales have also been fairly common in railways and in the retail food sector. By 1988, however, these arrangements had become increasingly unpopular and began to decline in frequency. Instead, an increasing number of firms and unions negotiated lump-sum bonuses that did not permanently increase the wage structure.

The growth of labour concessions such as wage cuts and two-tier wage scales has the effect of increasing local contract diversity, since such contract changes tend to be negotiated at plants and firms in a particularly unstable financial condition. Thus, a national union may have some locals (union branches) whose contracts still resemble an industry-wide pattern (or perhaps a firm-wide standard contract), and other locals that are forced to alter the contract significantly in the light of firm-specific or plant-specific economic problems. Bargaining in the auto, rubber, airline and meatpacking industries (among others), once based on patterns that helped workers achieve steady contract increases, now proceeds on a firm-by-firm and plant-by-plant basis. In 1986 the major steel companies bargained separately with the Steelworkers Union for the first time in over twenty years, and they have since continued to bargain separately. Industry-level bargaining, once conducted among the union(s) and employers throughout an entire economic sector, is now a rare event (Freedman & Fulmer, 1982). The determination of wages and working conditions is more and more linked to the performance of decentralised business units. Workers in the same industry, and even in different plants within the same firm, have been delegated significantly different wages and working conditions. Local collective bargaining contracts increasingly contain 'riders' modifying and adapting the national contract to the specific conditions of different plants and local business units (visible, for example, in trucking).

Another device for increasing labour-cost flexibility is contingent compensation, such as profit sharing and employee share ownership. The workers at many airline and trucking concerns, for instance, were granted shares in lieu of wage increases (and in most cases on top of wage cuts) during the early 1980s, when the impact of deregulation was so sharply felt in both of those industries. In some cases, the companies in question have gone bankrupt despite labour concessions, making the shares worthless, and leaving no profits to share. In other cases, however, the workers have materially aided the companies involved. At Western Airlines, for example, workers took substantial pay cuts in return for profit sharing and share ownership, thereby, perhaps, enabling the company to survive. Although the carrier is now owned by Delta Airlines, a larger, mainly non-union, company, the workers at least were able to maintain their jobs, restore some of their concessions through profit sharing, and see the value of their shares increase almost fivefold. At the time of the merger with Delta, most Western employees recovered an estimated 75 to 90 per cent of the wages they gave up in concessions (Wever, 1986). Similar share plans have been negotiated at other troubled airline carriers and trucking companies.

Whatever the effect on job security, the increase in the scope and degree of local contract diversity has produced sometimes bitter power struggles and political conflicts between, on the one hand, local unions —for whom flexibility and diversity are often associated with survival (as well as organisational autonomy)—and on the other, national union leaders—whose central authority and co-ordinating and standardising functions are threatened by this diversity. Conflicts of this nature have emerged over the last five years in such major unions as the Air Line Pilots Association, the International Association of Machinists and Aerospace Workers, the United Rubber Workers, the United Food and Commercial Workers and the United Auto Workers. For example, the Pilots Association has intervened in local contract negotiations to minimise particular kinds of concessions, and the Association of Machinists placed a local union in trusteeship, taking over all local functions, because of the local's willingness to grant contract concessions.

Partly because of these organisational struggles, and largely because of the more general decline in labour's power and influence, there have been relatively few strikes or lockouts since the beginning of this decade. Although the Bureau of Labor Statistics no longer collects the data needed to determine the total number of strikes occurring in a given year, trends in strikes involving more than 1000 workers are available, and these clearly suggest that industrial action has declined sharply in this decade. For example, the number of stoppages fell from 424 in 1974 to 145 in 1981, and 61 in 1985 (see table 2.12). Though the number rose to 69 in 1986, it again fell (to 46, the lowest figure of the decade) in 1987. The number of lockouts in 1986 (work stoppages initiated by employers), at 41, was also up 44 per cent from 1985 (*Daily Labor Report*, March 1987).

A number of highly visible and particularly prolonged and bitter labour disputes have occurred in the 1980s. Strikes at Continental Airlines and at Phelps Dodge (a large employer in the copper industry) symbolise the stakes involved. In both cases large wage cuts were imposed and at Phelps Dodge the dispute ended only with the

## 12 Work stoppages involving over 1000 workers

| | 1971 | 1974 | 1977 | 1980 | 1983 | 1985 | 1986 |
|---|---|---|---|---|---|---|---|
| of stoppages | 298 | 424 | 298 | 187 | 81 | 61 | 69 |
| of workers involved ('000) | 2 516 | 1 796 | 1 212 | 795 | 909 | 323 | 533 |
| of days idle ('000) | 35 538 | 31 809 | 21 774 | 20 844 | 17 461 | 7079 | 11 861 |
| ge of estimated days lost | 0.19 | 0.16 | 0.11 | 0.09 | 0.08 | 0.03 | 0.05 |

Handbook of Labor Statistics, Washington DC, Bureau of Labor Statistics, 1985; Daily Labor Report, Washington DC, Bureau of Labor S March 1988.

de-certification of the unions. In 1986–87, a lockout involving the Steelworkers and the USX Corporation, the industry's largest employer, illustrated an increasingly typical conflict. The company's management style was distant, and its business strategy was increasingly focused on expansion in non-steel areas and on increasing the use of subcontracting to reduce its labour costs. Meanwhile, the union was determined to reject any concessions to the company unless these were accompanied by a variety of new industrial relations programmes designed to increase communications between the parties and expand the scope of their relationship in the long term. These included profit sharing, enhanced job security against subcontracting, and a broadly co-operative forum for labour–management discussions. In other words, the fundamental industrial relations goals of the two parties were completely contradictory. In the end, the union settled on terms that did not achieve any significant change in the company's business strategies or labour relations policies.

Thus, the role of the strike has also changed in important ways in this decade. What once was an application of union bargaining power to achieve marginal improvements in employers' wage offers has now become a defensive battle over the basic principles, and sometimes basic survival, of the bargaining relationship.

*Union involvement in strategic and workplace management*

Measures to increase communication and co-operation between labour and management have generally occurred at two levels of the labour–management relationship other than that of traditional collective bargaining. First, in some cases unions have been involved in strategic management decision making (at a level above the normal reach of collective bargaining). Such involvement has taken the form of informal information-sharing and regular meetings (such as between Xerox and the Amalgamated Clothing and Textile Workers Union), and sometimes formal union involvement through seats on boards of directors (for instance, at several airline carriers and trucking companies) or permanent positions on plant management or steering committees (as at General Motors' Fiero plant, where the workers are represented by the United Auto Workers).

In 1989 another major conflict occurred when the machinists, pilots, and flight attendants went on strike against Eastern Airlines, demanding a change in ownership of the company as their price for making concessions needed to avoid bankruptcy. The eventual outcome will close an important chapter in the labour history of the 1980s.

Sometimes unions have become involved in the development of new mechanisms to regulate and facilitate the introduction and implementation of new technologies in a variety of sectors, ranging from communications and defence contracting to basic manufacturing. The Association of Machinists at Boeing, for example, has been able to gain some increase in leverage at the collective bargaining table. Union influence in the introduction of new technologies (and concerning the effects of such technologies on jobs) has been granted in return for labour concessions in some other area, such as flexibility in the utilisation of workers. Union involvement in technological decision making has, however, spread to only a limited number of settings, and it generally focuses only on adjusting to the effects of new technology. Moreover, union participation in the planning and design phases of technological change is still quite rare and experimental in nature.

Indeed, union participation in strategic management decision making is still limited in scope and impact, and highly experimental. Yet these limited experiments can have profound consequences, since they represent a fundamental departure from the New Deal idea that it was management's prerogative to make these decisions without union involvement. Given the range of choices contemporary firms face in determining their competitive strategies, investment decisions, location decisions, product sourcing, technology policies, and so on, and given the effects that decisions taken at this level have on employees' welfare, we expect labour representatives to continue to press for expanded influence at this level. However, to do so unions will have to overcome strong managerial resistance to the expansion of labour's role, and break with the long-standing business unionist principle of avoiding involvement in managerial affairs. Thus, while experimentation with new forms of participation and information sharing over strategic issues is likely to continue, such developments will continue to be the focus of considerable debate and conflict, both within and between labour and management groups.

A second new form of labour involvement in management decision making takes place on the shopfloor or at the workplace (below the level of collective bargaining). Experiments of this kind include Quality of Worklife programmes and autonomous work groups (as between the Clothing and Textile Workers and Xerox) and many less extensive programmes directly involving workers in decisions about how they do their jobs. While the initial focus of quality of worklife programmes initiated in the 1970s was to improve the climate of the workplace and the satisfaction and motivation of the workforce, more recently these efforts have been aimed more directly at increasing productivity and enhancing quality. Indeed, our own studies have shown that unless worker participation programmes address the basic economic needs of employers as well as enhancing the economic security and job satisfaction of the employees, they are destined to occupy comparatively marginal status (Kochan, Katz & Mower, 1984).

It is clear, however, that only a few comprehensive and lasting programmes exist for involving unions in such joint activities. One reason for this is that meaningful and sustainable participation efforts require a deep commitment on the part of both labour and management to co-operate at every level of industrial relations (MIT Industrial Relations Section, 1987). Based on the case studies our research group has tracked, we have concluded that unless participation and co-operation expand gradually over time to encompass broader issues, and unless they are reinforced through collective bargaining activities and at strategic levels of decision making, these experiments are unlikely to be institutionalised into continuing industrial relations practices. The most successful of these cases are ones in which the parties have moved beyond narrow Quality of Worklife programmes to pursue problem solving and participation processes that address more general issues. For example, in a number of cases we have been following, the parties have begun to make significant changes in the organisation of work and the use of new technology. In others, joint efforts have produced new forms of work organisation that emphasise the use of teams, fewer job classifications, and new compensation systems. But extensive use of participation and continuous union–management co-operation is, to date, found only in a minority of bargaining relationships in the United States.

## The range of management strategies

The ability of any union to become involved in workplace and strategic management decisions is strongly influenced by management's willingness to 'let the union in' to these new areas of industrial relations activity. In the United States, the range of managerial strategies in this respect is wide. Three typical and quite distinct approaches can be identified.

The first kind of management strategy towards increasing the scope of labour–management relations is generally found in companies that are heavily or entirely unionised, and that have experienced moderate to strong increases in competitive pressures in the 1980s. In these cases the costs to management of union avoidance are high, and therefore the firm needs co-operation from its union(s) if it is to meet its competitive challenges. Thus these employers often seek a (limited) partnership with the union(s). A typical example of such a relationship is that between the United Auto Workers and General Motors Corporation.

Since 1973, the United Auto Workers and General Motors have expanded what started out as narrow quality of worklife programmes in specific plants to encompass a broader array of joint activities. In 1982, for example, a joint Auto Workers – General Motors Human Resource Centre was established to administer a variety of worker and union leadership training and education activities. In a growing number of

General Motors plants the union and the company have experimented with new team-based work systems that are designed to increase flexibility. In 1983 the company and the union began jointly to plan for the design of the new Saturn Division to produce small cars in Tennessee. The industrial relations system in this new division calls for voluntary recognition of the union and participation of union representatives at all levels of the organisation, from the shopfloor to the top executive group and board of directors. This new level of union involvement is paralleled by a new compensation system, a team form of work organisation, and a commitment to the principles of co-operation and consensus decision making. An equally radical departure from the traditional New Deal model is found in the Auto Workers–Toyota–General Motors joint venture plant called the New United Motors Manufacturing Incorporated (NUMMI), in Fremont, California. Similar, but perhaps more limited experiments with a new industrial relations model are found in Ford and Chrysler, as well as a limited number of other highly unionised firms in the United States.

The second typical management strategy is quite different from the approach at General Motors. This second approach might be termed the successful union-avoidance strategy. Large and well-known companies approaching this model include International Business Machines (IBM) and Delta Airlines. The non-union (or union-avoidance) strategy is often, but not always, associated with a low level of unionisation throughout the industry. For example, the high-technology computer industry in which IBM is the leader is barely unionised at all. In such a sector the incentive to remain non-unionised is extremely high because of the need (among other things) to maintain flexibility and labour-cost competitiveness.

Delta Airlines, however, faces a somewhat different situation. This company operates in an industry that has long been (and continues to be) highly unionised. Although it is by no means entirely non-union, Delta has used a number of methods to keep unions out, including paying the highest wages in the industry, and aggressively resisting unions that have tried to organise portions of the workforce. Over the years, Delta has developed a reputation for being a leader in human resource management techniques that are associated with high levels of job satisfaction and company loyalty among many of its employees. Moreover, Delta, like IBM and many other companies following the non-union model, have worked hard to provide their workers with something approaching lifetime job security. The promise of such employment stability can serve as a strong impetus for employees to reject unionisation bids.

While few other non-union firms are as innovative in their human resource management policies as are Delta or IBM, enough non-union employers have adopted enough elements of this model to contribute to the decline in unionisation in the United States (Kochan, McKersie & Chalykoff, 1986). There is little reason to expect any significant change in the policies of these firms or in the results they achieve.

The third type of management approach to unions is found in cases where the company in question has some significant portion, but not all, of its facilities unionised. Examples include General Electric as well as the vast majority of other large, multidivisional American firms. In these cases management faces a choice. It can target corporate resources at its non-union facilities and to expanding in areas where the union(s) can be avoided. Alternatively, it can reinvest in and retrofit existing union facilities and 'let the union in' to new facilities on the basis of increased labour participation as well as a competitive and flexible set of production processes. The latter choice is clearly more difficult to make when competitors are entirely non-union, and the prevailing union/non-union labour-cost differential is high.

Firms in this category generally have been successful in separating their union and non-union establishments and strategies. Few union leaders have been willing to co-operate with management in existing establishments under these conditions, however. How this group of firms and union leaders responds in the future will have a critical effect on the type of industrial relations system that evolves in the United States in the years ahead.

## Changes within the union movement

The pressures outlined above, and the fundamental changes in industrial relations they have produced in the 1980s, have plunged the labour movement into what promises to be a sustained period of debate over its future strategies. The stakes involved in these debates appear to be every bit as profound as those of the 1930s between advocates of industrial unionism and those who favoured maintenance of craft unionist organising principles. In any case, it is clear that some new strategies for organising and for representing American workers will be needed if the labour movement is to reverse its long-term decline in membership, and to regain its reputation as a stimulus to innovation in working conditions.

One step in the direction of suggesting a broader agenda for future union activities was taken by the AFL–CIO's Committee On the Future of Work (1985). This committee was established by the AFL–CIO executive council in 1982, and charged with the task of evaluating the current state of the labour movement's strategies for promoting the economic and social interests of American workers. It brought together the presidents of about twenty major unions with AFL–CIO officers and staff to analyse data and discuss evidence on the state of the labour movement. The committee issued a lengthy report in 1985 suggesting possible strategies for the revitalisation of the labour movement. These include the possible extension of associate membership status (an individual membership option for workers who are not in a formal collective bargaining unit), financial and other services (designed to broaden the functions the union performs for its members), and a variety of more familiar ideas, including the use of 'corporate campaigns' (designed to neutralise employer opposition in organising drives or in contract disputes) and more positive media coverage. While the committee's suggestions have sparked considerable interest and internal debate, many of its ideas are difficult to implement. The net effects of the committee's efforts will not, therefore, be clear for some time to come. At this point, however, it is fair to say that there is no consensus among the top union leaderships in the country, within the AFL–CIO or among local union leaders as to a new set of strategies for the United States labour movement. Instead, we are likely to see a prolonged period of experimentation, change, internal political debate and conflict that will be consistent with the decentralised structure of the labour movement and the American industrial relations system.

The lack of consensus within the labour movement as to the appropriate line of action is one of many factors contributing to the limited diffusion of labour–management co-operation schemes in the United States. As noted above, no such arrangements have been established at the national level. There have been a few isolated cases of (usually short-term) union involvement in industry level productivity-enhancing programmes, involving for example the International Masonry Institute and the Joint Labor–Management Committee in the Retail Food Industry. However, the credo of both unions and managements in the United States has historically been to 'let management manage', so most managers as well as union leaders still approach these joint initiatives with a great deal of caution. Indeed, many of these experiments have been initiated primarily (or at least partly) in response to severe economic pressures, where union involvement in management decision making has been granted only in return for labour concessions. Sustaining and diffusing these joint activities will require that union and management leaders make the strategic choice to depart from these traditions.

A few unions have begun to take steps in the direction of re-educating their local leaderships and members in such novel forms of strategic planning and joint participation with management outside the arena of collective bargaining. One example of such a programme is an extensive and jointly funded United Auto Workers/General Motors Paid Education Leave programme, in which the entire General Motors local union leadership is being sent through four weeks of training concerning the economic, political and industrial relations challenges of the day. Not surprisingly, many unions (including the United Auto Workers) are undergoing a period of intense debate, intra-organisational conflict and political factionalism around a variety of potential strategic adjustment approaches. Training of this sort is clearly the exception rather than the rule.

## Government policy

Government labour policy is currently subject to the same measure of internal debate, uncertainty and contradiction as are the strategies of labour and management. On the one hand, labour policy in general and the National Labor Relations Board in particular have taken a decided turn toward a more conservative and pro-business posture, consistent with the philosophies of the Reagan and Bush administrations (Levitan et al., 1986; Morris, 1987). At the same time, within one branch of the Department of Labor some major new initiatives have supported innovations in industrial relations. The Bureau of Labor–Management Relations and Cooperative Programs has become increasingly committed to promoting labour–management co-operation, and to developing a network of professionals who share an interest in establishing a new agenda to include a prominent role for organised labour. This, however, is the extent of government involvement in the development of constructive adjustment mechanisms in the area of labour–management relations.

In another move, in the wake of a Congressional impasse, the Secretary of Labor established a labour–management task force to explore policies for workers permanently displaced because of plant shutdowns or large-scale layoffs (discussed briefly above). The task force recommended the enactment of a new US$900 million programme of enhanced training and labour market services for displaced workers. But while members of this group were able to agree that advance notice of plant closing is desirable, the management representatives could not reach consensus on whether such provisions should be required by law (Lovell, 1986). As noted above, Congress did enact a compromise Bill requiring sixty days advance notice of a plant closing and providing funds for helping workers affected to adjust to job loss. A general interest in a variety of labour and employment policy issues has again surfaced in the Congress, after a prolonged period of lack of attention to these problems. Hearings and debates are currently under way on such issues as the minimum wage, health insurance, and a variety of aspects of trade policies. This increased interest is largely due to the fact that the Democratic Party, as well as having a majority in the House of Representatives, regained a majority of the seats in the Senate in 1986. Labour and employment issues are at least temporarily elevated to a higher position on the national agenda. Whether this results in a visible or significant shift in the content of national labour or employment policy still remains to be seen.

Some limited adjustments to structural change have been undertaken by the government. The Job Training Partnership Act 1981 created the framework for a decentralised set of mechanisms for the development of local employment policies. The Act was designed to allow leaders in local government, industry and education to co-operate in the management of technological transition, thus minimising workers' job loss and displacement. But while the principle underlying these efforts is sound, and the goals are broadly shared, funding of the Act was reduced to only about 50 per cent of annual employment and training expenditures during much of the 1970s (Levitan et al., 1986). As such, its real potential efficacy has not been tested and its concrete value cannot be judged. Indeed, the federal government's General Accounting Office (GAO) admits to the very limited effects of the programme, citing that only about 7 per cent of those eligible for assistance have been able to avail themselves of the needed services (*Daily Labor Report*, March 1987).

## Conclusion

Whatever adjustments to industrial relations may occur in the short run, it is highly likely that the unionised percentage of the United States workforce will continue to decline as it has over the past few decades. The internationalisation of the United States economy has its severest impact on sectors that are most highly unionised. The movement of capital (either out of the country or from union to non-union establishments or divisions of American firms) will continue to have major effects on union employment (Bluestone & Harrison, 1982). The growth sectors, mostly in services, tend to create jobs that the labour movement has so far failed to organise, in part as a result of prevailing labour laws and labour's traditional organising strategies. The diffusion of new technology will continue to reduce the labour content required for many manufacturing processes. To avoid further reductions, union jobs would require a combination of economic growth fuelled by product innovation in manufacturing firms and service sectors, and new, successful union organising efforts.

While the AFL–CIO and some unions have identified a series of new measures for organising traditionally unorganised workers, few of these ideas have been implemented in practice, and many of them are the subject of much controversy within the labour movement. For instance, the AFL–CIO's consideration of associate membership is quite controversial. While this technique may increase membership, some claim that it will divide the ranks of workers and undermine worker solidarity.

Indeed, controversy characterises other issues touching the labour movement as well. Conflicts between local and national unions concerning the appropriate response to employer demands for concessions have flared up in the International Association of Machinists in 1982 and 1983, and in the Air Line Pilots Association in 1983 and 1984. In both cases the central leadership was less willing to make concessions than the local leadership. But in other cases (involving, for example, the United Food and Commercial Workers and the United Auto Workers, among others) the situation has been reversed. More subtle conflicts have emerged in major unions like the Communications Workers and the Auto Workers regarding the appropriate extent and nature of flexible approaches to work organisation and contingent wage mechanisms (some of which, as at General Motors' highly publicised Saturn plant, represent significant departures from traditional shopfloor labour–management relations and divisions of labour). There is no question that there is a substantial amount of controversy and debate within the labour movement as to the validity and desirability of various experiments with non-traditional labour–management relations.

Nonetheless, as noted above, quite a bit of change and innovation in these areas has already occurred. In a typically decentralised fashion —but also in a wide range of settings—unions and managements (and, sometimes, local governments) have engaged in new methods of dealing with each other in the process of negotiations, in shopfloor or workplace relations, and in the domain of strategic managerial decision making. In the 1970s such developments were sporadic and often not sustained. In the early 1980s they were often identified with the need to respond to severe economic crisis. But as we near the end of the decade, some of these developments appear to have taken on a more permanent quality, especially where they are integrated into a deeper transformation of management's business and technological strategies. In certain industries (as, for example, in auto manufacture), the question is no longer whether to adopt such innovations, but which innovations to adopt, and at what pace to adopt them.

It is still, however, entirely unclear whether these kinds of industrial relations changes can be diffused to permeate the economy and transform the fundamental nature of the relationship between the parties. Indeed, although systematic quantitative data are not available, our impression is that the rate of such diffusion may have slowed somewhat since the earlier part of this decade. The extreme decentralisation of American industrial relations and the historical reluctance of the government (especially at the federal level) actively and visibly to articulate a clear policy on these issues may inhibit the diffusion and institutionalisation of these developments. Therefore, we believe that these two features of American industrial relations—the decentralised locus of labour–management adjustments, and the *laissez-faire* approach of the government—need to change as necessary (but not sufficient) preconditions to the broader application of the developments discussed above. Put differently, local unions and managements need the support of their national counterparts and of the government in their efforts to adjust.

It will be difficult for many employers to make the necessary change. To begin with, top corporate executives will have to commit their firms to long-term business strategies capable of maintaining employment in the United States, rather than taking advantage of lower labour costs in other countries. Firms that do so will need to re-educate their managers to think of unions as institutions that (among other things) contribute to the productive process. The historical aversion to unions among United States managers will render this shift in outlook and strategy difficult. Indeed, all indications are that the current level of anti-unionism is more intense than it has been at any other time since the Great Depression.

Moreover, there is little doubt that management has been the dominant actor in forcing changes in American industrial relations in recent years. This trend began with more aggressive and sophisticated strategies to avoid unions in the 1960s and 1970s, and then continued in the 1980s with the introduction of changes in collective bargaining. This proactive posture on the part of management is likely to prevail at least in the near future, given the sustained competitive pressures and technological changes occurring in world markets, and given the relative weakness of American unions. The central question is what directions will managerial industrial relations initiatives take in the years ahead?

Given the historical aversion to unions that is so deeply ingrained in the culture of the American managerial community, there is no doubt that those firms that are currently not unionised, like those partially unionised firms that see viable opportunities for avoiding further unionisation, will continue to follow union avoidance strategies. No significant changes in management strategies are therefore likely in such firms. Likewise, firms with very high percentages of their labour force unionised that lack viable non-union options are likely to continue to press aggressively for changes and innovations in collective bargaining and industrial relations, along the model presented by General Motors and the United Auto Workers. They are likely to do this in concert at all levels of their labour–management relationship.

The pivotal settings will be those cases that fall in between these two extremes. Will partially unionised firms be willing to adopt policies that expand and sustain innovations that require a broader role for unions? Or will they increase their efforts to limit union influence, and channel more resources into union avoidance? The latter course is more likely, unless unions are able to raise the costs of pursuing this route and to promote and demonstrate the value of industrial relations changes that entail broader forms of worker and union participation at the workplace, in bargaining, and in strategic decision making. We believe the future of management policies in these partially unionised firms could be influenced by the strategies adopted by the unions that currently represent their employees. The more these unions cling to their traditional roles within the New Deal system, the more freedom and incentives management will have to pursue a union-avoidance strategy. On the other hand, the more aggressively unions promote new forms of participation in strategic and workplace issues, the more directly they will force employers to choose between greater co-operation, flexibility, and innovation versus greater confrontation and resistance to change.

Taking this latter course will not be easy for organised labour. Unions still face difficult strategic questions of their own. The need for political strategies has become evident with the increasing failure of traditional economic approaches. Still, questions and controversies abound as to which political strategies should be adopted, and what portion of the labour movement's scarce resources should be allocated to these endeavours. Important pieces of the collective bargaining process itself must also be preserved, in order for unions to be able to exert sufficient leverage to shape the new and non-traditional aspects of the labour–management relationship.

Much of the impetus for change will need to come from the unions, for it is the labour movement that faces the most immediate incentives to change the nature of United States industrial relations. Even assuming a vibrant and creative labour response to the current difficulties, however, it is not at all clear whether the changes enumerated above will (or how they would) come to pass. It is quite possible, indeed likely, that things will go on much as they have for most of this decade, with union membership continuing to decline. After all, the turmoil associated with the deep recession of the early 1980s appears to have passed without engendering much social, political or economic change. If the next seven years continue as the last seven years have gone, however, the chances for incremental and consensual changes will be increasingly diminished; more dramatic, more abrupt and less controlled changes would then be much more likely.

# 3

# The Federal Republic of Germany

## WOLFGANG STREECK

**Basic characteristics of the industrial relations system**

The state and the law have always played a strong part in German industrial relations. But legal intervention tends not to be direct, rather it is designed to strengthen the role and the organisation of the 'social partners' and allocate responsibility to them for effective industrial self-government. This has resulted in a 'neo-corporatist' pattern of both trade unions and employer associations assuming, in a variety of ways, a quasi-public status under which they exercise delegated regulatory authority with strong legal facilitation.

Trade unions and employer associations in West Germany have comparatively centralised and encompassing organisational structures. After the Second World War, the traditional political divisions of German trade unionism gave way to joint organisation of Social Democratic, Communist, Christian and Liberal currents in the Deutscher Gewerkschaftsbund (DGB, German Trade Union Federation). Today the DGB consists of seventeen industrial unions that organise both blue-collar and white-collar workers (*Arbeiter* and *Angestellte*) and that together cover the entire economy, including the public sector and the civil service. DGB-affiliated unions face competition from two other trade union centres, the Deutsche Angestellten-Gewerkschaft (DAG, German Staff Union), which organises only white-collar workers, and the Deutscher Beamtenbund (DBB, German Association of Civil Servants), which in principle represents exclusively tenured civil servants (*Beamte*). In both categories, however, the industrial unions of the DGB together have clearly more members than their competitors.

Employers are organised at the national level in the Bundesvereinigung Deutscher Arbeitgeberverbände (BDA, Federal Association of German Employer Associations), which is a federation of 47 sectoral employer associations (Bunn, 1984). The BDA specialises as an employer association and divides responsibility for the representation of business interests with a number of peak trade associations, such as the

53

Bundesvereinigung der Deutschen Industrie (BDI, Federal Association of Germany Industry). Owing to the almost complete organisation of the large artisan sector—whose peak employer association is affiliated to the BDA (Streeck, 1987c)—the latter represents between 80 and 90 per cent of private employers. It does not, however, cover the public employers, who conduct their industrial relations through a separate employer association (Keller, 1978).

Trade unions and employer associations interact with each other and with the state in a number of legally structured institutional settings and policy areas. The most important of these are the Labour Court system, and the systems of collective bargaining, co-determination and vocational training.

## The Labour Court system

Disputes over the application of labour legislation and collective agreements are adjudicated by a three-tiered system of Labour Courts (Blankenburg & Rogowski, 1986). A Labour Court is presided over by a professional judge specialising in labour law; its other members are representatives of trade unions and employer associations. Labour Courts have jurisdiction over both procedural and substantive matters, and over 'individual labour law' pertaining to the individual contract of work, as well as over 'collective labour law' regulating the rights and obligations of trade unions and employer associations, including strikes and lockouts. In the latter respect, the Federal Labour Court has become an important source of case law where the Bundestag has abstained from politically sensitive legislative intervention. (In spite of the strong role of the law in the West German industrial relations system, there is no trade union or strike legislation in West Germany, and arbitration procedures, where they exist, are regulated by collective agreement.)

## The system of collective bargaining

Collective agreements in West Germany are negotiated at the industry level, either nationwide or regionally (Streeck, 1984a). Regional negotiations are, however, closely co-ordinated by the national executives of the respective trade unions and employer associations, and variations between them are small. On the trade union side, collective bargaining is dominated, if not monopolised, by the industrial unions of the DGB, and in fact by only a few of them. The number of formally separate agreements is high, but a large majority follow the pattern set by a few key, or 'pilot', agreements, and although sectoral bargaining is not formally co-ordinated at the national level, inter-industry wage differentials are very low (Marsden, 1981:41). This is partly because some DGB affiliates are too small to pursue an independent policy.[1] The same applies to the DAG, whose bargaining activities in most sectors consist essentially of putting, at the invitation of the employers, its signature to the DGB agreements. The DBB and those public sector DGB unions that represent only tenured civil servants cannot formally bargain at all; while legally pay and conditions of tenured civil servants are unilaterally determined by the state, in practice they follow the master agreement for the public sector which is negotiated by the respective DGB union, the ÖTV (Gewerkschaft Öffentliche Dienste, Transport und Verkehr—Public Services and Transport Workers Union) (Keller, 1978). West German industrial agreements regulate in great detail a wide range of issues in addition to wages, including employment security, training and retraining, work organisation, and the rights and obligations of trade unions and employer associations (Streeck, 1981b). Agreements are legally binding on their signatories and their members, and they can in addition be declared binding by government decree on all firms in an industry, regardless of membership in the employer association. In effect, this makes for almost complete coverage. At the same time, it is important to emphasise that there has never been a statutory incomes policy in West Germany, and it is doubtful whether direct state intervention of this kind would be constitutional.

## The system of co-determination

This is the 'peculiar institution' of West German industrial relations (Adams & Rummel, 1977; Bundesminister für Arbeit & Sozialordnung, 1978; Streeck, 1984b). Employees in West Germany are represented, under the Works Constitution Act 1972, by works councils, which are elected every three years. All workers in a given establishment are entitled to vote and to stand for election, regardless of union membership. However, about 80 per cent of works councillors are elected from among candidates put up by the respective DGB trade union, and the works council has in effect become the organisational centre of industrial unions at the workplace. Works councils have legal rights to consultation and co-decision-making on a range of legally specified matters, and in large firms their *de facto* strength often exceeds their legal powers. Works councils are also legally charged with supervising the implementation of industrial agreements, and they are barred from negotiating on subjects that are settled by industrial agreements—particularly wages (Streeck, 1981b). In West Germany's 480 largest companies, which account for about 27 per cent of the national workforce and one half of total output, workers and trade unions also hold one-half of the seats on the supervisory board. In the case of a split vote, however, the chair, who always comes from the shareholders' side, has a casting vote. Works councils are not permitted to call a strike, but have to take recourse to mediation, arbitration and adjudication.

*The system of vocational training*

West Germany has a comprehensive vocational training system, important parts of which are jointly managed by employer associations, trade unions and the government (Streeck et al., 1987). Trade unions are particularly involved in the establishment of training profiles and curricula for the 420 recognised occupations throughout the economy. The vocational training system is one of the most important sources of the West German industrial consensus. The strong support of both trade unions and employers for vocational training and retraining reflects the dependence of the West German economy on world markets for quality rather than price-competitive products, and the corresponding need for a highly skilled and reliable workforce as well as for a co-operative relationship between management and labour on the shopfloor.

## Significant events and developments in the 1980s

Between 1980 and 1983[2], the West German unemployment rate rose from 3.7 to 9.3 per cent, and it has since remained almost constant (table 3.1). And in 1982, one and a half decades of Social–Democratic participation in the federal government came to an end when the Social–Liberal coalition of Helmut Schmidt lost its majority and had to give way to the Conservative–Liberal government of Helmut Kohl. Both developments represent dramatic changes in the economic and political environments of West German industrial relations. Industrial relations, however, have not as yet changed nearly as much, and on the whole the picture throughout the 1980s has been one of remarkable stability and continuity, albeit lately interspersed with mounting signs of gradual but fundamental transformation and growing pressure on all actors in the system to review their basic strategic orientation.

Trade union wage restraint (Flanagan et al., 1983) continued into the 1980s, although the 'Concerted Action', the German version of a voluntary incomes policy, had been formally disbanded in 1977. This was partly because the tight monetary policy of the Bundesbank left trade unions no alternative. But the unions themselves were also willing to accept stagnant or declining real wages (table 3.2) as a way of fighting unemployment or at least preserving employment. Unlike, for example, the British unions, they had in the German system of centrally co-ordinated collective bargaining an effective instrument to hold down sectional wage militancy. Real wage increases through the 1980s remained below the increase in productivity, in particular in the manufacturing sector, and this clearly helped the government's supply-oriented policy of rebuilding profitability.

Another reason for the unions' moderate wage policy was that the metalworkers' union, IG Metall, was saving bargaining power and strike funds for a major offensive on working hours. By the early 1980s, the West German trade union movement had placed its hopes for a reduction of unemployment on measures to limit the labour supply, given that the government was clearly unwilling to adopt a Keynesian strategy of fiscal expansion. Some DGB unions, notably the chemical workers (Industrie Gewerkschaft Chemie–Papier–Keramik, IG CPK), opted for an extensive early retirement programme; others followed the lead of IG Metall which, after some internal confusion, came out in favour of work-sharing by means of a general shortening of working hours. For

**Table 3.1  Economic conditions**

|      | Employment '000 | Unemployment '000 | % | Real growth % | Change in productivity % | Rate of inflation % |
|------|-----------------|-------------------|-----|---------------|--------------------------|---------------------|
| 1973 | 22 906 | 273 | 1.2 | | | |
| 1974 | 22 649 | 582 | 2.5 | 0.4 | (3.2) | 7.0 |
| 1975 | 22 014 | 1074 | 4.7 | – 0.2 | (3.3) | 6.0 |
| 1976 | 21 939 | 1060 | 4.6 | 5.7 | (7.2) | 4.5 |
| 1977 | 22 029 | 1030 | 4.5 | 2.6 | 4.3 | 3.7 |
| 1978 | 22 264 | 993 | 4.3 | 3.5 | 5.4 | 2.7 |
| 1979 | 22 663 | 876 | 3.7 | 4.4 | 4.8 | 4.1 |
| 1980 | 23 009 | 889 | 3.7 | 1.8 | 0.8 | 5.5 |
| 1981 | 22 869 | 1272 | 5.3 | 0.0 | 1.1 | 6.3 |
| 1982 | 22 436 | 1833 | 7.6 | – 1.0 | 1.1 | 5.3 |
| 1983 | 22 057 | 2258 | 9.3 | 1.5* | 4.4 | 3.3 |
| 1984 | 22 097 | 2266 | 9.3 | 3.0* | 4.2 | 2.4 |
| 1985 | 22 274 | 2304 | 9.4 | 2.5* | 3.0* | 2.2 |
| 1986 | 22 525 | 2228 | 9.0 | 2.5* | 3.0* | – 0.2* |
| 1987 | 22 700 | 2150 | 8.7 | | | |

*Notes:*  * provisional
Employment: wage earners, yearly average.
Unemployment: yearly average. Percentage unemployment: number of unemployed (column 2) as a percentage of employed and unemployed wage earners (columns 1 and 2).
Real growth: Gross National Product in prices of 1980 (1981–85) and 1970 (1974–80)
Productivity: manufacturing output per worker and hour; different basis for calculations 1974–76.
Inflation: consumer prices, percentage changes from previous year.

*Sources:* Employment: OECD (1986), WSI Mitteilungen 11/1986. Unemployment: OECD (1986), WSI Mitteilungen 11/1986. Real growth: *Statistisches Jahrbuch der Bundesrepublik Deutschland*, consecutive editions; WSI Mitteilungen 11/1986; own calculations. Productivity: *Sachverständigenrat* (1985); own calculations. Inflation: OECD Economic Outlook 39, May 1986; WSI Mitteilungen 11/1986.

a time this seemed to give rise to a major political and ideological split in the union movement, especially when the government sided with the proponents of early retirement and passed a law to subsidise early retirement schemes set up by collective agreement. But the law was regarded as insufficient even by those unions who would have been willing to make use of it, and in the course of events the issue turned out to be less divisive than many had expected.

**Table 3.2 Yearly changes in nominal and real wages and productivity, 1975–85**

| | Changes in gross wages and salaries per employee | | Change in productivity |
|---|---|---|---|
| | Nominal | Real | |
| 1974 | + 10.4 | + 3.4 | + 1.8 |
| 1975 | + 6.3 | + 0.3 | + 1.5 |
| 1976 | + 7.9 | + 3.4 | + 7.3 |
| 1977 | + 7.1 | + 3.4 | + 3.5 |
| 1978 | + 5.6 | + 2.9 | + 2.5 |
| 1979 | + 5.9 | + 1.8 | + 3.1 |
| 1980 | + 6.8 | + 1.3 | + 0.2 |
| 1981 | + 5.0 | − 1.3 | + 1.0 |
| 1982 | + 4.5 | − 0.8 | + 1.3 |
| 1983 | + 3.4 | + 0.1 | + 3.2 |
| 1984 | + 3.4 | + 1.0 | + 2.7 |
| 1985 | + 3.4 | + 1.2 | + 1.7 |

*Notes:* Real changes: nominal change minus rate of inflation (see table 3.1). Productivity: Gross Domestic Product per gainfully employed, discounted for inflation.

*Sources:* Real changes: *Sachverständigenrat* (1985); own calculations. Productivity: *Sachverständigenrat* (1985).

In the spring of 1984, IG Metall went on strike for a 35-hour week, without reduction of weekly pay, for the entire metalworking industry (Rosner, 1984a; Weber, 1985). The strike lasted nine weeks and was the biggest and probably the most bitter in the history of the Federal Republic. At its end, 455 000 workers were affected, of whom 58 000 were on strike; 147 000 were (partly in addition) locked out; and 250 000 were laid off owing to lack of supplies. The strike cost IG Metall about 500 million Deutsche Mark, one-third of its total reserves. A clearly higher amount, in the range of 800 million Deutsche Mark, was paid by the employer association to its members in strike and lockout support, and about 300 million Deutsche Mark were paid in unemployment benefit to laid-off workers (see also below). Agreement was reached only after mediation by a former Social–Democratic Cabinet member. The settlement provided for an average 38.5-hour working week and a modest wage increase. Since the employers had initially rejected any general cut in working hours, the outcome was widely perceived as a union victory. On the other hand, the union had to concede in return the possibility of different and more flexible working time regimes for different firms and, inside firms, for different groups of workers, to be negotiated under co-determination between employers and works councils. To this extent, it had to yield to the employers' counter-demands, during the strike, for more 'flexibility', reflecting the pressures exerted by new capital-intensive technologies on the traditional organisation of work.

The strike of 1984 and its settlement may well have been of formative importance for the future of West German industrial relations although, or perhaps because, its outcome is not unambiguous. The union movement had shown itself to be still a power to be reckoned with, in spite of highly adverse political and economic circumstances. The fact that the settlement had remained well inside the limit of the productivity increase--and thus had no inflationary or profit-squeezing consequences—restored the credibility of the unions and made it more difficult for the employers to resist further hours reductions in the future. The agreement also had a positive effect on employment, even though its exact size was debatable. Moreover, although the strike gave rise in its aftermath to a highly divisive political battle over the rights of trade unions and the role of the state in industrial relations (see below), IG Metall and its counterpart on the employers' side, Gesamtmetall, managed in 1984 to conclude at long last a joint project for a comprehensive modernisation of the vocational training scheme in the metalworking industry. In this respect at least, the traditional pattern of West German industrial relations—which has been aptly described as 'co-operative conflict resolution' (Jacobs et al., 1978)—has survived the strike intact.

On the other hand, reduction of working hours by industrial agreement was pursued by the unions also in order to protect traditional working-time regimes, and in this respect the union was clearly less successful. The 1984 settlement has established a pattern of give-and-take under which further reductions of working hours will have to be paid for with further concessions on 'flexibility'. In fact, in 1987 IG Metall won a further reduction of working time at full compensation of pay, to 36.5 hours by 1990. In exchange, it not only agreed to a wage settlement with a currency of three years, but also accepted further 'flexibility' provisions, the details of which have to be negotiated between individual employers and works councils. Second, in the West German industrial relations system, any differentiation of rules and regulations in individual establishments inevitably implies a transfer of jurisdiction, from the industrial agreement and the trade union to co-determination and the works councils. While originally the industrial agreement on working-time reduction was to bring working-time re-gimes back under central control, in effect it merely ratified the growing involvement of the works councils in their regulation (see below). One might also add that while the 1984 agreement did increase employment, the number of unemployed nevertheless continued to grow in 1984 and 1985, and in fact one lesson trade unions might learn from their relative success of 1984 is that more than just work-sharing is needed to fight unemployment.[3]

The Kohl government has on the whole resisted the temptation to roll back the unions' institutional position. The co-determination leg-islation of the 1970s was left untouched, and calls for decentralisation of collective bargaining by regions and firms, which came primarily from representatives of small and medium-sized businesses, were not heeded (cf., Rosner, 1984b). In the latter respect, it is remarkable that the BDA sided with the trade unions, arguing that the existing bargain-ing machinery offered sufficient flexibility and that its dismantling would make the labour market ungovernable (Knevels, 1985).

Trade unions in West Germany, unlike those in some other countries, did not have to defend themselves in the first half of the 1980s against a deliberate government policy of 'labour exclusion'. In part, this was accounted for by their unimpaired organisational strength, in spite of high unemployment, which in turn was related to the protection offered to them by the legal system. Major legal changes are difficult to accom-plish in West Germany with its tradition of four decades of consensus politics based on centrist coalition governments; a federal system in which the *Länder* (states) command significant powers; constitutional rights to group 'self-government'; and an elaborate body of constitu-tional law which can be forced on the legislature by a powerful judiciary. Thus, while the unions disagreed fundamentally with the Kohl govern-ment's strategy of fiscal consolidation, demanding instead a Keynesian policy of public spending programmes for employment creation, their role and status were, at least initially, not at stake. In fact, attempts were made on both sides to continue the high-level consultations between the chancellor and the trade union leadership that had been routine under Social–Democratic rule, and on several occasions such meetings did take place.

Nevertheless, relations gradually deteriorated, around the mid-1980s. This development began with the passage of the Employment Pro-motion Act 1985, which represents a moderate German version of labour market deregulation. In essence, the Act attempts to facilitate new recruitment by extending the probation period during which em-ployees can be dismissed without legal cause, and by widening the legal range of applicability of fixed-term contracts. The unions strongly opposed the Act, which to them appeared as a first major attempt to undermine their role in the regulation of the employment relationship. As with working-time reduction, the practical effects of the legislation in terms of its stated and, perhaps, unstated objectives are still difficult to determine (cf., Erdmann, 1986).

For the unions, the Employment Promotion Act may have been no more than what was to be expected under a conservative government, comparable to the various cuts in social welfare spending that were introduced early in the legislative period. Relations became highly politicised, however, when the government, under pressure from employer associations trying to make up for their defeat in the 1984 strike, proposed to amend the social security law to make workers ineligible for unemployment benefit if they were laid off because of lack of work during a strike, and if they stood to benefit directly from the industrial agreement at stake. This was in response to the strike tactic of IG Metall which, in order to spare its strike funds, officially struck only at selected establishments and counted on other firms having to shut down for lack of supplies (see below). Trade union opposition to the Act was strong and passionate; just as the campaign for shorter hours had dominated union activities in 1983 and 1984, the mobilisation against the so-called 'section 116' legislation almost absorbed all other union activities in 1985 and most of 1986. The unions regarded the Act as an attempt to change permanently the balance of power in the industrial relations system in favour of the employers, and references to the suppression of trade unions in the 1930s became almost commonplace. Unions also sensed an opportunity to bring down an unfriendly government over what for a time was a highly unpopular piece of legislation, either through the trade union wing of the Christian Democrats or at the polls in the upcoming election. But the government was undeterred and passed the Act in early 1986. Its impact on the collective bargaining system and its constitutionality are still untested.

It seems that, at some time in early 1986, the unions made themselves believe that, partly as a result of their mobilisation against section 116, the Social Democratic Party (SPD) had a chance of winning the general election in January 1987. Unlike earlier confrontations, unions made no effort to keep open a way back to a more peaceful working relationship with the conservative parties, and trade union support for the Social Democratic Party campaign build-up became more undisguised and unqualified than ever. The government retaliated, when under a smell of corruption, the Neue Heimat, the giant housing concern which was part of the DGB's business interests, came to the verge of collapse. The issue, and its amateurish handling by the DGB leadership, quickly eclipsed the section 116 conflict and created a flow of bad publicity, not just for the unions but also for the Social Democratic Party. There are also signs that it undermined the confidence of trade union members in their leadership. This was, of course, more than welcome to the government, which refused to come to the unions' assistance and bail out the Neue Heimat—not least to maximise the drain on trade union financial resources. By the end of 1986 the unions had to realise that their public reputation had been badly damaged and would continue to suffer from the Neue Heimat problem for years to come; that the inevitable reorganisation of their economic empire would cost them dear and might even impair their capacity to strike; and that above all they had grossly miscalculated the electoral prospects of the Social Democrats and were without a ready strategy of how to operate under four more years of conservative government.

Working-time policy, and the associated conflicts, have for a while helped unions hide their bewilderment regarding persistent high unemployment in a prosperous economy. In particular, they enabled them to shift the blame for unemployment to the employers and the government who resisted shorter hours for fear of higher labour costs and shortages in skilled sub-markets. Moreover, employer and government resistance offered the unions an opportunity to define unemployment politically in the traditional language of distributional confrontation when, behind the smokescreen, they had tacitly accepted the need to change the distribution of income in the favour of capital. Demands for shorter hours also responded to rising work intensity in a rapidly modernising production system and may thereby have helped the introduction of new technology. Not least, working-time policy reflected changing income–leisure preferences among certain highly visible and outspoken segments of the population, in particular the increasingly typical childless family with two wage earners, and it went down well with the feminist stream in public opinion, with IG Metall holding out a vague promise of the 30-hour week at the beginning of the next century creating the conditions for 'full equality between men and women'. Finally, it played to some of the post-industrial sentiment organised in the Green party but extending well into the new mainstream of Social Democracy, for which a reduction of unemployment through economic growth instead of redistribution appears unacceptable because of its expected negative consequences for the environment and the 'quality of life'.

However, as the marginal employment effects of the 1984 and 1987 agreements are becoming more difficult to hide, the usefulness of working-time policy as symbolic politics is bound to wear down. Indeed, having themselves actively endorsed the now widely accepted definition of unemployment as a problem of redistribution and solidarity between workers 'inside' and 'outside' employment, trade unions in early 1988 found themselves exposed to mounting public demands to be consistent and agree to working-time cuts *exceeding* productivity increases—cuts, in other words, that would result in lower incomes for their employed members. How vulnerable trade unions had made themselves became apparent during the 1988 wage round for the public sector, which, following usual practice, was to carry over the main elements of the 1987 metal industry agreement. Characteristically, it was not the employers or the government but ambitious Social Democratic politicians who took the lead in urging the unions to live up to their altruistic proclamations and renounce pay compensation, a move designed to steer clear of a perceived electoral liability of too-close association with 'old-fashioned' trade unionism, and also well-suited to hiding the SPD's own impotence in relation to unemployment. In the circumstances, the union's long-standing record of wage restraint was easily forgotten, also because the unions themselves had never publicly advertised it for fear of arousing internal opposition. And having in the past vigorously rejected the argument that the structure of the unemployed workforce ruled out any significant amount of work 'redistribution', unions suddenly found themselves defenceless, not least in relation to altruistically minded, middle-class segments of their own membership.

By the late 1980s, West German trade unions had manoeuvred themselves into an increasingly uncomfortable political corner where their opponents had little difficulty in picturing them, in a phrase coined by Ralf Dahrendorf, as a 'special interest organization of a declining social group'. Like their counterparts in other countries, West German trade unions are today facing an urgent need to find an equivalent for their Keynesian role as stabilisers of effective aggregate demand and as 'productivity whip' for marginal firms. This role had made it possible for unions to prosper because of the peculiar combination it entailed of distributive and productive functions, performed through a complex mixture of conflict and co-operation with employers and the government. While West German trade unions may have advanced further than most other union movements in assembling the building blocks of a post-Keynesian strategy, they have done so quite unsystematically, often unknowingly and always with a bad conscience, frequently leaving novel initiatives to the works councils under co-determination and sometimes accusing them later of class collaboration, or *Betriebsegoismus*, to appease the militants.

Rather than accepting a lower price of labour to clear the labour market, West German unions and works councils have, under the cover of their symbolic politics of working-time reduction, embarked on a variety of strategies to *raise the quality and productivity of labour*, so as to justify *ex post*, as it were, its present, downwardly rigid, 'excessive' price. This response to unemployment does not promise a fast and simple solution. Moreover, its logic runs counter to traditional trade union ideology which has always rejected the notion that a worker's wage cannot, in the long run, exceed his or her marginal productivity.

But while strategic thinking among German trade unions on their future role moves extremely slowly, actual behaviour clearly revolves around the idea of increased investment in, and better utilisation of, human resources, in an effort to rebuild and defend the competitiveness and long-term profitability of the West German economy. Important developments have recently taken place in this respect, but just as with wage restraint, unions have been reluctant to advertise them. The following three examples may serve as illustrations.

First, shortly after the 1984 strike, IG Metall and the employer association of the metal industry, Gesamtmetall, ended ten years of intense negotiations and joint research on an overhaul of the training scheme for the skilled metal occupations. The length of the average apprenticeship was extended to three and a half years; the number of occupations was reduced to eighteen to make curricula broader-based and less specialized; extensive training in micro-electronic technology was included in all curricula; and training standards were (further) raised. Remarkably, both sides were willing and able to protect their joint reform project over an entire decade against the repercussions of an increasingly tense industrial relations climate in the 1970s and 1980s, and even the 1984 conflict was not allowed to interfere with the completion of the extremely complicated negotiations.

Second, the chemical workers union, IG Chemie, in 1987 concluded long negotiations on a new framework agreement that is likely fundamentally to change the face of the German employment system. The agreement, called *Entgelttarifvertrag*, eliminates for all practical purposes the century-old distinction between blue-collar and white-collar workers (a distinction, by the way, that has always been unknown in Japan). In coming years, payment systems and job descriptions will be completely revised so that all employees are paid by identical criteria of skill, responsibility and effort. The integration of formerly separate pay scales and the merger of previously categorically different status definitions will both accommodate and facilitate continuing changes in the organisation of work, in particular in the relationship between direct and indirect labour and between conception and execution. Incidentally, the agreement will also protect the organisational basis of IG Chemie as an industrial union against the possibility of highly skilled manual workers who achieve white collar status leaving the union for a competing white-collar organisation.

Third, in early 1988, IG Metall signed a framework agreement in its 'pilot district', Nord-Württemberg/Nord-Baden, which is of no less historical importance than the *Entgelttarifvertrag* of IG Chemie or the reform of the metal industry training scheme. The event went almost unnoticed as the agreement was negotiated in complete consensus. The agreement, which redefines and homogenises the criteria of wage determination for blue-collar and white-collar workers, contains, according to a report in the pro-business *Frankfurter Allgemeine Zeitung* (*FAZ*, 13 February 1988):

> regulations on the maintenance and extension of the employees' qualifications. Under these, employer and works council are to determine jointly the skilling needs of the enterprise and the skilling interests of the workforce, and if possible bring the two in agreement. Incentives for further training are created in that employees who undergo training are guaranteed upgrading and higher pay . . . From the perspective of the parties which interpret the agreement in rare unanimity, this will facilitate the adjustment of enterprises to growing requirements of quality and flexibility; it will also improve work satisfaction and thus contribute to a better working climate. Already during the planning of physical investment and parallel to it, enterprises can now consider the further training needs of workers affected by technical change . . . With the agreement . . . the union can reject the charge that its wage policy has in the past been guided by a tendency to erode differentials. Now employees are to seek and receive a higher income through higher qualification.

Since, under the agreement, employers have to pay a worker who has acquired additional skills higher for at least eight months even if his or her enhanced skills are not used, the expectation is that employers will reorganise work in such a way that they can benefit from the human capital investment they are obliged to make under the agreement. 'Employers can expect from the agreement to be placed under pressure to train, and this effect *both parties* [my italics] actually intend to create' (*FAZ*, 13 February 1988). The agreement includes an understanding that on the basis of the anticipated extended training efforts, the two sides will move towards an *Entgelttarifvertrag*, as in the chemical industry; formal negotiations on this will start in 1991.

## Strategic realignment in the 1980s

### The West German economy

Despite its relatively small population, West Germany is still the world's largest exporter of manufactured goods, ahead of both Japan and the United States. About one-half of the production of German manufacturing industry is exported, with the export ratios of core sectors, such as chemicals, machine tools and automobiles, exceeding 60 per cent. Among the larger economies, the West German is, more than any other, exposed to world market pressures. It is only against this background that the high degree of stability and mutual co-operation in West German industrial relations can be understood, and it is this stability and co-operation that has in the past accounted for part of the country's competitive success in world markets.

The strong world market position of the West German economy is not based on low labour costs. The competitive advantages of West German manufacturing industry typically derive from high product quality, customised design and superior engineering, high reliability of delivery, and efficient repair and maintenance services. Moreover, the product range of German industry is highly diversified, and big companies can rely for specialised supplies on a large number of flexible and technically advanced small and medium-sized firms. Also, research and development expenditure is high, and this combines with the traditional long-term profit orientation of German capital, which is supported not least by the banking system (Cox & Kriegbaum, 1980).

West Germany's status as a classical manufacturing country is reflected in the structure of its workforce. In 1985, 41 per cent of the gainfully employed population were engaged in manufacturing (table 3.3). Although this was clearly fewer than at the beginning of the 1970s,

**Table 3.3 Distribution of economically active population over sectors**

|  | Gainful employment '000 | Agriculture % | Industry % | Services % |
|---|---|---|---|---|
| 1971 | 25 817 | 8.0 | 48.4 | 43.6 |
| 1975 | 25 810 | 6.9 | 45.3 | 47.8 |
| 1980 | 26 328 | 5.5 | 44.1 | 50.4 |
| 1985* | 25 531 | 5.4 | 41.0 | 53.6 |

Note: *provisional.
Source: Statistisches Jahrbuch der Bundesrepublik Deutschland (1986).

the level of industrialisation continues to be higher than in any other large country, and deindustrialisation has proceeded more slowly than elsewhere. While the service sector has increased in importance, the prosperity of the West German economy will for a long time continue to depend on the performance and competitive strength of its manufacturing industries.

The West German economy was badly hit by the massive increase in oil prices of OPEC 2 in 1980 and 1981, much worse than by OPEC 1 (table 3.1). For a time this gave rise to a widespread loss of confidence in the country's future ability to compete, especially with Japan. But by the middle of the 1980s, the German version of the 'Euro-Malaise' seemed to be on its way out. Investment was going up, including in modern sectors such as telecommunications, and there was a new optimism that the battle for the high technology markets of the future might not yet be lost. This was clearly reflected in the almost complete insignificance of unemployment in the 1986-87 election campaign. The changed mood had also left its impression on the trade unions, whose attitudes towards new technology were becoming comparatively protective and defensive in the early 1980s (Kubicek, 1986), but which now seemed to be more willing to explore a more forward-looking, aggressive approach to technological modernisation.

## Changing patterns of employment

The rise of unemployment in West Germany coincided with major changes in the functioning of labour markets and the pattern of employment. In part, these were connected with industrial relations. Overall labour force participation declined steadily in the 1970s and 1980s, from 69.4 per cent in 1970 to 65 per cent in 1985 (OECD Labour Force Statistics, 1986). The decline was strongest among young people aged between 15 and 24, whose participation rate fell from about 67 to 57 per cent, and it was quite dramatic among males aged between 55 and 64, whose participation rate of 77.8 per cent in 1970 fell to only 57.5 per cent in 1985. The former reflects the expansion of formal education whereas the latter was largely due to early retirement in response to unemployment (between 1980 and 1985 alone, that is, in the period when unemployment was highest, participation among men in the 55 to 64 age group declined by 8 percentage points). Early retirement was the preferred instrument of works councils and employers in trying to solve redundancy problems consensually. The only group whose participation rate increased was women, in particular those aged between 25 and 34 (with an increase from 49.1 per cent in 1970 to 60.3 in 1985) and between 35 and 44 (from 48.1 to 57.5). Overall, however, increased female participation was offset, and in a sense made possible, by the combined effects of extended schooling and early retirement.

The fact that unemployment increased steeply in spite of declining participation is indicative of the dimension of the present employment problem in West Germany. This holds in particular since, by the late 1980s, the potential for further early retirement or educational expansion is largely exhausted, for demographic as well as public finance reasons. The same seems to be true for two other trends that have in the past helped relieve unemployment: the decline in the number of foreign workers and the reduction of working hours. The share of foreign workers in the total number of wage earners, employed or unemployed, has declined steadily since the mid-1970s, although the decline was slower than is often thought (table 3.4). In the same period, the foreign population has grown relative to the population as a whole, indicating an increase in the number of family members, which makes re-migration less likely. The average number of working hours per year and worker, as determined by industrial agreements (tarifliche Arbeitszeit), declined by 9.1 per cent from 1898 in 1970 to 1726 in 1986, and actual hours worked fell by as much as 13.4 per cent, from 1885 to 1632 (Mitteilungen aus der Arbeitsmarkt und Berufsforschung no. 3, 1986: 380). German working hours have, as a result, become shorter than in most other countries and this is likely to place limits upon further reductions.

**Table 3.4 Foreign nationals and employment of foreign workers in Federal Republic of Germany 1975–85**

| | Number of foreign nationals | | Number of foreign workers | |
|---|---|---|---|---|
| | '000 | Percentage of population | '000 | Percentage of workforce* |
| 1973 | | | 2498 | 10.9 |
| 1974 | | | 2381 | 10.5 |
| 1975 | 4090 | 6.6 | 2061 | 9.4 |
| 1976 | 3948 | 6.4 | 1925 | 8.8 |
| 1977 | 3948 | 6.4 | 1872 | 8.5 |
| 1978 | 3981 | 6.5 | 1858 | 8.3 |
| 1979 | 4144 | 6.8 | 1924 | 8.5 |
| 1980 | 4453 | 7.2 | 2018 | 8.8 |
| 1981 | 4630 | 7.5 | 1912 | 8.4 |
| 1982 | 4667 | 7.6 | 1787 | 8.0 |
| 1983 | 4535 | 7.4 | 1694 | 7.7 |
| 1984 | 4364 | 7.1 | 1609 | 7.3 |
| 1985 | 4379 | 7.2 | 1568 | 7.0 |
| 1986 | | | 1570 | 7.0 |

*Note:* *number of foreign workers in dependent employment (column 3) as percentage of total number of workers in dependent employment (see table 3.1)

*Source: Statistisches Jahrbuch der Bundesrepublik Deutschland,* consecutive editions; OECD (1986); own calculations.

The incidence and distribution of part-time work has, by comparison, been stable. In 1976, 11.7 per cent of wage earners were part-timers; by 1984 their share had grown, but only to 13.6 per cent. About 90 per cent of the present part-time workforce are women, which compares with about 85 per cent in the early 1970s (Büchtemann & Schupp, 1986:42). Part of the expansion of female workforce participation can thus be attributed to increased opportunities for part-time work, although this effect has been much stronger in other countries. Full-time employment, with a standard working week, has remained the rule in

West Germany, much more so than elsewhere. It is difficult to say with any degree of certainty to what extent this is explained by trade union resistance to part-time work. It is true, however, that West German trade unions regard part-time employment with suspicion, arguing among other things that it is used 'as a rationalisation instrument with negative consequences for the quality and quantity of full time jobs'; that it perpetuates discrimination against women; and that it preempts union demands for a general reduction of working hours (WSI, 1984).

West German unemployment is highly structured. Regional unemployment rates differ widely, being clearly higher on average in the north than in the south of the country. Some regions, especially in Baden-Württemberg, can be said to have full employment—with an unemployment rate in Stuttgart, for example, of 4.4 per cent in October 1986—whereas others, like Bremen, have a rate of 14.4 per cent or more. This coincides with a decline in regional mobility during the 1970s and 1980s, which is also observed in other countries (OECD, 1986b:60). In addition, the risk of becoming unemployed is differently distributed among different categories of labour market participants.[4] By the mid-1980s, groups with a high risk ratio (calculated by dividing the group-specific by the general unemployment rate) were foreign workers (1.55) closely followed by female manual workers (1.52). The principal explanatory factor here seems to be low skill. Other high risk groups were young people aged between 20 and 25 (1.32) and male manual workers (1.22). Relatively low unemployment risks existed for male non-manual workers (0.44) and for workers, male and female, between 40 and 45 (0.62) and 45 and 50 (0.7). The unemployment rate for prime age males was 5.8 per cent in 1985 (OECD 1986a:15), which may explain in part why high overall unemployment has not been more of a political liability for the present government.

Another factor that has helped defuse unemployment as a political and industrial relations problem is relatively low youth unemployment. The risk ratio for young people below age 20 becoming unemployed is 1.02, in stark contrast to other western European countries. The difference is accounted for by the vocational training system which has been vastly expanded in the 1970s and 1980s to absorb increasing numbers of school leavers. Vocational training is not only seen as a temporary shelter from unemployment but also as a way of reducing the risk of becoming unemployed in the future. While it is true that this risk increases after the end of the apprenticeship period (see the risk ratio for the 20 to 24 age group, above), it is also true that those without formal occupational training are vastly over-represented among the unemployed. Throughout the 1980s, up to the present, about one-half of the rapidly growing unemployed population were unskilled workers. At the same time, there were and still are obvious skill shortages in many parts of manufacturing industry. There seems to be agreement that, to a significant extent, the present unemployment is due to declining demand for unskilled workers in a rapidly modernising economy, and a tripartite consensus seems to be emerging between government, employers and trade unions that a publicly supported training campaign may be a promising approach to relieving unemployment. On the other hand, this begs the question of what is to be done about those who are unable or unwilling to undergo training—a question that is difficult to answer for trade unions committed to modernisation as well as, among other things, low wage differentials.

With rising unemployment, especially in the 1980s, tendencies towards labour market segmentation and dualisation began to emerge, giving rise to growing concern. In 1981, 0.8 per cent of wage earners had been unemployed for one year or longer. In the following year this percentage increased to 1.6 per cent, and it has been rising ever since, reaching 2.7 per cent in 1985. In absolute numbers, this amounted to about 660 000 people who were on the brink of being permanently excluded from the labour force. It is obvious that this must pose a severe problem for a trade union movement that has always regarded itself as the representative of all workers. The problem is exacerbated by the fact that the external labour market in Germany is clearly less flexible than in comparable countries, which in part reflects strong employment protection and the growing role of internal labour markets. Thus, the average length of employment in West Germany is second only to Japan (OECD, 1986b:47), and adjustment of employment to changes in output takes longer than anywhere else except, again, Japan (OECD, 1986a:21). The emergence of internal labour markets with strong employment guarantees has clearly been advanced by co-determination and is in this sense a result of trade union strength. But as the 'social closure' of the employment system proceeds (Hohn, 1983; Hohn & Windolf, 1985), trade unions are faced with the dilemma that what has, in the past, served the interests of some of their members well may increasingly clash with the interests of other members or, more likely, of an increasingly unorganised marginal labour force.

## The role of trade unions and employer associations

Trade union membership has remained remarkably unaffected by the economic crises of the 1970s and 1980s (table 3.5). Combined membership of the three trade union groups is clearly above the level of the mid-1970s. Trade union density was at 38.7 per cent among the employed workforce in 1987, compared with 36.5 per cent in 1973. (For the total workforce, including the unemployed—which is now considerably larger than in the early 1970s—density has only slightly declined in the last decade.) Moreover, the relative strength of the three union centres has remained essentially unchanged, with the industrial unions affiliated to the DGB now representing 86 per cent of all trade union members. This is in stark contrast to the tendencies towards organisational fragmentation and dispersion that can be observed in other countries, notably Sweden. Nevertheless, there has for several years now been a decline in aggregate density, by 1.3 percentage point since 1983, among the employed workforce, and by 2.5 percentage points since 1979 among the total workforce. The effect is clearly more due to workforce expansion than to membership losses. However, if the trend continues it may at some point begin to impair the unions' public standing and legitimacy.

**Table 3.5 Trade union membership (in thousands) and density, 1973–85**

|      | DGB  | DAG | DBB | All  | Density | |
|------|------|-----|-----|------|------|------|
|      |      |     |     |      | 1    | 2    |
| 1973 | 7168 | 483 | 718 | 8369 | 36.5 | 36.1 |
| 1974 | 7406 | 492 | 720 | 8618 | 38.1 | 37.1 |
| 1975 | 7364 | 470 | 727 | 8561 | 38.9 | 37.1 |
| 1976 | 7400 | 473 | 804 | 8677 | 39.6 | 37.7 |
| 1977 | 7471 | 475 | 794 | 8740 | 39.7 | 37.9 |
| 1978 | 7752 | 482 | 801 | 9035 | 40.6 | 38.8 |
| 1979 | 7844 | 488 | 824 | 9156 | 40.4 | 38.9 |
| 1980 | 7883 | 495 | 821 | 9199 | 40.0 | 38.5 |
| 1981 | 7958 | 499 | 820 | 9277 | 40.6 | 38.5 |
| 1982 | 7849 | 501 | 813 | 9163 | 40.8 | 37.8 |
| 1983 | 7746 | 497 | 801 | 9044 | 41.2 | 37.3 |
| 1984 | 7660 | 498 | 795 | 8953 | 40.5 | 36.7 |
| 1985 | 7719 | 501 | 796 | 9016 | 40.5 | 36.7 |
| 1986 | 7765 | 496 | 782 | 9043 | 40.1 | 36.5 |
| 1987 | 7757 | 494 | 786 | 9037 | 39.8 | 36.4 |

Notes: 1 as percentage of employed workforce.
2 as percentage of workforce including the unemployed.
DGB: Deutscher Gewerkschaftsbund
DAG: Deutsche Angestellten–Gewerkschaft
DBB: Deutscher Beamtenbund

Source: Statistisches Jahrbuch der Bundesrepublik Deutschland, consecutive editions; own calculations. (For employment and unemployment see table 3.1.)

Part of the stability of West German trade union organisation is explained by the stability of the country's industrial structure. In 1986, 67 per cent of the members of DGB unions were still blue-collar workers; 69 per cent worked in the private sector; and 48 per cent were employed in industries exposed to world market competition. The respective figures for 1975 were 73, 71 and 47 per cent.[5] The essentially unchanged composition of the leading trade union centre in terms of membership and member interests has spared union leaders the need to make major policy changes. It has also ensured that the interests of the export-intensive manufacturing sectors, mainly represented by IG Metall, continue to take first place in the formulation of trade union policy.

The organisational robustness of West German trade unions in part reflects the fact that the economic crisis was less severe in West Germany than elsewhere. But it is also related to trade union gains in institutionalisation at the workplace in the 1970s, mainly through the legal extension of co-determination, which enabled unions to make more extensive use of check-off arrangements and various forms of quasi-obligatory membership. In addition there was, beginning in the late 1960s, a wave of organisational change in trade unions, involving in particular a rationalisation of administrative procedures that had previously been responsible for high membership turnover. These developments have been analysed elsewhere in detail (Streeck, 1982).

West German trade unions, in particular the DGB and its affiliates, are well-financed and well-staffed. In the late 1960s and early 1970s, subscriptions paid by members of DGB affiliates were raised to an effective 1 per cent of wages before taxes. Since then, they have remained at this level. The financial strength of the union movement was an important factor in the 1984 strike, and it is not by accident that the two major political conflicts involving trade unions in the early 1980s—the section 116 measure and the government's refusal to rescue the Neue Heimat—had directly to do with trade union finance.

While trade union income from subscriptions continues to be high and steady, the once large industrial empire of the West German union movement is presently being dissolved. In the mid-1980s, the unions' giant housing concern, Neue Heimat, was on the verge of bankruptcy. When the government, in the aftermath of the 1984 strike and during the run-up to the general election of January 1987, refused to assist the unions in the reorganisation of the company, Neue Heimat had to be refinanced to be divided up and sold off to local communities and *Länder*. To raise the necessary cash, the unions had to sell other firms as well, in particular their bank, BFG, which had once been the fourth largest private bank in the country, and a large union-owned insurance company. By the end of this operation, West German trade unions will have ceased once and for all to be owners of major business enterprises.

In spite of their exceptional stability, West German trade unions do face organisational problems similar to those of other trade union movements. The difference—which is important enough—is that, as yet, they can approach these problems from a position of relative strength. One such problem is indicated by the decline in overall density by about 2 percentage points since the early 1980s, reflecting the division of a growing workforce between a safely employed core group and an increasing number of long-term unemployed. The existence of an unorganised marginal labour force may expose trade unions to the potentially damaging charge by their opponents that they have become organisations of 'job owners', whose selfish opposition to labour market deregulation keeps the unemployed out of work.

Second, among those in employment, trade unions have always, and everywhere, had difficulties organising young people, women and white-collar workers. In the past this has often led to predictions of imminent organisational crisis, which turned out to have been somewhat exaggerated. Today, however, the changing demographic composition of the workforce, the increased participation rate of women, and the (comparatively slow) transformation of the industrial structure may indeed have given the matter a new urgency (Hemmer, 1985; Niedenhoff & Wilke, 1986). It is true that the industrial unions of the DGB have a degree of experience in organising white-collar workers—including first-line supervisors such as *Meister* (Lawrence, 1980)—and the principal service sector union, Handel, Banken und Versicherungen, HBV, has long been the DGB's fastest-growing affiliate. Nevertheless, profound changes in policy and 'organisational culture' may be required to attract, for example, the rising number of highly skilled technicians in modern factories who are unlikely to be sympathetic towards warnings against the dangers of new technology, defence of rigid working-time regimes, and an ideological rhetoric that, as in the section 116 campaign, tries to revive the battles of the 1930s. While West German unions may have a better starting position and more time than others to accomplish the necessary organisational adjustments, they are debating whether the inclusion especially of highly qualified cadres will pledge them permanently to a co-operative policy, or whether they may be able to re-educate their new members in a traditional trade union mould.

West German employer associations have always been strong organisations, in relation to their members as well as in representing their interests. In the 1970s they built up an extensive, centrally co-ordinated system of strike funds to support firms or sectors singled out by the unions for selective strikes or breakthrough settlements. In addition, they have shown several times that they are able to require their members to take part in lockouts. At the same time, and apart from its support for the section 116 measure and the Employment Promotion Act, the BDA has always emphasised that it is in principle committed to the present system of centralised collective bargaining and joint regulation. In fact, some of the legislative attempts of the early 1980s to weaken the unions were publicly opposed by the BDA and its most powerful affiliate, Gesamtmetall. Whilst the BDA has joined the call for more 'flexibility'—not least because of the growing difficulties of many of its affiliated associations in securing acceptance for general agreements from members facing increasingly divergent regional and sectoral, as well as technical and economic conditions—it would like to see this negotiated through the existing machinery, rather than imposed by law. For this reason, the BDA has been criticised for lack of initiative and imagination by representatives of smaller firms, such as the Working Group of Independent Entrepreneurs (ASU, Arbeitsgemeinschaft Selbständiger Unternehmer) who would prefer a tougher stand being taken against trade unions.

## The collective bargaining system in transition

While central features of the West German system of collective bargaining have remained in place—in particular, the practice of interconnected industry-wide agreements and the 'strike monopoly' of industrial unions, making for relatively low wage drift and low wage differentials between firms, industries and regions—there have also been significant changes. However, since these have proceeded gradually and along the lines of evolutionary tendencies that have been present for at least two decades, they are not always obvious. Nevertheless, in effect they add up to a cumulative transformation of the system, in the course of which the centre of gravity of collective bargaining has shifted from industry to establishment and enterprise level, where workers are not represented directly by trade unions but by elected works councils.

By the mid-1970s at the latest, West German trade unions had given up whatever 'money illusion' they may once have entertained, and they had understood that their only realistic objective under high unemployment and a non-accommodating monetary policy was to defend existing wages against inflation. In holding nominal wage increases down and forgoing real wage increases, trade unions contributed strongly to rebuilding the profitability of the West German manufacturing sector, in the hope of higher investment to relieve unemployment. This, however, did not materialise, and the largest part of the growing after-tax profits went abroad, mostly into the New York money market, where it helped finance the United States budget deficit.

While trade unions used centralised bargaining successfully to protect the traditionally low wage differentials in West Germany between firms, industries, skill groups and regions, their implicit acceptance of important elements of supply-side economics made it difficult for them to continue to use the redistributional rhetoric that had in the past made the yearly wage negotiations ideal occasions for raising the spirits of the membership and, in particular, the activists. Wage settlements that follow or remain below the productivity increase are not likely to generate much enthusiasm, and neither is redistribution from better-placed to less well-placed categories of workers taking the place of redistribution from employers to wage earners. As a consequence, the significance of wage negotiations for the self-presentation and self-perception of West German unions declined in the 1970s and 1980s. Since wage bargaining has traditionally been one of the main activities at the sectoral level, its decline raised—as it were, by default—the relative importance of other, lower levels of joint regulation.

A parallel development which also started in the early 1970s was the growing role of so-called 'qualitative' bargaining matters (Streeck, 1981b). A new concern with working conditions and work organisation in the 1970s resulted in several key agreements on 'humanisation of working life'. These were followed by initiatives to protect workers from the impact of technical change (*Rationalisierungsschutz*, protection against rationalisation), and later by efforts to place under central regulation the emerging new, more flexible working-time regimes. In all these cases, the subjects at stake were too complicated to be regulated comprehensively and uniformly at industry level. The solution adopted was to insert in industrial agreements clauses charging works councils and individual employers with negotiating, inside the institutions of workplace co-determination, the detailed application of the general principles agreed at the industrial level. This development was seen with considerable ambiguity by the unions. However, it seems to have been so irresistible that even the 1984 and 1987 agreements on working hours added to the decentralisation of collective bargaining, although they were originally intended to re-establish control at the sectoral level (Bartel & Falk, 1986; Schmidt & Trinczek, 1986).

Today, the institutional setting of co-determination has turned into a second, decentralised bargaining system with what amounts to a *de facto* closed shop (legal representation of the entire workforce by the works council), a monopolistic bargaining agent (the works council), a prohibition on strikes, and compulsory arbitration (through, ultimately, the Labour Courts). Obviously, this system corresponds closely to the growing importance of internal labour markets and the increasing complexity and diversity of technical, organisation and economic conditions at the workplace. Its gradual emergence—which was in part of the unions' own making—exerts pressure on industrial unions to review their organisational structures and bargaining strategies, and to redefine the role of sectoral agreements. The evolutionary trend, predating the crisis but precipitated by it, seems to be for industrial unions to turn into centres of external organisational support for, and mutual co-operation between, works councils representing workers in more and more autonomous workplace bargaining units, instead of imposing general and uniform rules on entire industries. Among other things, this may lead to further concentration of private sector unions on the large firms with strong works councils and supervisory board representation, which may raise difficult problems for the representation of workers and union members in smaller firms.

West German trade unions are beginning to recognise the need to refer a growing number of problems to joint regulation by works councils and individual employers. While central agreements, also on non-wage matters, are here to stay, they may become limited to giving guidance to negotiators at the plant and enterprise level, charging them with regulating centrally specified subjects, circumscribing their range of discretion, and possibly offering them a set of alternative solutions among which they can, and have to, choose ('cafeteria' or 'menu' agreements). Such decentralisation of collective bargaining may afford firms more internal flexibility for adjustment and restructuring and may thus help contain pressures for neo-liberal deregulation of the external labour market. Contributing to internal flexibility may require trade unions to agree to custom-made forms of work organisation and working-time regimes, workplace-specific systems of participation, worker involvement and retraining, and new payment systems capable of enhancing competitive performance in volatile markets for quality goods and services. The resulting pattern would in certain respects come close to a form of enterprise trade unionism, under the umbrella of a functionally redefined system of industrial-level 'framework bargaining', a pattern already very much in place in the chemical industry.

## Coping with structural and technological change

West German manufacturing firms have in the past had little difficulty in getting their workforces to accept technical innovation, and comparative studies have shown German workplaces to be highly flexible in responding to technological change (Hotz-Hart, 1987; Jacobs et al., 1978; Sorge et al., 1983). In part, the workers' low resistance to technical change in West Germany is accounted for by the co-determination system, which provides for legally based comprehensive interest representation at the establishment and enterprise level.[6] While this places the articulation of sectional interests at a disadvantage and promotes the identification of workplace representatives with the economic well-being of the enterprise, it also gives workforces effective means to protect themselves from negative effects of technical change. Board-level co-determination has added to this in that it has strengthened the manpower management function in large firms. This, and the extended rights of works councils to co-determination on recruitment, dismissals, retraining and redeployment, has promoted a more circumspect and long-term workforce and human resource policy in large firms (Hoff, 1984), which has enabled firms to make up for strong and increasing employment rigidities through internal adjustment. The result is a pattern of sometimes considerable rigidity in the external labour market together with high flexibility of internal labour markets, in strong contrast to the Anglo-Saxon pattern of external flexibility and internal rigidity (Marsden, 1981:18).

Increased employment security in internal labour markets has enabled works councils and trade unions to continue to support technical change and organisational flexibility. Instead of demarcating job territories and imposing restrictive practices, West German industrial agreements on 'protection against rationalisation' provide, for example, for wage maintenance for workers allocated to a new job in the course of technical change; employment protection, especially for older workers; strengthening of the internal labour market by requiring employers to offer displaced workers alternative jobs upon retraining; and new payment systems which emphasise knowledge and ability rather than jobs actually performed. This is in keeping with the traditional awareness of German trade union leaders of the exposed position of their manufacturing industries in the world market and the need to remain technologically competitive, an attitude which, incidentally, always kept union demands for foreign trade protection within narrow bounds.

Another important factor making for the low resistance to change in West German industrial relations is the skill structure produced by the vocational training system. German firms use more skilled workers than their foreign competitors and this accounts in part for their more flexible work organisation (Maurice et al., 1980).[7] Works councils have considerable influence, especially on retraining and further training programmes, and have always used this to press for extended training efforts. One result was that, in the 1970s, the number of apprentices in the German manufacturing sector increased strongly, even in years when total employment declined. The resulting supply of broadly based skills is likely to constitute a major asset for industrial restructuring and may be a stabilising factor for the 'productivity coalition' between management and labour at the workplace.

With rapidly rising unemployment in the early 1980s, the positive attitude of West German trade unions towards technological change appeared for some time to come under pressure. Theories of 'technological unemployment' became more popular among trade union activists[8] and gave rise to demands for what was called 'social control of new technology' and would in effect have meant restrictive 'technology agreements'. But in practice, and apart from the printing industry, the national leaderships, in line with the attitude of the works councils, continued to look for compromises between the needs of firms for technological adjustment and the interests of their members. This 'conservative' approach was borne out by the experience of sectors such as automobiles which, after a decade of intensive modernisation of their production technology, today employ more workers than in the early

1970s, as a result of higher competitiveness (Streeck, 1986). By the mid-1980s, trade union thinking seemed to be on the verge of return to the earlier position that if there is such a thing as 'technological unemployment', it is unemployment due to technical backwardness. There is also a growing conviction that in order to use new technology to safeguard and increase employment, it is essential to adjust and enlarge the skills of the workforce. In this respect, unions seem to be increasingly regarding their strong position in the training system as an appropriate instrument to promote industrial modernisation and thereby enhance employment, seen, for example, in the reform of the training scheme in the metal sector. Unions have also successfully demanded that the surplus funds of the Federal Employment Office, where the unions are represented on a tripartite basis, are used to finance additional training programmes. Indications are that a national 'qualification offensive' would be more likely than any other approach to unite trade unions, employers and the government in a joint effort to fight unemployment.[9]

On the other hand, technical and organisational modernisation creates tensions even in an industrial relations system as flexible as West Germany's. While in the past co-determination has facilitated adjustment to technical change, there seems to be a degree of incompatibility between existing institutions of workplace representation and certain new forms of work organisation often associated with the new technologies. Devolution of managerial functions to semi-autonomous work teams may involve matters, such as job allocation, determination of manning levels, working-time or wage setting principles, that are subject to works council co-determination. Works councils may, therefore, perceive the introduction of organisational methods of this kind as undermining their legal power, and they have in fact for this reason vetoed it on several prominent occasions. If it is true that the full exploitation of some of the new technologies depends on their being used in a decentralised work group structure, co-determination in its present form may become a liability rather than an asset for workplace flexibility and, subsequently, economic performance. The possibly disturbing implications of technical change for co-determination have led the DGB to mount a campaign for 'co-determination on the shopfloor', which is designed to bring work groups, and quality circles where they are introduced, under the control of the works council (DGB, 1985). But legislation to this effect will not be available in the near future, and trade unions will have to find an answer to new forms of participation in its absence.

At the national level, West Germany is a country without a tradition of 'industrial policy', 'sectoral policy', or 'selective intervention'. The Ministry of Economic Affairs has always strongly believed in a combination of forceful domestic competition and free international trade, and it has never subscribed to singling out 'national champions' or future 'winners' for special support. There are, therefore, no tripartite institutions comparable to the National Economic Development Council in Britain, although the unions have long demanded the creation of 'industrial councils' (*Branchenrate*) to oversee, co-ordinate and guide investment in the private sector (Markovits & Allen, 1984).

At the same time, a host of initiatives have been used to promote technological innovation, not just by the federal government and its Ministry for Research and Technology but also by the *Länder* and local communities. Programmes for 'technology transfer' are, in addition, conducted by trade associations and chambers, some of them in close co-operation with government agencies. Even trade unions have recently begun to set up offices for technology transfer. Nevertheless, formal institutions of labour–management co-operation in technology policy above the enterprise level do not exist (Czada, 1985), and the tripartite 'technology dialogue', which was started under the Social–Liberal government, was discontinued. In line with both the government's free market principles and the continuing decentralisation of the collective bargaining system, institutionalised co-operation between labour and management in industrial modernisation is limited to the enterprise-level framework of co-determination. The policy area in which trade unions at industrial and national level come closest to playing a major initiating role with regard to structural change is still industrial training, which is becoming increasingly important, owing to the human resource and workforce implications of new technology.

The situation is somewhat different in declining sectors, which, especially if regionally concentrated, like steel and shipbuilding, have attracted considerable government subsidies. The practice of subsidisation has continued under the present government, although with greater ideological misgivings than in the past. Under the Social–Liberal coalition, the trade unions played a major role in the management of the steel (Esser et al., 1983) and the shipbuilding crisis (Stråth, 1986), but their influence has since declined.[10] Here, too, the role of trade unions is likely in the future to be confined to the enterprise level, also because it is becoming more difficult for them to mobilise solidarity from those parts of their membership that are in prosperous, non-subsidised sectors (Stråth, 1986).

*Patterns of industrial conflict*

The West German pattern of strikes and lockouts is a direct reflection of the centralisation of collective bargaining and of the strong role of trade unions and employer associations at the industry level. Strikes can be called only by the national executives of industrial unions, and they are legal only after an industrial agreement has expired. As a consequence, strikes are rare and working days lost are negligible in most years. But about every five years there is one major conflict, always in the metalworking sector, and recently as a rule accompanied by a parallel dispute in the printing industry. (As the private, export-oriented sectors of the economy continue to dominate trade union policy, public sector strikes are infrequent.) These conflicts are typically long-lasting and involve a large number of workers. They are normally not, or not primarily, over wages, but rather over employment protection, working conditions and working hours. About one-half of the affected workers are not called out by the union but are regularly locked out by the employers. The settlement that results from such disputes is in ensuing years gradually diffused throughout the economy, including the public sector. This pattern has remained unchanged in the 1980s, except perhaps that, since 1980, strike participation has been extremely low in normal years and extremely high in the conflict year, 1984.

Strike strategies of trade unions and employer associations are to a large degree determined by financial considerations. DGB unions pay their members strike benefit amounting to about two-thirds of take-home pay—roughly equivalent to the rate of public unemployment benefit. Since strikes can normally be called only in pursuit of an industry-wide agreement, the number of workers that may have to be supported is always high. As a consequence, unions have to save funds for a number of consecutive years. Even so, a union like IG Metall, with over 2.5 million members, cannot afford to call out all its members at the same time, and the high art of West German strike tactics is to concentrate on a limited number of selected establishments for maximum impact (which is referred to as the 'minimax strategy'). For this reason, IG Metall has always negotiated formally separate regional agreements, which makes it possible to limit a strike to one 'pilot area'. To get, nevertheless, uniform conditions for the entire country, the union depends in effect on the ability of the national employer association to make its other regional affiliates sign identical agreements. This has, with a few exceptions, always been achieved, although it has sometimes been accompanied by considerable tensions inside Gesamtmetall and has once even led to a (short-lived) secession of several regional affiliates.

Even within the pilot region, however, IG Metall normally strikes only at a few selected firms. To enable employer associations to distribute the burden of conflict more equally among their members, without which they would find it difficult to convince a majority of their membership to agree to a settlement that inevitably involves concessions, the law permits them to impose a 'retaliatory lockout' in a bargaining district where the union has gone on selective strike. The number of workers that are locked out must be 'in proportion' to the number of workers on strike. Since trade unions pay locked-out members strike benefit, the lockout is essentially a device to increase the costs of the strike for the union and deplete its funds.

While this system has been functioning for some time, in the mid-1980s its rules of the game were more strongly contested than ever. Unions have long campaigned to have the lockout declared illegal. Since this is unlikely to happen, the intention probably was and is to tighten up the legal restrictions on its use, especially in terms of timing and size. This was partly in response to the improved ability of employer associations to compensate their members for the costs of industrial disputes, through their reorganised strike insurance system. Unions are also testing new strike tactics, such as centrally co-ordinated, short warning strikes, which cost them less, involve fewer members, and are less legally regulated (called 'new flexibility' in union jargon).

In addition, IG Metall in the great dispute of 1984 used a new variant of the minimax strategy, which employers found particularly threatening. While the strike was (initially) limited again to one region, Nord-Württemberg/Nord-Baden, the firms that were selected were crucial suppliers to the car industry. Because of reduced (kanban-type) stock-keeping, this resulted in an almost immediate shutdown of this industry in the entire country, including regions where the union had not yet struck. There, the employers were legally barred from locking out in retaliation. The laid-off workers, however, were entitled to unemployment benefit. For the employers, the calculated use of this effect amounted to an attempt to turn the social insurance system into a second strike fund. It was this situation that gave rise to the section 116 legislation, which excludes workers from unemployment benefit if they are laid off for lack of work during a strike, and if this strike is for demands that are at the same time also being raised on their behalf.

As has been said, the impact of the new law is far from clear. One possible effect could be a more dispersed pattern of industrial conflict, with negative consequences for the comprehensiveness of the collective bargaining system and the organisational cohesion of employer associations (Weber, 1986). Unions may find themselves constrained to raise different demands for different bargaining regions to protect the right of laid-off members to unemployment benefit. This would be likely to undermine the practice of pilot agreements, at the expense of the governability of the collective bargaining system that has been so economically beneficial in the 1960s and 1970s (Flanagan et al., 1983). It would also give rise to potentially unmanageable solidarity problems among employers and make for erratic differences between regional agreements, something German employers and their associations have had good reasons to avoid in the past. Moreover, if employer associations can no longer offer their members equal protection, the latter may find it more in their interest to conduct their industrial relations on their own. The same consequence might result from the 'new flexibility' of trade union strike tactics. While it is too early to make predictions, there is a high potential for fragmentation in the 1980s' turmoil over the rules of industrial conflict.

## Problem areas, strategic options, and likely futures

Such are the conditions facing industrial relations decision makers in West Germany at the end of the 1980s. Gradually, and continually as they have developed, they have quite unexpectedly given rise to a degree of uncertainty unknown for a long time. All three participants—government, employers and unions—suddenly find themselves confronted with choices of potentially dramatic importance. It is quite conceivable that the choices that will be made will reaffirm traditional patterns of institutions and practice. But reaffirmation there needs to be, as the present system will no longer reproduce itself, as it were, by default and as a matter of course. This is, by definition, a moment of realignment, and as West German industrial relations enter a new formative period they will for some time be more precarious and unstable than they have been for decades.

Why is it not a foregone conclusion that an industrial relations system as apparently successful as the West German one will persist as it is? The difficulty, in a somewhat but not overly simplified description, is this. Industrial relations, in West Germany as anywhere else, can be conceived as a game with three participants, each of which has essentially two strategic alternatives, a co-operative and a non-cooperative one. When the West German industrial relations system was formed, all parties settled on a co-operative strategy, and they have stuck to it ever since, almost as a matter of routine. While this has made a major contribution to economic performance, it has not prevented unemployment, and it has above all invited a process of technical, economic, political, institutional and social change, as a result of which the participants in the co-operation have themselves changed. As businesses restructure towards new product and production strategies, trade unions adjust to a changing member base, and political parties face a more volatile electorate with new and unpredictable concerns (to mention only a few of the changes that have taken place), they discover new problems, interests and opportunities that each of them has to consider all the more carefully since they know that the others are doing the same.

Cost–benefit analysis of alternative political strategies is always difficult, but it seems that, today, the players find it particularly hard to establish how the pay-off matrix of their choice between co-operation and non-cooperation is laid out. Here, the still vivid memory of the past successes of co-operation could help, and indeed, if players could allow themselves to follow their instincts, they would probably end up still co-operating. But there is also a greater awareness than in the past that co-operation may result in heavy and potentially lasting losses—of position, power and face—unless it is reciprocated by each of the two other sides, and that it is enough for co-operation to be impossible if just one participant refuses to take part. This is, with some modifications, a classical 'prisoner's dilemma'.

A 'prisoner's dilemma' can be resolved, to everybody's benefit, by mutual confidence in the other parties' co-operative intentions, and such confidence indeed constitutes the most important asset in the management and resolution of conflict. If only one participant loses it, a downward spiral of low trust may ensue, which will make co-operation impossible. In fact, for a crisis to start it is enough that just one participant ceases to expect that co-operation will be achieved, or has come to believe that one other participant believes that he will be better off without co-operation. In other words, the problem lies in the asymmetry that, if one side chooses conflict, or believes that another side will, conflict will ensue, while co-operation requires that all three parties opt for co-operation at the same time, each knowing that if just one fails to choose co-operation, those who do choose it will lose heavily. Today there is considerable suspicion among the players in the West German industrial relations game that at least one other player expects greater pay-offs from conflict than from co-operation, and that he will, therefore, exploit rather than reciprocate co-operation.

Trade unions, as so often in industrial relations, face the most critical and difficult choice. As the gloom of the early 1980s and the disappointment with the last years of the Schmidt government have receded into the background, a new outlook has gradually been emerging, which might provide a basis for rebuilding co-operation. The theory of technological unemployment has been losing ground, and illusions about the potential of work redistribution through cuts in working hours as an instrument against unemployment are dwindling. A new thinking has begun about the role of central industrial agreements in an age of growing technical and social complexity; flexible working time regimes are no longer anathema; a co-operative retraining strategy is being considered, as well as the idea of using further cuts in working hours for retraining at the workplace rather than additional leisure time; quality circles and team working are no longer perceived necessarily as devices to undermine trade union loyalty; and the need is being felt to open up the unions' organisational culture to groups of potential members who care little for traditional ideologies. Above all, a generational change in the leadership of the trade union movement, especially in IG Metall, has been taking place, which may make organisational and ideological renewal easier and faster to accomplish.

Trade unions will never be entirely comfortable partners in industrial and institutional restructuring. There will always be a left wing that will oppose too intimate and consensual relations with employers and a conservative government. Nor will West German trade unions ever co-operate with neo-liberal projects to increase external labour market flexibility by chopping away at employment security; to use part-time work on a large scale to reduce unemployment; to introduce downward flexibility of wages; and to increase significantly the variability of wages and conditions by industries or regions. Accepting these and similar recipes would not be co-operation for West German trade unions but capitulation, and pressed too hard in this direction they would undoubtedly prefer to fight. This fight they may not win, but to defeat them would take time and be likely to cost the economy dear. Moreover, on the way the precarious development of a renewed commitment to co-operation would be stopped dead in its tracks. It is true that West German trade unions have begun to move away from the 'simple consumptionist views' that dominated their economic policy proposals in the mid-1970s, towards recognition of 'the need for adaptation and modernization of German capital in the face of more difficult international circumstances' (Gourevitch et al., 1984:379). But this move is still a precarious one, and its advantages are to be had only at the price of their potential partners once and for all resisting neo-liberal temptations.

The kind of co-operation that West German trade unions could offer would essentially consist of active support for higher organisational flexibility, and of participation in the modernisation of skills, technology and work organisation. That this is highly conducive to successful performance in quality competitive markets, and that the latter is compatible with, if not conditional on, trade union strength and co-determination, is an important lesson of the recent history of the car industry (Streeck, 1986). Continuation and extension of this approach would involve further wage restraint to safeguard firms' investment, and research and development capacity. It would also include support for the emerging, highly diversified and specific regulatory regimes in individual workplaces, which would rule out attempts to reverse the continuing decentralisation of 'qualitative' collective bargaining and curtail works council autonomy. As part of this policy, trade unions would have to permit the introduction of new and complex working-time regimes that would make it possible to separate worktime and machine time and thus help raise productivity. They would also have to participate in good faith in experiments with decentralised forms of work organisation, including semi-autonomous working groups and quality circles. Moreover, co-operation would involve support for the modernisation of skills through extensive retraining, and if necessary it would be up to the unions to explain to their members the need to upgrade and update existing skills.

For German trade unions a productivistic modernisation strategy would in many ways be a continuation of past practice, but it would also involve considerable risks. Above all, the employment effect of a 'qualification offensive' against unemployment, even if combined with a moderate reduction of working time, is uncertain. While this would apply to all other strategies as well, for a co-operative approach trade unions would find it impossible to reject co-responsibility. Moreover, active promotion of industrial modernisation might turn unions into exclusive representatives of the skilled and the skill-able, and there would be no easy answer as to where the unskilled remain in the co-operative system. Other problems are the need to accept higher wage differentials between skilled and unskilled workers to motivate retraining, and a lower position in the wage structure for declining industries, both of which would give rise to conflicts between unions and groups of union members. Moreover, trade unions acting as agents of training and retraining may well alienate members who find it hard to adjust to change. Most difficult of all, perhaps, would be the explicit recognition that the emphasis of trade union policy has shifted from the demand-side to the supply-side, from a primary concern with distribution to one with production, and from the macro-level to the micro-level. Such recognition, and the associated ideological reorientation, would, on the one hand, just bring to the surface elements of West German trade union policy that have always been present and that may even have grown in importance in recent years. But the problem is that while it will increasingly become impossible to hide the role of trade unions as co-managers of industrial change—if they are willing to assume such a role—this may give rise to fratricidal ideological conflict with quite uncertain consequences.

Given the external constraints and opportunities facing the West German economy, trade unions may nevertheless be prepared to confront all these risks. But their willingness to do so will greatly suffer if, in the critical period, government or employers attack existing institutions of co-determination, which are the single most important source of assurance for trade unions that they will be able to protect their members from undue hardship and later to extract their share of the benefits of industrial change. Similarly, the redefinition of the role of industrial agreements—which is as such difficult enough—may become too hazardous for trade unions if their right or ability to strike at the sectoral level is simultaneously undermined. Also, the critical problems raised by semi-autonomous working groups for co-determination and trade union presence on the shopfloor will be even harder to resolve at a time when co-determination rights have to be defended against restrictive government legislation. And the shift in unions' organisational centre of gravity to the new white-collar groups, which is an inevitable element of any co-operative modernisation strategy, will become still more precarious if at the same time special representative committees for these groups are set up by employers or through legislation. Trade unions can solve the problems of a renewed commitment to co-operation only from a position of strength, otherwise their leaders will have to yield to pressures for simpler alternatives.

It is probably true that, if unions choose conflict, it would in the long run damage important economic interests of their members. But it is also true that, at present, non-cooperation would be ideologically less demanding, more in line with traditional rhetoric although not practice, and easier to explain to the activists. Above all, it would not be dependent on the uncertain support of others. Just like the contours of a renewed co-operative strategy, those of a new antagonistic policy are already present in the unions' internal debate, its main elements being a restrictive approach to new technology and a redistributive reaction to unemployment. At the bottom would be a narrow and enticingly simple definition of the role of trade unions. Management would be ascribed exclusive responsibility for efficiency, with unions defending the interests of their members through, for example, technology agreements, as in the public sector. Government would be charged with responsibility for full employment, and unemployment would be blamed on the government's refusal to reflate the economy and its legislative attacks on trade union rights at the workplace. Trade unions would define their contribution to higher employment exclusively in terms of a redistribution of work through further cuts in working hours, defending their members against ensuing increases in productivity and work intensity through restrictive work rules ('social control of new technology') and leaving it to management and the government to worry about economic competitiveness. In the course of this strategy, the opportunities offered by new, more flexible warning strike tactics, and the new constraints of section 116 would be thoroughly tested. The rising level of conflict would offer some hope that works councils can be whipped into line with external union policy—indeed they have been to some extent in the implementation of the 1984 agreement. As a welcome side effect, this would in part reverse the continuing decentralisation of the collective bargaining system. Training and retraining would still be supported, but primarily as a short-term—redistributive—device to hide unemployment, with an exclusive emphasis on egalitarian entitlement as distinguished from economic efficiency. No risks at all would be taken with regard to workplace co-determination, and new forms of work organisation would be judged exclusively in terms of their contribution to a reduction of work effort. As has been said, the ideological trappings for this line of action are already in place, and so are its potential protagonists, whose prospects of taking control of trade union policy were never better in the past two decades.

The way the unions will solve their strategic puzzle will be closely observed by the conservative government in devising its own strategy.

The Christian Democratic Party (CDU) is clearly much closer to business than to labour, and this holds even more true for the Free Democrats. At the same time, the CDU has always cultivated a small group of Christian trade unionists, who were given some degree of influence in the party, in exchange for the DGB giving them enough influence in turn to prevent the union movement turning entirely Social-Democratic. This complicated deal may no longer work. In the section 116 conflict, the Christian trade union group seems to have lost its influence in both the Christian Democratic Party and the DGB. For the government, there may also be economic reasons for attacking trade union power in the coming years. If the government no longer wants to subsidise ailing industrial sectors—agriculture, of course, being sacrosanct—it may have to exclude the unions altogether from the co-management of industrial decline. The consolidation of the social security system might also be easier to achieve if trade unions are weakened. And even though unemployment played virtually no role in the 1987 election campaign, at some stage the government might consider it necessary to do something about it. Unwilling to give up its ambitious goals of fiscal and monetary stability, it could try to put at least part of the blame for unemployment on the unions through further initiatives for more flexibility of the external labour market.

Of course, the government is more likely to choose an antagonistic strategy if employers believe that they can manage structural change without union co-operation, or that they will have to do so since such co-operation will be refused. Under the rules of the tripartite 'prisoner's dilemma' game, if employers are not willing to wait for trade union co-operation, the government will not be able to force them to do otherwise.

Also, up to a point, they can engage in conflict as well as co-operation, since they can hope to get the latter in spite of the former. Flexibility in external labour markets is as desirable to them as flexibility in internal labour markets, and the recent coincidence of the Employment Promotion Act with growing decentralisation of collective bargaining towards the works councils may give them the best of both worlds: a marginal labour force that can be hired and fired as necessary, as well as a well-integrated core labour force. Some employers are likely to rely primarily on the former, others—the large firms in particular—will prefer to rely on the latter, although they have little reason to object to the additional possibilities afforded to them by more fixed-term contracts.

This list could easily be prolonged. The weakening of external unions at the national and sectoral level is welcome to employers as long as it does not result in shopfloor wage bargaining—which it is unlikely to do—and the same holds for a piecemeal curtailment of co-determination rights. A critical point would be reached where external political conflict would threaten to undermine the domestic peace in the large, world-market-oriented firms that have, up to now, determined the policy of the leading employer associations. An antagonistic trade union strategy would amount to an attempt to withdraw this indispensable resource by making works councils refuse co-operation on technical and structural change. Whether trade unions are capable of this is an open question, and today there may be employers who are willing to take the risk and find out. They may place their hopes on the growing numbers of skilled employees whose aspirations may well be satisfied with a liberal and long-term enterprise human resource policy on the model of, for example, the chemical industry. It is not impossible that works councils, rather than falling in line with union conflict strategy, would be willing to administer such a policy. But if they are not, it could perhaps also be done without them, in the context of a strategy of 'unionism without unions', which would be the most likely response of German employers to a strategic withdrawal of trade unions from co-operation.

As has been said, there are strong temptations for each side to start a new, antagonistic game, and the short-term sacrifices and opportunity costs of continued co-operation are sizeable. The conservative government would have to disappoint some of its most faithful supporters, and it may even have to leave out a chance to reshape the political landscape fundamentally in its favour. Employers would have to continue to live with significant limitations on their right to manage and, in particular, to hire and fire, and they might have to help the unions organise the new and growing group of white-collar technical workers. And, finally, the unions would have to accept responsibility for technical change and industrial modernisation in a time of high and stable unemployment. On the other hand, there are undoubtedly high potential gains to be reaped from co-operation, and conflict may entail economically disastrous consequences. But the blame for these can always be laid at the other party's doorstep, and in any case, given the present high plateau of prosperity, the negative economic effects of lost consensus will take time making themselves felt. The problem is that it is not just economic rationality that counts but also political rationality, and it seems that, for the first time in the history of postwar German politics and industrial relations, the two will not easily coincide.

**Notes**

I am grateful to Winnetou Sosa for research assistance.

1 Two-thirds of all DGB members belong to the four largest unions (Visser, 1985).
2 On the 1970s, see Streeck (1987a).
3 The increase in employment ensuing from the 1984 agreement in 1984 and

1985 was estimated by the Federal Labour Office to be in the range of 100 000 jobs over two years.

4 Unless otherwise indicated, the following statistics were calculated using data from the official periodical of the Federal Employment Office, ANBA.

5 Slightly different figures are given in Visser (1985:table 4).

6 The situation is quite different in the protected public sector (Kubicek, 1986).

7 About 60 per cent of male manual workers in German manufacturing industry are skilled (Marsden, 1981:41).

8 For a convincing case against this theory, see Krupp (1985).

9 Although there are still important 'traditionalist' reservations on the trade union side (Kuda 1986; Malcher 1986).

10 One result of the strong trade union role in those sectors was that their relative position in the national wage structure improved between 1970 and 1980 (Krupp, 1984).

# 4

# France

## YVES DELAMOTTE

## Overview

### Trade unions

The oldest of the central labour organisations in France is the Confédération Générale du Travail (CGT, General Confederation of Labour), which was founded in 1895. Profoundly influenced during its early years by the doctrine of syndicalism, the CGT before 1914 supported the idea of 'direct action' and general strikes as a means of overthrowing capitalism, distrusted political parties, and was opposed to any kind of labour legislation. The First World War and the Russian Revolution led to changes in ideology and internal conflict. In 1921 the dissidents broke away and formed the Confédération Générale du Travail Unitaire (CGTU), which became a member of the Komintern in 1923. In 1936, with the left in power (Front Populaire), the two organisations reunited under the banner of the CGT.

In 1948 another split occurred: the dissidents within the CGT, unwilling to submit to Communist domination, formed the Confédération Générale du Travail–Force Ouvrière (CGT–FO, Workers' Strength, usually known simply as FO). The Fédération de l'Education Nationale, in order to avoid rifts amongst its members, opted for independence.

Christian trade unionism was yet another movement. It began as a white-collar movement, closely linked to the Catholic Church. The Confédération Française des Travailleurs Chrétiens (CFTC, French Confederation of Christian Workers) was founded in 1919. After the Second World War a change took place in the membership, with a growing influx of blue-collar workers, and in the philosophy of the movement, marked by a desire for independence from the Church. The outcome was that in 1964 the CFTC became the Confédération Française Democratique du Travail (CFDT, French Democratic Confederation of Labour). However, a minority, opposed to the abandonment of all reference to the doctrine of the Church, carried on under the banner of the CFTC.

Alongside these labour organisations, unionism also existed amongst managerial and supervisory staff, particularly after 1936. In 1981 the Confédération Générale des Cadres became the Confédération Française de l'Encadrement–CGC, (French Management Confederation), the change in name reflecting a desire to enlist some grades of junior staff without managerial status. Managerial and supervisory staff can, if they wish, join any of the other labour organisations.

In the elections of judges to the labour courts (*conseils de prud'hommes*[1]), these tribunals, whose origins date back to Napoleonic times, are composed of equal numbers of employers and workers and adjudicate disputes concerning individual contracts of employment. In the last periodical elections of *prud'hommes*, which took place in 1987, the CGT obtained 36.3 per cent of the votes, the CFDT 23.05 per cent, the CGT–FO 20.49 per cent, the CFTC 8.3 per cent and the CGC 7.43 per cent. This gives some idea of the 'constituency' of each of these confederations, although it gives no hint of the enormous fluctuations in membership that can occur as the economic and political climate changes.

*Employer associations*

The first national employer organisation was set up shortly after the First World War under the name of the Confédération Générale de la Production Française. It was succeeded in 1945 by the Conseil National du Patronat Français (CNPF), which is a flexible organisation with social as well as economic aims, grouping together a number of powerful federations (the most important being the Union des Industries Métallurgiques et Minières, UIMM).

Alongside the CNPF, there is also an organisation representing small and medium-size enterprises, the Confédération Générale des Petites et Moyennes Entreprises (CGPME), founded in 1944. The CGPME claims to be representative of those employers who not only run, but in many cases also own, their own business (as distinct from salaried managers). Even though the CGPME is separate from the CNPF, the two organisations are in constant contact and invariably join forces in negotiations with the government or trade unions on matters that concern employers as a whole.

*The role of the state*

France's labour legislation is extremely elaborate, but increasingly the tendency is to facilitate collective bargaining.

Labour legislation covers employment contracts (of various types), termination of employment, the minimum wage, working hours and worktime patterns, health and safety regulations, trade unions and workplace organisations (works councils, staff representatives). The legislation also defines the levels and subjects for collective bargaining, as well as its coverage (e.g. the possibility of the 'extension' of such agreements by means of an order issued by the Minister of Labour). For many years the tendency has been for such negotiations to be industry-wide, national, regional or local.

The legislation also lays down procedures for the peaceful settlement of industrial disputes, but more often than not it is the Labour Inspectorate that acts as a conciliation service, the Labour Inspectorate in France performing a far broader function than simply that of enforcing safety regulations. Although extremely detailed in other respects, France's labour legislation has very little to say on the subject of strikes.

Once a firm has reached a certain size,[2] it has, operating alongside one another, union representatives designated by each union that has members working in the firm, (statutory) employee representatives elected on a basis of proportional representation—in principle, from union lists—and (statutory) works council members elected in the same way. The union representatives negotiate the company agreements. The staff representatives submit employees' individual and collective demands to management. The works council is a body of elected workers' representatives, presided over by the managing director, who is required to provide it with a wide range of information (the legislation stipulates what sort of information this should be and how frequently it should be provided) and to consult it on certain types of project. The council manages many of the welfare arrangements of the firm. In addition there are workplace committees on health, safety and working conditions.

The CGT, the CGT-FO, CFDT, CFTC and the CGC for managerial and supervisory staff are all national organisations. Their constituent industry-based federations take part in negotiations on an industry-wide basis. At the level of individual firms, the unions affiliated to one or other of these confederations are, *ipso facto*, considered to have a representative character within the firm (even if they do not meet the main criterion regarding the number of union members in the firm) and accordingly can nominate representatives and present lists of candidates for the staff representative and works council elections. The number of representatives and councillors depends on the size of the firm and they may belong to one, two, or more trade unions.

## Developments in the first half of the 1980s

The legislation enacted throughout 1982, following the election of François Mitterrand and the formation of a socialist government in 1981, gave practical form to a policy that was designed to achieve a number of aims:

- to curb the increase in unstable employment by restricting the conditions under which an employer was allowed to hire temporary workers or workers on short-term contracts;
- to reduce working hours while encouraging negotiated agreements on the redistribution of working time (it was hoped in this way to increase the number of persons in employment through a system of 'work-sharing');
- to promote collective bargaining, particularly at the level of the individual firm, and at the same time increase the powers and prerogatives of the representative bodies, such as the works council, and the committees on health, safety and working conditions; and
- to give workers the opportunity to express their opinions directly on their working conditions and the organisation of their work.

At the same time, major reforms were put in train: the regionalisation of government departments, strengthening of elected regional councils, and the nationalisation of a number of industrial and financial undertakings.

*Government policy on wages*

The government decided that, with effect from 1 June 1981, the statutory minimum wage should be raised by 10 per cent, despite the fact that the price index had risen by only 3.33 per cent since the last adjustment. This was all part of a policy based on the idea that stronger growth and lower unemployment could be generated by stimulating consumer demand—in sharp contrast to the policies adopted by France's main trading partners. The effects of this 'go-it-alone' policy were not long in making themselves felt in the form of a substantial trade deficit and an increase in inflation (13.5 per cent from July 1981 to June 1982, compared with 8.4 per cent for OECD countries as a whole). In mid-1982 this policy was abandoned and this brief spell of demand stimulation was followed by a phase of austerity that is still more or less in force today.

A devaluation of the franc was coupled with a number of other measures, the most radical of which was a price and wage freeze for the period from June to November 1982. The government's objective was to bring price inflation down to 10 per cent in 1982, and to 8 per cent in 1983; this price freeze would be phased out through the negotiation of 'regulatory agreements' with business and industry. The government recommended that the phase-out of the wage freeze should be negotiated on the basis of mechanisms allowing for periodic readjustments rather than systems of indexation that tended to perpetuate the effects of inflation.

Whereas previously most wage increases were negotiated on the basis of linking them to recent increases in the price index, the wage agreements entered into in conjunction with the phasing-out of the freeze were geared to a forecast rise in prices (coupled with a much stricter contractual price policy). In most cases this involved phased increases (e.g. 2.25 per cent on 1 December 1982, 2 per cent on 1 February 1983, and so on) geared to price rises in line with government targets (10 per cent in 1982, 8 per cent in 1983). These agreements contained escape clauses allowing for an adjustment of wages at the end of 1983 which, according to the Minister of Labour, would ensure that average real earnings would be maintained.

At the same time as these guidelines were being drawn up for the private sector, the government was applying similar principles in the civil service and public sector undertakings. At the start of the year a timetable was drawn up for wage increases on the basis of the expected rise in prices. At the end of the year, if need be, there would be an adjustment in order to maintain average real earnings. This new approach marked the demise of a long-established practice which had survived despite being forbidden by law, namely, the indexation of wages on prices.

### Employers' wages policy

During the years following the lifting of the freeze, wage bargaining in the private sector was governed by the CNPF's guidelines, which were followed by the employer organisations in the individual industries, the object being that wage increases should each year be slightly lower than in the previous year, this wage restraint keeping pace with the slowdown in inflation.

The obligation to negotiate[3] in the case of industries applies only to organisations that have already entered into an industry-wide agreement and such negotiations have to cover wages. (Industry-wide bargaining has long been the practice in France.) The negotiations take place every year, but there is no requirement that a settlement must be reached. In the case of individual firms, this obligation applies only to those with at least 50 employees, when at least one union has designated one delegate, and the annual negotiations cover actual wages, the actual number of hours worked and the pattern of working hours. Here again, although the legislation gives indications as to how such negotiations should be organised, it imposes no obligation to reach a settlement.

According to the figures given in the *Bilan annuel de la négociation collective* (Annual Report on Collective Bargaining) for 1983 and 1984, published by the Ministry of Labour, out of the 299 national collective agreements in force, 53.5 per cent had at least one wage increase in 1983 and 48 per cent in 1984. Clearly, the obligation to negotiate on an industry-wide basis has not revived collective bargaining in those areas where it had become dormant (but where outdated agreements frequently still exist). In most cases where negotiations took place and where agreements were reached (often with only one or two unions), the CNPF guidelines were generally followed, with respect to either the number of wage increases during the year (which declined from 1983 to 1984) or the scale of wage increases (which in the case of industry bargaining are minimal wages far below actual wages in most cases).

As regards the statutory obligation on individual firms to enter into negotiations, this has certainly led to a considerable increase in wage bargaining at this level since, according to the report for 1983, two-thirds of the firms required to enter into negotiations had effectively done so and nearly two-thirds of these had reached a settlement. However, the increases ratified in these agreements (which in this case concern actual wage levels) are usually in line with CNPF guidelines. The report notes that with few exceptions employers had refused to compromise on the level of the proposed increases, using as their argument the government's recommendations, the CNPF guidelines, or the provisions contained in industry-wide agreements—an attitude that led to the failure of a number of negotiations. The unions in these negotiations were mainly concerned to get the timetable for the increases changed plus the promise of a review at the end of the year. The report (paragraph 23, page 52) also notes that on the whole this wage bargaining had not aroused a great deal of passion amongst workers and only in very rare cases had a breakdown in negotiations triggered off a dispute.

*The evolution of real wages*

Since 1983, with these changes in the conditions governing wage negotiations, wage increases have no longer been leading systematically to an increase in purchasing power. Between 1980 and 1985 average real earnings of wage earners in both the public and private sectors fell by 1.8 per cent, calculating this on the basis of an unchanged pattern of employment by category. However, taking into account the industrial restructuring and the job reclassification that have taken place (which have reduced the number of unskilled workers), average net real earnings rose by 1.2 per cent between 1980 and 1985 (*Economie et Statistique*, May 1986:3).

Over the same period the average annual increase in the price index was 13.5 per cent in 1980, 13.4 per cent in 1981, 11.8 per cent in 1982, 9.6 per cent in 1983, 7.4 per cent in 1984, and 5.8 per cent in 1985.

*Negotiations on working time*

Apart from wages, the main subject for negotiation during the early part of the 1980s was working time (in terms of both the number of hours and worktime patterns). This was the outcome of the Act regarding negotiations within individual firms, which stipulated that the compulsory annual negotiations should cover actual working hours and worktime patterns, and also of the Ordinance of 16 January 1982, which had a twofold effect. First, by stipulating that the statutory working week should be reduced from 40 to 39 hours, it obliged the employer organisations and unions at industry level to negotiate arrangements for reducing actual working hours. Second, the Ordinance left it up to industry-wide negotiation (or, failing that, to negotiation within individual firms) to decide the practical arrangements for the redistribution of worktime, which was now made legal (e.g. adjustment of working hours around an average, and weekend shifts).

By 15 June 1983, 97 such agreements had been signed at national level, concerning 86 industries. These agreements provided for an immediate reduction in actual working hours, ranging from one hour to two and a half hours, depending on the industry. These agreements had also to deal with the tricky problem of compensating for the loss of earnings that this reduction in hours implied. With few exceptions, no deduction was made for the first hour.

As for the possibilities of adjusting worktime provided for under this Ordinance, the extent to which these have been made use of varies: the possibility of arranging worktime around an average for the year that does not exceed 39 hours a week has been used on a wide scale, whereas weekend shifts have not proved very popular.

It would seem that these industry-wide agreements, once drawn up, have not required renegotiation, except for the occasional minor detail. In most cases they have been extended.

The combined effect of the Ordinance and these agreements was to reduce the working week by 2.5 per cent in 1982. However, the idea of 'work-sharing', which the unions saw as underlying this policy, has proved somewhat unrealistic, and it was very soon recognised that the effects of this reduction in working hours, in terms of job creation, had been slight.

As for the agreements within individual firms, in response both to the January 1982 Ordinance on worktime and the November 1982 Act on collective bargaining, these initially either applied or adapted the provisions of the industry-wide agreement to their firm. It was only later that the possibilities offered by the Ordinance would be really made use of.

*Emergence of the concept of flexibility in 1984*

The Ordinance of 16 January 1982 on worktime, which was very closely modelled on a national inter-industry agreement of 1981, contained provisions that paved the way for greater flexibility, and the policy of wage de-indexation, introduced by the Socialist government at the end of 1982, marked a major step in this direction.

In July 1984 discussions on flexibility were begun at national, inter-industry level (this being the level at which a number of agreements had been drawn up in the 1960s and 1970s on job security, worktime, vocational training, and the payment of wages on a monthly basis, not to mention unemployment insurance and supplementary retirement pensions).

A draft agreement was drawn up in December 1984 after six months of discussions. It dealt with a number of aspects: technological changes (staff representatives would be more closely associated with the intro-duction of new technologies in firms), working hours and the adjust-ment of worktime (the number of hours worked in a year would be negotiated on an industry-wide basis), redundancies (shortening of the time limit for consulting the works council and for the Labour Inspec-torate to authorise or reject a redundancy proposal, the preparation of a 'social plan' to deal with redundancies, and so on), and 'differentiated employment' (a relaxation of the conditions governing the use of fixed-term contracts, temporary and part-time work). Some of these provisions would mean amending current legislation.

It was known that the CGT would not sign this agreement, but it was expected that the CFDT might, as it was more inclined to accept changes to existing legislation if these were likely to have a beneficial effect on employment, and the executive committee of the CFDT even made a statement to this effect. However, this immediately aroused a violent reaction from its regional bodies and some major unions and the committee had to give up the idea of signing the agreement. The CGT–FO as well as the CFTC had already come out against it and the CGC, once the CFDT had backed off, declined to be the only organ-isation to sign it.

### Management's new style, 1980–84

These setbacks in collective bargaining did not prevent managements from pursuing a policy whose aims and methods became more clearcut as the 1980s wore on. 'Personnel management' began to be superseded by what is termed 'human resources management': a good manager is one who knows how to detect and exploit his employee's potential. In the case of managerial and supervisory grades, increasing emphasis is placed on setting objectives and annual performance reviews. Individual initiative is encouraged and rewarded. In many high-tech firms gradu-ates with similar qualifications and recruited at the same level find themselves ten years later occupying positions within the firm that differ widely in terms of job interest and financial reward.

Quality circles begin to be increasingly common, and in many firms they exist alongside the statutory discussion ('workers' expression') groups initiated by the legislation of 1982, whose purpose is to discuss the organisation and conditions of work. However, there is little in common between quality circles, with their economic and technological functions and which management can adopt as they see fit, and discussion groups, imposed on them by law and by and large not supported by the unions. The way things are developing, the future must inevitably be on the side of quality circles.

In the period 1980–84 management strategy became the most important factor in shaping industrial relations. There was very little industrial unrest (see the statistical appendix at the end of this chapter) and the level of union membership, which during the early 1970s was still around 20 per cent for non-agricultural workers, slipped to a figure probably in the region of 15 per cent (and certainly much lower if the public sector is excluded). The drop would seem to have been particularly marked in the case of the CGT (see the results of works council elections in the appendix).

This period is also one that is rich in paradoxes. The November 1982 Act, on the obligation to negotiate, was published during the price and wage freeze. The individual firm, which, according to traditional socialist doctrine, was the root of all exploitation, was rehabilitated as a job-creating unit and a source of innovation. Unions' bargaining power had never been so weak, even though legislation had never been more in their favour. Firms in the main found no great difficulty in shouldering their new legal obligations.

### Unemployment and changes in the pattern of employment

The number of unemployed (using the International Labour Organisation definition), which had represented 2.8 per cent of the labour force in 1974, amounted to 7.3 per cent in 1981 and 8 per cent in 1982 (*Données Sociales*, ed. 1984:56). By March 1985 the unemployment rate had risen to 10.2 per cent—an increase of 8.2 per cent on March 1984. This increase was less than that for the previous year (18.6 per cent), but the rate of growth was nonetheless higher than that for the years 1981–83 (*Economie et Statistique*, No. 183, December 1985:24).

The unemployment rate for young men in March 1985 was 24.5 per cent, and that for young women, 30.5 per cent. In March 1985, 42.7 per cent of unemployed men and 50.5 per cent of unemployed women had been out of work for a year or more. Given such rates, the unemployed are prepared to accept insecure or part-time jobs. The number of persons in part-time jobs was 1 979 000 in April/May 1982 and 2 327 000 in March 1985 (out of a total employed labour force of 21 319 000); the majority of these part-time workers were women. The

number employed on fixed-term contracts rose from 306 000 in April/
May 1982 to 315 000 in March 1985, although this figure was down to
256 000 in March 1984. This type of contract affected only 2.4 per cent
of white-collar workers in the private sector in March 1985, but was
gaining ground, primarily among blue-collar workers.

Over the period 1980–84 (*Economie et Statistique*, no. 187, April
1986:4), employment in industry fell by an average of 2.3 per cent a
year, with the figure for 1984 being 3 per cent. The hardest hit were the
steel and automotive industries. Employment in the traded services
sector rose by an average of 1 per cent a year over the same period. In
total, employment decreased (by 0.3 per cent on average for the period
1980–84 but by 0.9 per cent in 1984).

The government took measures throughout this period to encourage
early retirement, youth employment, part-time work, and so on. A
reform of the unemployment insurance scheme, dictated by the growing
seriousness of the employment situation, was introduced in 1984.

## Adjusting the labour market to the economic crisis

This is the area in which the greatest variety of solutions have been
proposed, at all levels, both by the government and the negotiating
partners, to deal with the problems posed by reconstruction to ensure
competitiveness.

### The iron and steel industry, shipyards

This is not the place to more than touch on the case of the iron and steel
industry, already in difficulty before the economic crisis descended on
Europe. As early as 1967, a 'social pact' containing various measures to
pave the way for job re-location and early retirement had been concluded. Today, the industry is covered by a general social plan agreement concluded in July 1984 (plus a rider for engineering and professional staff approved in June 1985) between the metal trades employers
and all of the workers' unions with the exception of the CGT. The
document defines the terms under which workers aged 55 and over may
opt for early retirement, and provides for the state to pay them a
monthly 'resource payment' equal to 70 per cent of their gross salary.
The contract provides also that workers aged under 45 whose jobs are
abolished should be offered 'job conversion leave' of up to two years.
For the period of this leave, the worker would receive from the state a
monthly resource payment equal to 70 per cent of his or her gross
salary. At the expiry of the leave, the employer would be obliged to offer
the worker the choice of two posts of indeterminate duration.

Similar provisions were decided upon for the shipyards (agreement of
9 November 1984). A complex welfare plan was worked out also in the

shipbuilding industry for a company facing particular difficulties (see the Normed case below).

### State assistance for early retirement

State assistance is available for companies in sectors other than iron and steel and shipyards. The Ministry of Labour manages a system of appropriations under the title of the Fonds National Pour L'Emploi (FNE, National Employment Fund). Set up in 1963 when the world economic situation was very different from what it is now, the fund began by helping labour, then rather scarce, to adapt to technological change. These days its main role is to avoid lay-offs (by providing aid to make short-time working possible) or permit early retirement.

To qualify for the FNE early retirement scheme, a worker must be employed in a company that has signed a contract with the Ministry of Labour. Early retirement is available to employees aged 56 years and 2 months or more who are laid off for economic reasons and who subscribe to the contract (it is thus a voluntary matter). Until the moment when they become eligible for their full old age pension, such early retirees are entitled to a guaranteed benefit equivalent to 65 per cent of their gross salary within the ceiling[4] applied by the Social Security scheme (in 1989, 477 francs a day, 10 340 francs a month) and to 50 per cent of any part of their gross salary in excess of that ceiling. The FNE early retirement scheme is financed by the retiree (to a small degree), by the employer, and, mostly, by the state.

### Agreements concerning mass lay-offs

National collective agreements on what is rather coyly named 'employment security' were signed in 1969 and 1974. The 1974 agreement, technically a rider to that of 1969, mainly required (article 12) that, when the management of a company was contemplating an economically necessitated collective dismissal, it had to supply the works council not only with the mandatory information concerning the number and type of workers liable to be laid off, but also with a draft 'social plan' consisting of such measures as transfers, modification of working hours, training, re-employment, FNE early retirement scheme, and so on. The agreement has resulted in the frequent establishment of social plans, with the more or less express approval of the workers' delegates, in a large number of companies. Their main planks were FNE early retirement (in nearly all cases), training initiatives, and assistance in finding other jobs.

In the public works industry, where the number of workers fell from 280 000 to 205 000 between 1974 and 1984, an industry-wide welfare plan was drawn up providing for job training for redundant workers under 55 years of age, early retirement for workers aged 55 and over employed in irksome or dangerous work, and assistance for resettlement in their home country for immigrant workers.

Other large employers of immigrant labour (Citroën and Renault, for example) have offered lump sum payments to ease repatriation. A Decree dated 27 April 1984 regularised the system, setting out the terms of eligibility, the various forms of aid, and the sources of funds (the state, unemployment insurance, the employer). Some firms have offered lump sum payments to workers who give up their jobs voluntarily, irrespective of nationality. In July 1986, for example, the government-approved social plan of Boussac (Textile) made provision for 579 FNE early retirements out of the 1461 redundancies and six to eight months' job conversion leave (on 65 per cent pay) for the other 882 employees involved. Those who did not opt for job conversion leave would receive the sum of 25 000 francs in addition to their severance pay. This amount was lower than that offered to workers at the Normed shipyards (6800 employed), an undertaking ordered into receivership in June 1986. Employees were offered job conversion leave of up to two years or a lump sum of 200 000 francs. Social plans on this scale obviously need government support.

## Statutory measures, 1985

The idea of job conversion leave made its first appearance in the social plan agreements signed in 1984 in the iron and steel, and the shipbuilding industries and in certain corporate pacts. Towards the end of June 1985 national collective negotiations (the first since those on flexibility broke down in December 1984) were organised by the Ministry of Labour with a view to the idea's general adoption, but they too failed. The government then introduced a Bill, which was passed by Parliament as the Act of 5 August 1985.

The Act instituted a new allowance, the job conversion allowance, to be financed by the FNE. Like early retirement, it was restricted to employees of an undertaking that had signed a contract with the Ministry of Labour who accepted the job conversion leave offered to them by the management. The minimum length of the leave was four months. The beneficiary would receive a monthly allowance equal to no less than 65 per cent of gross average earnings over the previous twelve calendar months (and in no case less than 85 per cent of the minimum wage). The state would finance half of the allowance up to twice the Social Security ceiling. State assistance would be limited to a period of ten months.

The employment contract of the worker on job conversion leave would be suspended. During leave, the worker would attend courses to acquire suitable training for the new jobs that the employer was supposed to be seeking out, and possibly training in new technologies. (Here again, the state would finance half the cost of the courses.) If, at the end of this leave, the employee failed to find work, he or she could be laid off, with their unemployment benefit backdated to the beginning of the job conversion leave.

## Developments in industrial relations 1986–89

No major change has taken place in the last few years. Wage negotiations have continued to be constrained by austerity. Negotiations concerning working hours have been aimed more at rearranging working time than reducing it. The government headed by Jacques Chirac, from March 1986 to May 1988, took some measures in order to promote more flexibility (notably in alleviating the administration's control on lay-offs), but did not touch the major Socialist Acts of 1982.

### Wage negotiations

According to the Ministry's annual report for 1987 (the latest report available), forward planning of wage increases according to a set timetable is becoming normal management practice.

For the years 1987 and 1988, the Conseil National du Patronat Français (CNPF, Employers' Confederation) reports that 53 national agreements were concluded between April 1987 and the end of 1988. It should be remembered that many of these agreements cover industries with a small number of employees. According to the Ministry of Labour, in May 1986 only 54 out of the 183 industries employing over 10 000 workers had concluded wage agreements, and about 3 million wage earners were covered by these accords (out of 11 800 000 employed in the private sector). In 1987 and in 1988, according to the CNPF, most agreements have included a calendar of rises of minimum wages (for instance, 1.5 per cent on 1 March, 0.75 per cent on 1 July, 0.5 per cent on 1 October). The wage increases scheduled in these agreements are not above the 3 per cent, which is the government's inflation objective, and probably also the goal of the CNPF, even if the CNPF does not any longer deliver precise guidelines. Not surprisingly many of these agreements are signed with one or two workers' federations (the CGT does not sign most of them).

In the private sector, where there is a duty to bargain on effective wages for companies with more than 50 employees, 72 per cent of these companies conducted a negotiation in 1987. In 89 per cent of such companies having negotiated, an agreement was reached (Annual Report for 1987). In nearly 80 per cent of these agreements, this raise was between 1 and 3 per cent (Annual Report, p. 61). Many agreements included some form of individualisation of wages (according to merit) or special measures to deal with low wages.

Overall, wages have barely grown over the past five years in real terms. But in many firms, especially those of small and medium size, profit-sharing schemes add to the employees' income.

In November 1985, the chairman of the CNPF labour relations committee circulated a recommendation to affiliated federations concerning the wage policy to be pursued in 1986. It emphasised the need to fix overall wage increases with reference to the economic situation of each industry and company, to keep industry and company decisions in perfect step with one another, and to take personal merit into account within the company. The CNPF also recommended associating workers with the company's success, in particular through production bonuses. It stressed the vital role of professional and executive staff. Their duties and remuneration needed to be studied separately. It gave some guidance as to figures: 'In 1986 increases in the total wage bill should be inferior to those granted in 1985'. In passing on these recommendations, the metal trades employer association (l'Union des Industries Métallurgiques et Minières) suggested that companies required to conduct annual wage negotiations should take into account both corporate and individual performance and hold increases in average gross real wages to less than 3 per cent throughout 1986.

In the public sector, various agreements have been concluded in 1988–89: Civil service (November 1988), Banque de France (January 1989), Electricité–Gaz de France (December 1988), French Railways (December 1988). These agreements, as in the private sector, define a calendar of rises (two or three in the year), but usually foresee a meeting at the end of the year to compare the evolution of the wages to the evolution of prices.

The general impression is that the policy of wage restraint, as conceived by the government (Socialist or Conservative) and by the employers, has not been threatened by the collective bargaining developments.

*Negotiations on working time*

The Ordinance of 16 January 1982 had opened new possibilities, at the industry or at the enterprise level, in the area of the redistribution of worktime, including adjustment of working hours around an average (*modulation* in French) and weekend shifts. This Ordinance was modified in order to make room for more 'flexibility' by an Act of 28 February 1986, the last piece of social legislation to be enacted by the Socialist government. And when the Conservatives came to power in March 1986, a new Bill was prepared, which became the Act of 28 June 1987. This Act, of a bewildering complexity, defines the conditions under which the new formulae can be introduced by industry or company agreements, the type of compensations which should be defined for the workers (in lieu of paying a premium on hourly rates) and so on.

Instead of analysing this Act, let us look at some agreements which were concluded in this legal framework.

The industry-wide agreements concern mainly the so-called *modulation*. An example is the agreement concluded in 1987, in the meat packing industry. This agreement allows individual companies to adjust the working time around the legal 39 hours a week, but without exceeding 41 hours. Hours above 39 carry a premium of 25 per cent. The agreement also provides for company-level agreements. In this case the maximum limit can be raised to 46 hours by the agreement, instead of 41. No overtime premium is then paid for hours above 39 a week. But the agreement must define the compensations granted to the employees, such as supplementary paid rest periods, reduction of the working time, and periods of training with pay.

In April 1989, according to the CNPF (*Liaisons sociales*, number 6235, 9 May 1989), 21 agreements had been concluded on the basis of the Ordinance of 1982 and 14 on the basis of the Act of 1987. Negotiations were pending in eleven branches (notably insurance, building trades, textile industry).

Since the Act of 13 November 1982, which imposed on enterprises with more than 50 employees a duty to bargain on wages and working time, working time is second only to wages as the most frequent item of negotiation.

In 1985, for the first time, negotiations over the pattern of working hours outnumbered those over the length of working time. According to the annual report of the Ministry for 1987 (p. 72), out of a total number of 5966 agreements concluded in 1987, 251 dealt with the reduction of working time, and 2272 with the pattern of working hours. Most of these agreements have to do with long weekends, holidays and flexible hours. However, according to the report (p. 72) the new formulae are spreading: *modulation*, weekend shifts, night work for women, and 'the agreements aiming at lengthening the period of utilisation of equipments are more and more frequent' (p. 73).

In France, the search for 'flexibility' has led to an exploration of what could be done in the area of working time, unlike, for instance, the United Kingdom, where 'flexibility' has meant principally trying to eliminate or lessen the rigidity of the internal labour market (demarcation between crafts, for example).

## Government action under Chirac

In March 1986, the national legislative elections saw the victory of the Conservatives. François Mitterrand designated Jacques Chirac as Prime Minister. The main measures taken by the right-of-centre Chirac government, in the area of social issues, aimed at easing restrictions placed on employers and promoting flexibility.

Concerning working hours, the Act of 28 June 1987 went a little further in this direction than the Act of 18 February 1986 (prepared under Socialist rule). An Ordinance of 11 August 1986 made it easier to resort to fixed-term contracts and temporary labour.

The main initiative was the preparation of a Bill, which became the Act of 30 December 1986. The government wanted to abolish the need for an enterprise to obtain authorisation from the Ministry of Labour services for any economically motivated lay-off, whether individual or collective. Such a requirement is rare in OECD countries. Before preparing the Bill the government invited the CNPF and the major workers' confederations to negotiate in order to determine some compensations for workers for the suppression of this protection. The agreement, signed on 20 October, fixed new rules concerning information and consultation of works councils about the lay-off to come, job conversion contracts, social plans to be prepared at company level. The Act of 30 December 1986 embodied and institutionalised procedures and remedies that were first defined in the October agreement.

The Act stipulated that, where they are not obliged to establish a social plan, companies involved in lay-offs, for economic reasons, of less than ten employees must offer job conversion contracts to the laid-off workers, on the condition that the latter have been employed by the company for at least two years. If the employee accepts the contract (which must be put to him or her individually and in writing), the employment contract is considered to be terminated by common accord and not by lay-off. The contract is valid for a period of five months. During the job conversion period, the worker receives a special allowance equivalent to 70 per cent of his or her former gross salary. The allowance is financed jointly by the state, the unemployment insurance fund, and the employer. The worker forfeits two months' wages in lieu of notice, but receives a payment equal to what he or she would have been entitled to if laid off; this is not, however, to be called severance pay as no lay off has occurred. Another provision of the agreement incorporated in the same Act calls for the management of a company employing 50 or more workers that intends to lay off 10 or more workers for economic reasons in the space of 30 days to submit a *social plan* to the works council. The plan may contain various measures, listed in the agreement and in the Act, notably FNE (National Employment Fund) early retirement and job conversion contracts, although these are not in this case mandatory. The early retirement measures form part of a strategy to combat unemployment, since they have the effect of removing older workers from the labour market. In 1981, even before a reform of old-age insurance enabling a worker insured for 150 quarter-year terms to retire on full pension at the age of 60 took effect in March 1982, the proportion of actively employed workers in the 60–64 age group was only 26.6 per cent.

Lastly, it should be noted that the Chirac government never contemplated repealing the 1982 legislation concerning collective bargaining, representative structures, and workers' expression.

## Current situation, unresolved issues

### *Inflation on the wane, but unemployment unabated*

Thanks to wage restraint and tough fiscal and exchange rate policies, inflation has been on the wane. In 1986 the rise in the consumer price index fell to 2.7 per cent, the lowest rate in the last twenty years. In 1987 and 1988, mainly on account of external factors (higher cost of imported oil, exchange rate of the US dollar), the rise was 3.1 per cent for both years. As of April 1989, the year-on-year rise (April 1988 to April 1989) was 3.6 per cent, suggesting a slight threat of renewed inflation. Significantly, the gap between West German and French inflation rates has regularly decreased. At 3.6 per cent, the French rate is half a percentage point more than West Germany's. In 1983, the gap was about 6 points.

Less progress has been made with unemployment, which remains high at 10.3 per cent (United Kingdom 8.5 per cent; West Germany 6.2 per cent). Demographic factors have certainly had some impact: there are more newcomers entering the job market than in West Germany. Employers put forward some rigidities in dismissal procedures as a reason, but the suppression in 1986 of the need to obtain government authorisation for economically motivated lay-offs had little effect on hirings. The national minimum wage is of course a factor of rigidity for the job market, but even during the conservative interlude (March 1986 to May 1988) its suppression was not envisaged.

### *New patterns at the enterprise level*

At the enterprise level and very succinctly, the situation offers the following characteristics:

- Very little social strife. The number of working days lost through strikes has fallen greatly (see table 4.2 at the end of this chapter). There are still occasional clashes, however, mainly linked to the employment situation in individual companies.
- A search for new methods of organising output and working hours within companies. The aim is to adjust more quickly and cheaply to fluctuations in demand or (by an increase in the number of shift-work teams or weekend teams) to put plant and machinery to more intensive use.
- The frequent inclusion of these new methods in company-level agree-

ments. These agreements are new to France, in that they embody concessions made by the unions and workers, and tend to address management problems. They address more issues (and their side effects) and are more independent than before of negotiations at other levels.

- Even in firms that have not concluded formal agreements, the new methods of organising production and working hours cannot be decided upon without lengthy discussions with the workers concerned, since their consent is essential. That is to say that a new bargaining partner has entered upon the classic industrial relations scene.

### Trade union problems

It is undoubtedly the trade unions that are faced with the most serious problems. Some of these problems are similar to those facing unions in other industrialised countries: changes in the structure of the economy are causing a shrinkage in the traditional areas of union strength; the economic conditions are putting a damper on their members' militancy; and the values and ways of life of the younger generation place more emphasis on life outside the workplace.

The growing diversification of workers' status and situation is probably more marked in France than in many other industrial countries. Workers' situations differ widely, ranging from that of civil servants and employees in the public sector at one end of the scale to those in so-called 'unstable' employment at the other. The former, who have virtually complete job security, are more or less guaranteed a steady increase in their pay over time and they enjoy a whole range of fringe benefits. The latter have intermittent jobs and rarely progress from one to the next. It is this great range, which is accentuated by the fundamental distinction between those who have a job and those who do not, that makes it extremely difficult to formulate demands behind which trade unionists can unite in the traditional manner of the French trade union movement. (A union's relations with the workers in a firm are further complicated by the fact that certain of the workers' motivations and aspirations are being catered for in other ways: some of the job satisfaction as far as skills and efficiency are concerned, for example, is being derived from the discussion groups and more particularly the quality circles that have multiplied in recent years.)

To quote the words of Edmond Maire, former Secretary General of the CFDT, in this sort of context, if the confederation backs the action undertaken by a particular union on behalf of a section of the labour force, not only will it not succeed in enlisting support from the other sections but it will often be considered as acting against their interest. For example, if the confederation comes out strongly in favour of improving unemployment compensation, those in employment will be afraid that they will have to pay higher unemployment contributions; if the confederation backs the civil service unions in their wage negotiations, this is likely to annoy workers whose jobs are under threat, who believe that the trade union movement has something better to do than fight for the 1 or 2 per cent difference between the government's and the unions' proposals (*Syndicalisme Hebdo*, 2 May 1985).

In addition to this difference in 'status' there are the differences that result from the tailoring of the working hours and wages of individuals, which is done deliberately by many employers, as well as cultural differences—large numbers of workers in industry, for example, are Muslim immigrants. This whole problem makes itself felt when it comes to drawing up programmes and deciding priorities.

Problems of a second kind are caused by the increasing inappropriateness of the usual forms of action. As we have seen, militancy has never been at a lower ebb. Nonetheless, in accordance with tradition, 'days of action', that is, strikes, in the public sector—e.g. SNCF (French Rail), Electricité de France—are periodically organised by the unions. Although the strikes are only for a short time (generally one day), they disrupt social and economic life and are becoming increasingly unpopular amongst the public, who do not hesitate to make their views known. Consequently, the leaders of both trade union confederations and individual unions are endeavouring increasingly to limit the inconvenience caused by strikes. There have even been strikes without work stoppages. In Brittany, for example, the regional branch of the CFDT, having decided to call a strike on the railways, got permission from the SNCF to run its own rush-hour commuter trains for workers and schoolchildren. The wages of these railwaymen were paid into a solidarity fund for the unemployed (*Syndicalisme Hebdo*, no. 2134 of 23 October 1980). What is more, great care is taken to explain to the public that the strike is aimed at preserving the efficiency of a public service, that is to say, the interests of the public themselves. At a demonstration in Paris on 21 October 1986, the CFDT unions in France's gas and electricity industry (EDF–GDF) carried banners announcing 'No cuts between EDF–GDF staff and the public' and 21 October was to be subsequently described in the CFDT press as 'the consumers' day'.

However, the broader problem would seem to be that the tradition of unselfish militancy is beginning to lose ground. The militant (that is, union activist) need not necessarily be a union official, but it was on his or her allegiance and faith (which frequently stemmed from the hope of a radical change in society) that French trade unionism has traditionally been based. The fact is that there are fewer and fewer militants, which should oblige unions to behave in a more business-like manner and, indeed, there are certain signs that this is already happening (e.g. they are attempting to find ways of ensuring that their members pay their dues regularly). Nevertheless it is clear that a satisfactory remedy for this decline in militancy has not yet been found.

A further problem is that of the relations between unions belonging to the same confederation and the relations between union leadership and members. In essence the question is the double-edged one of representation, with, on the one side, the mandate and, on the other, the instructions issued.

The problem of the mandate arises when it comes to putting a seal on negotiations by signing an agreement, particularly in the case of national and inter-industry negotiations. The agreement reached late in 1984 on flexibility remained unsigned because of the reaction from regional unions and certain federations within the CFDT. However, the lesson had been learnt by the time it came to finalising the October 1986 agreement on employment, when, throughout the final session, numerous internal consultations took place during the adjournments. Negotiators try to obtain a clear remit from their members in order to avoid being left out on a limb, but this would seem easier to do at the level of a single industry (e.g. the negotiation within the metal trades industry in 1986 of an agreement on worktime) than at the national–central level.

The other side of this question of representation is the instructions that are issued. It has quite often been the case that local unions refuse to accept and apply instructions issued by their confederation, particularly with regard to adjustments to worktime. Noting the number of cases in their area where employees have agreed to proposals made by the management of a particular firm, they consider that they are better placed to assess the suitability of an agreement than distant officials in Paris.

The problems facing unions were highlighted at the end of 1986 when a particularly large-scale strike brought to an abrupt end a period of several years during which unrest, measured in terms of the number of days lost through strikes (see the statistical appendix at the end of this chapter), had been at an unprecedentedly low level. It all began a week before Christmas on the railways with employees of SNCF coming out on strike in protest against the management's proposals concerning wages (which would have increased the merit element in wage payments). The strike spread very rapidly to include the entire rail network, the Paris metro and the electrical power industry, and led to violent reactions from users (private individuals, shopkeepers and so on). The strike began to peter out in the second week of January, after management had made a few, relatively minor, concessions. What was remarkable about this strike was its spontaneity. Although under French law trade unions are not seen as the ones who instigate strikes (the right to strike is vested in the individual and not in an institution) and the concept of a 'wildcat strike' has no special relevance in the French context, there is, however, some justification for using the term 'wildcat strike' to describe this sudden outburst that took the unions, who had not been expecting it, completely unawares. As always in these cases, they tried to take over the leadership of the movement, but even in this they were unsuccessful, with the non-union 'co-ordinating committees' keeping them out, as if a strike were far too serious a matter to be left to the unions. The strikes, it should be noted, were confined to the public sector, the sector where there is virtually complete job security as well as the highest level of trade union membership. The strikes were evidence of the crisis in the relations between unions and the workers.

## The emerging structure of collective bargaining

The Employers' Confederation (CNPF) has become clearly the main force shaping the evolution of collective bargaining. The emerging pattern includes three levels of negotiations.

First, at the top, that is, the national inter-industry level, where the CNPF itself directly negotiates, negotiations deal with such matters as the social security institutions, for example, insurance against unemployment, or complementary old-age pensions. Such institutions have been created by national inter-industry agreements, concluded by the CNPF and the major workers' federations, to fill the gaps of the state social security system (which does not cover unemployment) or to add a complement to the benefits paid by the systems. The negotiations concerning these institutions deal with for instance the rate of contributions, the duration and rate of allowances, and more generally the adjustment of the institution to changing economic circumstances.

At this level questions that are expected to become the subject of a Bill would also be discussed. Then the agreement concluded would be used as a basis for the Bill by the government, which could announce in Parliament the 'consensus' of the social partners upon the text submitted. This pattern has been followed for such questions as economically motivated lay-offs (in 1986 and now) and working time (in 1981).

A third type of national inter-industry agreement would define guidelines and approaches for dealing, at the industry level, with certain questions. Typical from this point of view is the agreement on working time signed in March 1989 by the CNPF and the managers' union, the CGC. This *accord de méthode* stipulates that negotiations will begin at the industry level within six months. The industry agreements should improve the quality of working life for the employees; they should also make for a longer utilisation of equipment and machines, and for the adaptation of the length of working hours to economic fluctuations. The reduction of the working time should be obtained through an arrangement of the working time, without increasing labour costs. The agreement defines also more restrictive conditions governing the use of shift work. Other *accords de méthode* such as this one have been concluded concerning technical mutations, and the adaption of the personnel to these mutations.

Second, negotiations at the industry level would not involve the CNPF, but the employer organisations of the industry and the corresponding workers' federations. At this level would be negotiated minimum wages, job classifications, working time, and training, for instance. Certain orientations of the wage policy could be also defined at this level.

The purpose of industry-wide negotiations would be to establish an appropriate general framework within which firms could identify their own requirements and from which they could extract the elements they need in order to put together a package that best suited their present and foreseeable development. This last phrase calls to mind a type of bargaining that we saw is becoming more common and which tends as much to solve management's problems as it does to satisfy workers' aspirations.

Third, at the enterprise level the two main subjects of negotiations would be, as imposed by legislation, effective wages and arrangements of working time. Wages should take into account the results of the company. Working-time arrangements should take into account the wishes of the employees, and the pressures of the market. This policy means an increased decentralisation of the negotiating processes, combined with impulsion and control coming from the top level. It implies also that at each level the employers find valid interlocutors. Some observers are sceptical about the future of collective bargaining.

### A Socialist government again

Since the re-election of François Mitterand, in May 1988, the dissolution of a National Assembly, and the return to power of a Socialist government, headed by Michel Rocard, no major measure has been taken in the field of labour relations, a big difference from the first years of the Socialist rule in 1981 and 1982. The market-oriented policy is maintained with a high degree of wage restraint. A new Bill under discussion by Parliament in June 1989 concerned economically motivated lay-offs, but it aimed mainly at improving the job-conversion contracts, without re-establishing the government's power to veto a lay-off. Reduction of unemployment is the major goal of the government.

The present Socialist government tries to conciliate economic pragmatism (profits of companies have never been so high) with the respect due to workers' rights. In the years to come, any French government will try to maintain this equilibrium at the level of the European Economic Community against those who in France and elsewhere see in Europe only a common market.

## Statistical Appendix

### Trends in trade union membership

Trustworthy data do not exist in this area, which in France is compli-cated by the rapid membership turnover and the vagueness surrounding the very concept of membership (owing to the irregular payment of union dues). Table 4.1, referring to works council elections, gives some idea of the trend in size of the major 'confederations'.

### Extent of coverage by labour agreements

*Industry-wide negotiations.* The Ministry of Labour's target is to extend labour agreement coverage to all industries. The Report on Collective Bargaining in 1983 noted (page 1) that 'in the last two years, an extra 500 000 wage-earners have received labour agreement coverage. A fur-ther 1 200 000 are concerned by negotiations under way.'

What really matters is the 'vitality' of these industry-wide agreements (as evidenced by the number of riders attached to the basic accord concluded in a particular year). The Report for 1985 remarks (page 11) that 'while national labour agreements devoid of riders over a period of five years form 16 per cent of the total number, they concern only 2 per cent of wage-earners covered by such agreements', and 'Out of every three wage-earners covered by a labour agreement, two were affected in 1984 and 1985 by the signature of at least one rider.'

*Company negotiations.* According to the Annual Report for 1985 (page 21), 15 per cent of wage earners (as against 8 per cent in 1983 and 12 per cent in 1984) in all sectors were covered by company agreements registered with the departmental Labour Directorates. The percentage varied widely from sector to sector.

### Table 4.1 Works council elections

|               | 1979 | 1985 | Change 1979–85 |
|---------------|------|------|----------------|
| CGT           | 34.4 | 25.9 | − 8.5          |
| CFDT          | 20.5 | 20.8 | + 0.3          |
| CFTC          | 3.1  | 4.7  | + 1.6          |
| CGT–FO        | 9.7  | 13.0 | + 3.3          |
| CFE–CGC       | 5.8  | 6.7  | + 0.9          |
| Other unions  | 4.8  | 5.1  | + 0.3          |
| Non-unionised | 21.2 | 23.8 | + 2.6          |

*Disputes*

**Table 4.2 Number of workdays lost owing to labour disputes (agriculture and government services excepted)**

| Year | Workdays lost | Year | Workdays lost |
|------|------|------|------|
| 1976 | 4 054 900 | 1982 | 2 250 499 |
| 1977 | 2 434 400 | 1983 | 1 320 969 |
| 1978 | 2 081 000 | 1984 | 1 316 820 |
| 1979 | 3 172 300 | 1985 | 880 000 |
| 1980 | 1 511 300 | 1986 | 567 700 |
| 1981 | 1 441 228 | 1987 | 511 600 |

*Source:* Tableaux Sociaux, *Liaisons Sociales* no. 10329, 3 November 1988.

*Rise in prices for 1986 and 1987*

In 1986 average consumer prices rose by 2.7 per cent; the change for the year was an increase by 2.1 per cent (quoted from *Liaisons Sociales*, no. 9909, 12 February 1987). The difference between these two indices of inflation is the result of two different methods of calculation:

- for *change for the year*, INSEE calculates the relation between the index for December 1986 (163.7 over base 100 in 1980) and that for December 1985 (160.3); and

- for the *average for the year*, INSEE compares the average index for the whole of 1986 (162.2 over base 100 in 1980) with the average indexed for 1985 (158.0). The average index is calculated by INSEE from a set of twelve monthly indices, themselves revised (but not published) to take account of seasonal changes in six categories of fresh produce.

The rise in terms of change gives an accurate picture of month-by-month variations, whereas the rise in terms of average rather portrays the trend. In a period of declining inflation, such as the one we are currently experiencing, the rise in terms of change for the year is lower than the rise in terms of average (the reverse being true when inflation is rising).

In 1987, change for the year was + 3.1, and the average for the year was also + 3.1 (Tableaux Sociaux, *Liaisons Sociales*, no. 10329, p 81).

**Table 4.3 National Consumer Price Index (base 100 in 1980)**

| | Average for year | | Change for year (December to December) | |
|---|---|---|---|---|
| | Index | Percentage change | Index | Percentage change |
| 1980 | 100.0 | + 13.5 | 105.1 | + 13.7 |
| 1981 | 113.4 | + 13.4 | 119.7 | + 13.9 |
| 1982 | 126.8 | + 11.8 | 131.3 | + 9.7 |
| 1983 | 139.0 | + 9.6 | 143.5 | + 9.3 |
| 1984 | 149.3 | + 7.4 | 153.1 | + 6.7 |
| 1985 | 158.0 | + 5.8 | 163.7 | + 2.1 |
| 1986 | 162.2 | + 2.7 | 163.7 | + 2.1 |
| 1987* | 167.3 | + 3.1 | 168.8 | + 3.1 |

*Note:* *The official target for 1987 was a rise of 2 per cent in terms of average and 1.7 per cent in terms of change.

**Notes**

1 The *conseils de prud'hommes* are composed of lay judges (employers and employees in parity), elected every five years on a basis of proportional representation. For the employees, the major workers' confederations present lists of candidates, so that the results of the election show the relative influence of each confederation.
2 Eleven employees for staff representatives; fifty employees for union delegates and works councils.
3 The act of 13 November 1982, imposes an obligation to negotiate each year on wages (minimal) at the industry level and on wages (effective), length and organisation of working time at the enterprise level.
4 The social security contributions are a certain percentage of the wage in the limit of a 'ceiling'.

# 5

# BRITAIN

## LAURIE HUNTER

### Overview

In its analysis of the British industrial relations scene twenty years ago, the Donovan Commission (1968) left a clear impression of a system dominated by voluntarism, a term that implies a preponderant reliance on a voluntary (rather than legal) basis for the organisation and conduct of management and union activities, including their interaction in collective bargaining. Where law was used in this voluntarist system, it was primarily to provide safeguards, for example, the Factories Act, Wages Council legislation and, more recently, equal pay and equal opportunity legislation. In the past twenty years, despite Donovan's affirmation of the virtues of voluntarism, successive governments have eroded the voluntarist approach, introducing over time and with differing objectives an expanding body of legislation to regulate both organisations and behaviour. Most observers would probably agree that the essentially voluntarist character of the traditional British system is still dominant, but there is no doubt that the role of law in industrial relations has increased substantially.

Alongside that change, two other shifts of major importance have occurred. First, within the voluntarist system, there was a great deal of informality and reliance on custom and practice as a means of conducting relationships. While adjustment to change could undoubtedly be achieved through custom and practice methods, the very concept is rooted in precedent and the traditional way of doing things. New products and processes frequently demand new methods of working, and reliance on traditional and conventional forms of organisation may inhibit investment in change, or slow its diffusion, or simply make the outcome less efficient than it should be. Perhaps in response to growing competitive pressures for change, and perhaps in part as a reflection of more formal legal structures in certain areas of industrial relations, informality, custom and practice have been increasingly displaced by a greater reliance on formal, codified provisions governing procedures

115

and agreements. That is not to say that informality has disappeared: a strong element of informality is always likely to be present as a lubricant to maintain the formal mechanisms in good order.

The second additional factor has been a change in the structure of collective bargaining on pay and conditions of employment. Donovan described a system that was essentially that of private manufacturing industry, the sector in which Britain's industrial relations problems were then seen to be most severe. Donovan deplored the schism between the formal system, dominated by multi-employer bargaining at industry or national level, and the informal system represented by fractional bargaining within the workplace. In the last twenty years, private manufacturing has increasingly moved towards single-employer bargaining at plant or company level, but the industrial relations problem is no longer dominated by manufacturing. In part this reflects the sharp decline in its employment share and the expansion of service employment (table 5.1). Equally important, the public sector has proved to be a source of growing industrial relations difficulties, though for the most part this sector is characterised by centralised, industry-wide bargaining over pay and principal conditions of employment.

**Table 5.1 Changes in industrial composition of employees in employment, United Kingdom, 1977-88 (June)**

| | Percentage share of employees in employment in | | | | |
| | Manufacturing | Services | Other industries | Total | No. of employees in employment ('000) (not seasonally adjusted) |
|------|------|------|------|------|------|
| 1977 | 32.4 | 57.4 | 10.2 | 100 | 22 126 |
| 1978 | 32.0 | 57.9 | 10.1 | 100 | 22 273 |
| 1979 | 31.4 | 58.6 | 10.0 | 100 | 22 638 |
| 1980 | 30.3 | 59.6 | 10.1 | 100 | 22 458 |
| 1981 | 28.5 | 61.5 | 10.0 | 100 | 21 386 |
| 1982 | 27.5 | 62.7 | 9.8  | 100 | 20 916 |
| 1983 | 26.3 | 64.0 | 9.7  | 100 | 20 572 |
| 1984 | 25.6 | 65.1 | 9.3  | 100 | 20 741 |
| 1985 | 25.0 | 65.9 | 9.1  | 100 | 21 006 |
| 1986 | 24.3 | 67.1 | 8.6  | 100 | 21 089 |
| 1987 | 23.7 | 68.0 | 8.3  | 100 | 21 317 |
| 1988 | 23.3 | 68.7 | 8.0  | 100 | 22 074 |

*Source: Employment Gazette*, Historical Supplement no.1, February 1987, plus corrections provided by Department of Employment and updated from *Employment Gazette* May 1989.

These changes have taken place against a background of economic uncertainty, particularly in terms of a rising level of unemployment, large numbers of long-term unemployed, and a growing sensitivity to inflation. The effects of these factors have pervaded much of industrial relations attitudes and conduct, and have conditioned the character of change in relation to many of the specific issues discussed in this chapter.

### The labour market and industrial relations since 1980

In Britain, 1980 makes a convenient watershed, since it was in this year that the first effects of the new Conservative administration, which came to power in 1979, began to appear. For industrial relations, the significance of the change of government was more than the traditional shift of emphasis when a government of one complexion is replaced by one of a different complexion. This was a more radical, reforming administration, committed not only to curbing inflation by means of strict monetarist policies, but also to coming to grips with the problems it saw as underlying inflation, including inefficiency and inflexibility in the labour market and an imbalance of power between the parties to industrial relations.

This commitment and the link between overall economic policy and industrial relations reform underlined the Conservative government's belief that the industrial relations system was an important factor in holding back the performance of the economy. In itself, this was not new—concern about the interaction between industrial relations and economic performance was one of the reasons for the 1964 Labour government setting up the Donovan Commission. What distinguishes the recent experience from much that has gone before is the government's rejection of a consensus approach, and its greater readiness to take action—by legislation if necessary—in former 'no-go' areas that it regarded as important industrial relations obstacles to greater economic efficiency, such as picketing, lack of strike ballots, closed shop provisions and the legal immunities of trade unions. In 1989, Parliament dismantled the National Dock Labour Scheme, which had provided a statutory monopoly for 9400 registered dockers.

The main features of labour market and industrial relations development in the period from 1980 to 1987 are summarised in the following two sections.

### Labour market

The twin problems of wage inflation and unemployment, which had dominated the 1970s, continued to hold sway in the eighties. Unemployment in the United Kingdom had reached a postwar peak by 1980,

**Table 5.2 Employed labour force and unemployment rate in United Kingdom, 1977–88**

|      | Employed labour force (1980 = 100) | Unemployed as percentage of working population* |
|------|------|------|
| 1977 | 99.2  | 4.8  |
| 1978 | 99.4  | 4.7  |
| 1979 | 100.7 | 4.3  |
| 1980 | 100.0 | 5.4  |
| 1981 | 96.6  | 8.5  |
| 1982 | 94.7  | 9.8  |
| 1983 | 93.9  | 10.8 |
| 1984 | 95.5  | 11.1 |
| 1985 | 96.9  | 11.3 |
| 1986 | 97.5  | 11.5 |
| 1987 | 99.1  | 10.3 |
| 1988 | 102.7 | **   |

*Note: *Unemployment rates are expressed in terms of the seasonally adjusted claimant series, excluding school leavers, on the current basis allowing for changes in coverage due to administrative changes.*
\*\*Statistics no longer published on this basis. A crude estimate suggests a 1988 value of 8.3.
*Source: Employment Gazette.*

but the next three years saw a doubling of the rate to around 11 per cent (table 5.2), despite rapidly expanding programmes to provide relief from unemployment, especially for young people. The employed labour force shrank by over 6 per cent between 1980 and 1983; there was some recovery in 1984–86, but without any dent being made in the unemployment figures. Despite the high level of unemployment, average earnings generally continued to rise more sharply than retail prices: only in 1982 did real earnings fall slightly. Price and wage inflation, however, both dropped rapidly from their peaks of 18 and 20 per cent respectively in 1980, to 5 and 7 per cent in 1984 (table 5.3); increases in average earnings subsequently hovered around the 8 per cent mark, while retail prices began to increase again from 1987 and currently remain a matter of serious concern to government.

Control over inflation was achieved by means of a strict monetarist policy, which, in conjunction with the 1979 rise in oil prices and the subsequent world recession, led to a fall not only in employment but also in gross domestic product—down by over 3 per cent in 1979–81—and, especially, in manufacturing output, which fell by 15 per cent in the same period. Productivity (output per person employed), which had stagnated in the late 1970s, began to rise steadily, increasing

by 16 per cent between 1980 and 1986. In large measure this was due
to the shake-out of labour in the production industries, amounting to 20
per cent in the same period, and was reflected in a productivity growth
rate of 41.6 per cent (over the period).

**Table 5.3 Year-on-year changes in retail prices and average earnings,
1977–88**

|      | Retail prices % | Average earnings % |
|------|-----------------|--------------------|
| 1977 | + 15.8 | + 9.0 |
| 1978 | + 8.3 | + 13.0 |
| 1979 | + 13.4 | + 15.5 |
| 1980 | + 18.0 | + 20.2 |
| 1981 | + 11.9 | + 13.0 |
| 1982 | + 8.6 | + 9.4 |
| 1983 | + 4.6 | + 8.4 |
| 1984 | + 5.0 | + 6.1 |
| 1985 | + 6.1 | + 8.5 |
| 1986 | + 3.4 | + 7.9 |
| 1987 | + 3.4 | + 7.9 |
| 1988 | + 4.9 | + 8.7 |

*Source: Employment Gazette.*

In contrast to the 1960s and 1970s, the counter-inflation strategy
eschewed the use of incomes policy, viewed by the Conservative government as both ineffective and inhibiting to market forces. Strict control was exercised, however, over public sector borrowing and expenditure, which in turn had a strong influence on public sector pay and
employment levels. Forward public expenditure plans typically included
a level of cash provision for pay increases below current price inflation,
which implied either low pay settlements or further employment retrenchment. In effect, these elements of general economic strategy
operated as a highly effective incomes policy for the public sector and
its consequence both for pay and employment coloured government–
union relations.

*Industrial relations*

It was a central part of the Conservative government's policy when it
came to office in 1979 that the industrial relations system should be
reformed in a number of respects, with the aim of curbing trade union

power, increasing democratic control within trade unions, and tackling problems posed by the closed shop, violent mass picketing and the invoking of strike action without adequate testing of workforce opinion. In contrast to the Heath government's Industrial Relations Act 1971, which attempted wholesale legal reform, the Thatcher government proceeded by means of separate but progressive pieces of legislation: the Employment Acts of 1980 and 1982; the Trade Union Act 1984; and the Employment Acts 1988 and 1989. Among the main features of this legislative package were:

- a narrowing of the definition of a 'trade dispute' so that it covers only issues directly concerned with terms and conditions of employment, discipline and dismissal, work allocation and the operation of negotiating and consultative machinery;

- reduced scope for the immunities of trade unions and their officials when secondary industrial action takes place;

- new provisions relating to the maintenance and operation of the closed shop, requiring approval by secret ballot for the continuation of closed shop arrangements;

- restrictions on the circumstances in which lawful picketing can be undertaken;

- compulsory secret ballots of trade union members about prospective industrial action as a condition of trade unions and officials retaining their immunities against civil action in the courts; and

- changes in the law regarding the election of trade union executive bodies, requiring unions to adopt certain democratic practices, which in practice entailed amendment to union constitutions and procedures.

In addition, the government introduced a number of deregulation measures: from June 1985, employees wishing to lodge a complaint of unfair dismissal required two years of service rather than the previous one year and the earlier six months; the Wages Council system for regulating low pay was simplified, particularly by removing young people from the scope of council regulation; and the Truck Acts, regulating how wages can be paid, were repealed. Statutory procedures for trade union recognition embodied in the Employment Protection Act 1975 were also abolished in 1980.

This substantial legislative programme, together with tight monetary control of the economy and public expenditure constraints, was backed up by a firm government stance on a series of industrial disputes in which it featured, at least indirectly, as employer. The example par excellence was the long-running dispute in the coal-mining industry, ending without settlement in March 1985 after twelve months' industrial action. Other prominent examples include disputes in British Steel, the civil service, water supply and among schoolteachers, not all of which were 'won' by the employer. And there were some where the government chose not to become overtly involved or chose to take a more flexible attitude to pay adjustment, for example in disputes concerning local authorities and electricity generation.

As we shall see in more detail below, these developments had important implications for trade unions, management and government–industry relations. In brief, the Trades Union Congress (TUC) remained fundamentally opposed to the evolving legislative programme, and considerable debate continued about the proper response of member trade unions to changes in the law on union government and immunities in the course of industrial action. The trade union movement's ability to resist both the general changes and the more specific shifts in the margin of control was, however, restricted by the adverse labour market situation and falling trade union membership as a result of declining employment in the production industries—the traditional stronghold of manual trade unionism. Falling membership meant falling income, and a number of unions began to face serious financial difficulties, which tended to accelerate existing tendencies to mergers and rationalisation; strike benefit for large numbers of members over a prolonged period was often impossible, and this influenced strike tactics as well as strike propensities.

If the TUC felt frustrated at its loss of influence on government strategy, the Confederation of British Industry was almost equally frustrated, arguing unsuccessfully for some amelioration in the harsh application of monetary controls, high real interest rates and a continued squeeze on profits. At enterprise level, however, management increasingly used their bargaining power, enhanced by greater legislative support and the struggle for economic survival, to cut costs and introduce change in working practices. Despite speculation about the growing importance of 'macho' management, the evidence suggests that comparatively few cases of extreme exploitation of bargaining advantage occurred. Firmer management control was still, in general, consistent with the recognition of trade unions and the pursuit of joint agreement through the procedures of collective bargaining; evidence exists, also, of some compensating increase in effort by management to develop greater employee participation. Among the more difficult areas of management –union relations were some examples of technological and organisational change, the most notable of which affected provincial newspapers and Fleet Street, London, the traditional home of the national press.

In summary, the period from 1980 to 1988 saw a major change in the economic condition of the labour market, which adversely influenced trade union bargaining power, while the industrial relations system moved towards greater legal regulation. The mainstream procedures of

collective bargaining and consultation do not appear to have been radically disturbed in form or utilisation, though their character has undoubtedly been influenced by change in the legal and economic environment.

## Analysis of change

### Employment structure and patterns of work

The relative contraction of manufacturing employment and the expansion of service employment in recent years has already been noted (see
table 5.1). Manufacturing decline has not, of course, been even. Substantial productivity growth has seen rapid expansion of output in high-
technology industry, but without employment increases. Elsewhere, the
rundown has been severe, especially in engineering; this has been reflected in plant closures, high levels of compulsory redundancy, and
progressive reductions in the employment size of many of the largest
plants. The employment most severely hit by this decline has been
full-time male manual employment, and to a lesser extent female manual employment. Conversely, the growth in services has been over-
whelmingly female employment, mainly part-time, resulting in a substantial shift in the structure of the labour force. Table 5.4 shows a 4
percentage point decline in the share of male employment over a ten

**Table 5.4 Male, female and part-time employment, United Kingdom,
1977–88. Percentage share of employees in employment:
seasonally adjusted, September figure**

|      | Male | Percentage of whom part-time | Female | Percentage of whom part-time |
|------|------|------------------------------|--------|------------------------------|
| 1977 | 59.1 | n.a. | 40.9 | 16.3 |
| 1978 | 58.7 | n.a. | 41.3 | 16.1 |
| 1979 | 58.2 | n.a. | 41.8 | 16.8 |
| 1980 | 57.9 | n.a. | 42.1 | 17.5 |
| 1981 | 57.3 | 3.4  | 42.7 | 17.9 |
| 1982 | 57.1 | n.a. | 42.9 | 18.1 |
| 1983 | 56.6 | n.a. | 43.4 | 18.4 |
| 1984 | 56.0 | 3.7  | 44.0 | 18.7 |
| 1985 | 55.6 | 3.8  | 44.3 | 17.1 |
| 1986 | 55.0 | 4.0  | 44.0 | 18.8 |
| 1987 | 54.5 | 4.1  | 45.5 | 20.0 |
| 1988 | 54.3 | 4.1  | 45.7 | 19.3 |

Source: Employment Gazette, Historical Supplement no.1, February 1987, plus Department
of Employment; Employment Gazette April 1989.

year period, absorbed by a like expansion in the female share, but more strikingly, part-time employment now accounts for over 23 per cent of all employees in employment, most of them female workers, very largely married women. In addition, a growing fraction of the employed labour force is on some form of temporary work contract; for example, staff on a fixed-term contract, supplied by agencies, or subcontracted self-employment. A recent study, admittedly of larger companies, indicated not only that this practice was increasing, but also that it accounted for as much as 8 per cent of employment in these companies (Atkinson & Meager, 1986). If this could be added to the volume of part-time employment, it might seem that between one-quarter and one-third of those in work are now part of what has been termed the 'non-core' labour force, as opposed to the 'core' of regular employees (Hakim, 1987). This is, however, almost certainly at the top end of the range of estimates.

It is not yet clear how far this development is the result of a deliberate long term strategy on the part of employers or whether it is the outcome of a shorter-run, precautionary approach to the recruitment of core staff in the face of economic uncertainties and cost pressures. The employment protection legislation of the mid-1970s (Employment Protection Act 1975) is also thought to have contributed to this trend, most notably with respect to unfair dismissal provisions, which, if upheld at law, can be costly to erring managements. What may be more certain is that an increasing number of employers have been pursuing one or more forms of labour force flexibility, whether it be quantitative (as in the case of part-time workers replacing full-timers or fixed-term contracts), functional (in the sense of achieving multi-skill craftsmen or fusion between blue-collar and white-collar functions) or 'distancing' (contracting out of tasks, subcontracting self-employment, home-working).[1] While these particular forms of contractual relationship are not in themselves new, the scale and extent of their use does appear to have increased. While some of the increase is attributable to relative expansion of sectors that have always used such contractual forms, some traditional industries have shown signs of experimenting along these lines.

A further reflection of flexibility is the continued reliance by managements (and wage-earners) on high levels of overtime. Where fixed employment costs are perceived to be high, it pays to use existing employees intensively, especially to meet peaks in demand. In practice, average hours worked have remained virtually static over 1980–86, with the exception of a small decline in the case of manual male workers in 1980–81. Although in principle it would seem possible to convert the substantial overtime into additional jobs, it seems to be in the interests neither of employers, who gain the benefits of flexibility, nor of overtime workers, who get the benefit of premium payments, to embark on the conversion.

Taken in combination, these changes in work organisation represent for the time being an appreciable shift in employer manpower strategies and practices. As well as the direct benefits perceived in terms of the ability to cut off expenditure in labour costs at short notice and to avoid the penalties associated with claims for unfair dismissal, the peripheral labour force is typically much less prone to unionisation, often implying lower wage costs and less need to negotiate or pay for acceptance of change, whether technical or organisational. The consequences for trade union membership of this trend, as well as the structural industrial shifts eating into the heartland of traditional manual unionisation, are potentially severe, and, as we now see, may have contributed to changes in trade union organisation.

*Trade unions and employer associations*

Both employer associations and trade unions have faced increasing difficulties since 1980, largely reflecting the severity of the recession, but also the government's rejection of a consensus approach to policy. Employer associations, additionally, have suffered some loss of coverage and influence as more employers have moved to independent company bargaining (see below). The Confederation of British Industry, the main representative voice of employers, also lost membership for similar reasons, but it remains by far the most influential spokesman for employers as a whole.

The problems for trade unions have been even more severe.[2] The number of trade unions continued to decline in the 1970s, as it had in the previous decade, but the growth of union membership continued until 1979, when there were 13.3 million members in 453 unions. Since then, mergers and transfers, commonly involving local and craft unions joining national unions, had reduced the number of unions to 335 in 1986, by which time membership had fallen to 10.5 million. The heaviest declines in membership have been in manufacturing-based unions and those organising manual workers. The scene is increasingly dominated by large unions: over 53 per cent of total members are now in eight unions, mostly general, multi-industry organisations. Long-term decline in employment, especially in manufacturing, has signalled the need for rationalisation into bigger union groupings if an effective voice and membership service is to be maintained. Increasing numbers of unemployed members, or lapses because of unemployment or job change, have reduced union income from dues and enforced internal reorganisation to achieve staff economies. In the service sector, efforts have been made to recruit in expanding employment areas, and continued pressure for recognition has been maintained, but the largely female composition of employment growth and management's strong bargaining position have tended to nullify these efforts.

Such pressures have increased tendencies for some unions to adopt a more competitive strategy to maintain membership. Where major new production facilities are being set up, unions have been more willing to offer complete packages in response to management's wish for single union recognition agreements, cutting into occupational areas that have been regarded as another union's province. Such employers have been concerned to avoid the problems that may arise from multi-unionism[3] at plant level, and the package typically includes an information agreement, scope for employee participation in decision taking, straight-choice arbitration as the final stage in a comprehensive disputes procedure, and often a no-strike clause. In December 1985 the Trades Union Congress General Council approved a ban on these 'new style' agreements where they were reached without the consent of other unions involved, revealing its concern about the ways in which such agreements were being arrived at, and their implications for inter-union relations. Continued difficulties have been experienced in this area, culminating in 1988 in the expulsion of the Electricians Union (EETPU) from the TUC for failing to comply with TUC Dispute Committee rulings against the union.

Unions have been beset by other problems, too. The passage of new statute law has posed direct threats to the former legal immunity of unions and officials, and has required internal organisational change, while increasing use has been made by employers of older civil law. Unwillingness to co-operate with government legislation has shown itself more in demonstrations and brief industrial action than in outright opposition.

Public sector unions have faced some particularly difficult problems, many of them associated with the absence of any clear-cut set of principles attaching to the determination of pay in the public non-trading sector (e.g. civil service, health, local government and education). But throughout long disputes with steelworkers, coal-miners, civil servants and teachers, the government has appeared to give strong support to the employers, to whom its legislative measures (especially on secondary picketing and the more restrictive definition of a trade dispute) have proved helpful by constraining union choice of tactics.

Finally, unions have faced the difficulty that employers have increasingly adopted a policy of directly communicating with employee-members of unions with which they are in dispute. This in itself does not indicate employers' unwillingness to negotiate through regular machinery, which has remained largely intact, but suggests a more cautious approach by management to the use of shop stewards as a channel of communication with employees; shop stewards in some cases have also found the range of facilities made available to them by their employer being curtailed, for example, office space and services, and time off for union duties.

In summary, then, while both employer associations and trade unions have had an uncomfortable ride through the 1980s, the biggest challenges by far have been posed to the unions, not only by the greater bargaining advantage of employers, but also by the direction of legislation and the increased need for open accountability to rank and file membership. Despite this, there has been a continuing working relationship between employer associations and trade unions in a variety of spheres, including training bodies, industrial development committees and sector working parties.

## Collective bargaining

As noted earlier, bargaining structure in the United Kingdom is complex and has been undergoing change since the late 1960s. Patterns of pay bargaining differ considerably among private manufacturing, private services, public administration and the nationalised industries. Also, bargaining over non-pay matters varies considerably, both as to level and content. Thus it is difficult to encapsulate recent trends in short compass, and the following is no more than a sketch of the main developments. Factual information in the remainder of this section is drawn from the 1984 Workplace Industrial Relations Survey,[4] as the most thorough, up-to-date record of British industrial relations behaviour patterns at workplace level.

The evidence for 1980–84 is that important changes have continued to occur in some aspects of collective bargaining. Overall, there has been a tendency for pay to be determined by collective bargaining in a higher proportion of establishments, but employee coverage has declined. The reason is that as the proportion of manufacturing workplaces declined significantly, the share of workplaces in public services increased, and the latter are nearly all covered by collective bargaining. Thus the major changes here are caused by structural change in industry.

Within the public sector, there has been little change. Pay continues to be determined at national level, but this is generally synonymous with company or single-employer bargaining. Both public administration and nationalised industries are characterised by heavy centralisation of pay bargaining. There are, however, increasing signs that the government is anxious to develop greater decentralisation and differentiation in regional settlements, which it believes would contribute to employment expansion.

The biggest changes have occurred in private manufacturing, where establishment coverage for manual workers has declined from 65 to 55 per cent between 1980 and 1984. The proportion of manual employees working in covered establishments has also declined, though it still remains high at just under 80 per cent, a similar figure to that for non-manual workers. So far as the level of bargaining about pay is concerned, national bargaining remained the most important level for 40 per cent of manual workers, compared with less than 20 per cent for non-manual workers. But for the remainder, company and plant bargaining were most important, with company or divisional level bargaining increasing in importance, particularly for non-manual staff. Plant bargaining remained highly important in larger-scale plants, in the engineering industry and among foreign-owned companies. If anything, then, the drift away from industry-wide bargaining continued, mainly towards higher levels of negotiation within the company, a trend consistent with the desire of corporate management to keep a tighter grip on overall changes in pay.

In private services the coverage of collective bargaining for pay purposes increased slightly, especially for manual workers. The main determinant here has been organisational size, rather than establishment size as in manufacturing. As in manufacturing, company bargaining increased for non-manual workers, growing at the expense of industry-wide agreements. Of particular significance is the observation that, in organisations characterised by more advanced technology, bargaining was more likely to be establishment-based, perhaps suggesting that this sector of services is becoming more like manufacturing.

Non-pay issues present a slightly ambiguous picture. The overall amount of collective bargaining about non-pay matters appears to have declined since 1980, especially at workplace level, and the decline was most marked in private services and private manufacturing. However, there does seem to be some fluidity in negotiation on non-pay matters, in the sense that certain issues may be brought into the ambit of bargaining on an irregular basis—sometimes negotiated, at other times not. The evidence is at least consistent with management's retraction of their willingness to negotiate on non-pay issues, because of their greater ability to resist union pressure for joint regulation of matters such as re-deployment, manning levels and redundancy.

An overview of collective bargaining suggests that, although the public sector has remained relatively unchanged, and dominated by strong central pressures, especially on pay, the private sector has witnessed some rolling back of the frontier of bargaining on pay and non-pay measures, to the advantage of management. Collective bargaining remains by far the most significant method of pay determination in establishments employing a great majority of employees, and national or industry-wide bargaining is still important for many employees in manufacturing. But the trend towards plant and company bargaining, particularly the latter, appears to be continuing. Further insight into the significance of collective bargaining will emerge in the following section, where the adjustments to structural and technological change are discussed.

*Structural and technological change and adjustment*

In addition to coping with the problems of a substantial shift in employment between manufacturing and services, the labour market has had to absorb a widespread diffusion of new technology, much of it related to information technology, which has not only created new products but has also had a major influence on processes. The implications for industrial relations tend to vary, according both to the economic health of the product market concerned, and to the nature of the change in technology itself.[5] Generalisation is, accordingly, somewhat hazardous.

For the present purpose, perhaps the central issue is the way the parties to industrial relations have approached the problems of technological change. The trade union line, at least, was clear in intention. The TUC (1970) launched an Employment and Technology initiative in which it accepted and welcomed change, but sought to secure a trade union role in design and selection of new technology, rather than just involvement in implementation. To this end it advocated model 'new technology' agreements, which would provide for participation in planning, as well as providing safeguards to those affected; and this line was widely adopted by affiliated unions. Discussions between the Trade Union Congress and the Confederation of British Industry produced a draft 'framework for technological adaptation' in 1980, which argued that employment security could be compatible with changes in job structure and skills, recommended that compulsory redundancies should be avoided where possible, and stressed that joint understanding on the distribution of benefits could provide a satisfactory platform for introducing technological change. Opposition from within the confederation led to its employment policy committee being unwilling to endorse the proposals, so that unions were left to try to secure agreements in a context where managements were facing a severe recession and were anxious to find ways of cutting costs—and were, therefore, particularly interested in reduced manning and greater labour force flexibility.

It is not surprising, then, that only a small fraction of the workforce are covered by new technology agreements, and those who are frequently find them falling well short of the TUC ideals. Certainly few have won rights for their union to be involved in selection and design stages—and the evidence likewise indicates that personnel management have had little influence either. White-collar unions have been more successful than blue-collar unions, but even then, most agreements relate to implementation, for example, the avoidance of compulsory redundancy, provisions for training and redeployment, and specification of remuneration. With fewer new agreements being signed since 1983, the original TUC conception would seem to have failed. Even where advance information has been provided, union representatives have not always been able to make the best use of it, for reasons such as lack of technical expertise, lack of resources and the nature of union organisation (TURU, 1984). Significantly, most unions have been particularly backward in their own adoption of information technology, both for administration and for analysis.

Since a good deal of new technology has been introduced, what has been the trade union stance in practice? Once the technological choices and design have been settled, there remains the implementation stage, which can be approached either by outright resistance, by bargaining to improve the terms of change, or by active participation in advancing change. Despite significant exceptions in both directions, British trade unions have tended to be adversarial but not obstructive, and the main method of handling this has been through collective bargaining— probably the traditional British approach to the adjustment to change. Thus negotiation is common on such matters as manning levels, re-deployment, the acceptability of multi-skilled craftsmen, and the pay increases required to make the change palatable.

More direct opposition has occurred in some areas, notably in the national press (Fleet Street) and parts of the civil service. In each of these areas, however, other factors may have helped to focus union resistance, and the same may well be true of other localised instances of resistance. At the other extreme, there are significant examples of new technology on greenfield sites, which have led to single-union agreements incorporating acceptance of new technology, flexible working practices and interchangeability of skills, as well as the other features of such agreements discussed above. Where such agreements feature the recognition of a trade union operating beyond its traditional boundaries, we are in part observing the effects of changing technology itself, as microprocessor technology offers scope to re-draw industrial and craft boundaries, and blur the conventional lines between white-collar and blue-collar activities.

The general conclusion from this rapid survey is that the trade union movement as a whole has been willing to adopt a participative approach to the introduction of new technology, but has found it difficult to make progress, as it has been largely excluded from the early stages of decision making. Unions have then fallen back on the more traditional approach of bargaining over change at the implementation stage, softening the employment effects on members, and seeking improvements in remuneration. Managements appear to have reached the technological decisions at high organisational levels and without significant involvement of unions or of personnel management. The combination of new technology, especially the microprocessor varieties having a widespread effect on production processes, and a cost-sensitive, competitive economic environment has been used to redefine the boundaries of production control in favour of management, and to achieve a significant increase in flexibility in work organisation and working practices.

*Work stoppages*

Table 5.5 shows that the number of stoppages due to industrial action has declined significantly, by over 50 per cent, since the late 1970s, but that the number of working days lost remains highly variable from year to year. Underlying this apparent paradox is a strong indication that the pattern of strike activity has changed. In the 1960s and 1970s Britain's 'strike problem' was characterised by a high percentage of short stoppages, largely unofficial and unconstitutional, and typically involving relatively small numbers of employees directly. More recently, the percentage of unofficial and unconstitutional disputes has fallen, but the 'average' stoppage tends to involve more workers or to last longer than in the 1970s as a whole. Thus, in any given year, a major long-running dispute, such as that in coal-mining in 1984–85, can accumulate a very high number of days lost. The other significant change is that, whereas in the past the 'strike problem' was largely associated with manufacturing industry, the main sources of stoppages now arise in the public sector. This in itself is significant, for the largely centralised bargaining processes of the public sector mean that large numbers of employees are potentially included, and even where union tactics include national one-day stoppages or selective strikes, the days-lost figure can quickly mount.

**Table 5.5 Stoppage of work and working days lost in stoppages, United Kingdom, 1977–88**

|  | No. of stoppages beginning in period | No. of working days lost in stoppages in progress during period ('000) |
|---|---|---|
| 1977 | 2703 | 10 142 |
| 1978 | 2471 | 9 405 |
| 1979 | 2080 | 29 474 |
| 1980 | 1330 | 11 964 |
| 1981 | 1338 | 4 266 |
| 1982 | 1528 | 5 313 |
| 1983 | 1352 | 3 754 |
| 1984 | 1221 | 27 135 |
| 1985 | 887 | 6 402 |
| 1986 | 1053 | 1 920 |
| 1987 | 1004 | 3 546 |
| 1988 | 725 | 3 687 |

*Source: Employment Gazette* (incorporating September 1988 revisions).

The fall in manufacturing strike activity is readily explained by the well-recognised contra-cyclical pattern of strikes: the ability of unions to acquire and sustain membership support during recession is clearly limited. In the public sector, the underlying factor is the constraints imposed by government on public expenditure and the forward provision of a pay factor in budget estimates that is typically well below current rates of inflation. Public sector management is thus required to exercise pressure on pay improvements or on manpower, but often on both. Concern about public sector pay lagging behind, or about job loss, has led unions to take strong industrial action. Government's substantial and continuing programme of privatisation of public sector activity has likewise led to resistance, partly political but also reflecting concern about job security.

The Trade Union Act 1984 may also prove to be a significant element in the future pattern and volume of strikes. Trade unions wishing to retain immunity at law when taking industrial action are now required to hold a secret postal ballot of their members that results in a majority in favour of the proposal. At the end of the first full year, the (public) Advisory, Conciliation and Arbitration Service (ACAS, 1986) reported knowledge of 94 cases of ballots, resulting in a majority vote for action in 68 (72 per cent) cases and against in 25 cases (one vote was tied). On the one hand this suggests that only a minority of the 800 or so strikes in 1985 were protected by the ballot provision, and comparatively few injunctions were taken out by employers to restrain action. On the other hand, the use of the ballot provision would appear to have gained a substantial foothold and the popular view is that employees widely approve of the principle. It is too early yet to predict what long-term effect this will have on strike incidence, but the signs are that the pre-strike ballot may become an important tactical weapon when employer–union relations are threatened with breakdown. For example, a union that has ballot support from its membership for strike action may choose not to strike at once but to use the evidence of support as an extra weapon in the bargaining process.

The main causes of stoppages show little variation. Pay and conditions account for at least half of all stoppages and typically for about two-thirds of working days lost. Redundancy issues have been significant in recent years, while dismissal, disciplinary and recognition issues also regularly feature. Issues arising from resistance to technological or organisational change do not emerge as prime causes, but since the adjustment process is commonly bound up with compensation questions, disputes that are ostensibly about pay may conceal difficulties of adjustment to change.

Lastly in this connection, mention is due to the role of the Advisory, Conciliation and Arbitration Service, which provides an independent third-party route to dispute avoidance or resolution. Many of the formal procedures for grievance handling, especially those dealing with pay, provide for third-party involvement, and the service is commonly brought in either to provide conciliation or, more rarely, to arrange arbitration. In issues of individual rights, the service provides a statutory conciliation function before a case can be taken to an Industrial Tribunal. In collective disputes, resort to the service is voluntary, but, significantly, almost 50 per cent of the collective issues referred to the service derive from a joint employer–trade union initiative. Through its conciliation and arbitration functions, the service undoubtedly contributes both to the avoidance and to the curtailment of many disputes, and it appears to occupy a position of stability and trust within the industrial relations framework.

### Employee participation arrangements

Two opposing views have been expressed about recent trends in employee participation in Britain. The first maintains that managements, spurred on by competitive pressures and increased bargaining power, have adopted a more aggressive approach, have been much less willing to engage in negotiation or consultation, and have been more intent on developing direct links with employees, rather than going through the representative channels. The opposing view would be that, although negotiation over pay and staffing requirements has been conducted more forcefully, the general practice has been to maintain the institutional processes of negotiation and consultation. Although examples of the first approach can be discerned, the balance would seem to lie in favour of the second.

So far as formal consultation is concerned, the traditional British institution is the joint consultative committee, dating back to the Whitley Committee at the end of the First World War, which provides a separate machinery for consultation at works level, and frequently at a higher level in the organisation. Historically, formal joint consultation has waxed and waned, and after a period of decline, but by no means disappearance, in the 1960s, there were signs of resurgence in the late 1970s. In addition, the 1960s and 1970s witnessed a substantial amount of productivity bargaining at plant level, in which the consultative machinery was often fused with negotiations over changes in working practice, and in these cases the consultative committees enjoyed a resurgence. Participative arrangements relating to productivity have continued to have a high profile through such devices as quality circles. The latest evidence suggests a current phase of stability, with almost one-third of all establishments having joint consultative committees, their presence being positively related to establishment size (Millward & Stevens, 1986). Within this context, however, three notable features deserve attention. First, there are signs that trade union representation on the committees is becoming slightly eroded, as representation is increasingly drawn from employees in general, rather than solely through union channels. Although there has always been a tradition in British joint consultation that employers need not rely on union nomination of consultative committee members, the latest figures show that in less than half of all cases is there no union nomination of representatives (Millward & Stevens, 1986:145). Second, it is becoming clearer that elements of negotiation are now commonly undertaken within the consultative mechanisms, a reflection, perhaps, of the difficulties of keeping negotiation and consultation entirely separate, especially if consultation is to deal with significant problems. Third, although production issues remain at the top of the agenda discussed in consultative channels, pay and conditions, and future trends have declined in importance, while employment issues and topics in industrial democracy and participation have increased in significance (Millward & Stevens, 1986:146–7).

It is perhaps too early to ascribe long-term significance to these tendencies, but they are consistent with other evidence that managements are anxious to develop channels of communication with their employees other than those controlled by the trade unions, and they are adopting a more experimental approach to employee participation. This experimentation carries over into new forms of approach to employee involvement, outside the joint consultative mechanism itself. Thus, according to the latest evidence, more attention is being paid to two-way communication between management and employees, in place of the former one-way process from management to workers, and the innovations that have been undertaken tend not to be structural but to relate more to process and content.

The tentative conclusion may then be drawn that, although formal consultation procedures continue to play an important complementary role to joint regulation, consultation is being developed increasingly as an alternative to formal union–management relationships, and there is some interest—and initiative—from management in extending the range and form of consultation. This could be a reflection of the requirement in the Employment Act 1982 that company annual reports should include a statement about initiatives to develop employee involvement, although analysis of these statements would suggest this is unlikely. More probably, managements, finding themselves better able to exercise control than for some years, are anxious to soften the hard edges by bringing employees, but not necessarily trade unions, more fully into the picture. Even this conclusion has its limitations, however, for the amount of information conveyed to employees, especially manual workers, about changes in working methods or work organisation is far from comprehensive (Millward & Stevens, 1986:157–8).

*Profit sharing and share ownership*

Since the 1970s, a succession of legislative measures have been designed to encourage employee share ownership by means of tax exemptions for Inland-Revenue-approved schemes, and each successive piece of legislation has produced its own stimulus to the number of schemes. It is estimated that, by 1984, nearly a quarter of workplaces in industry and commerce were in employing organisations operating a share ownership scheme; the highest participation was in financial services, and rapid expansion was taking place in retail distribution and the growth sectors of the engineering industry. Despite this, the actual coverage of employees remains small, partly because many schemes are confined to selected groups of employees, but mainly because of comparatively low take-up options by the generality of employees: one estimate for 1984 is a coverage of only 7 per cent of employees (Millward & Stevens, 1986).

The significance of this should not, however, be minimised, for growth has been rapid, and events since 1984 are likely to have contributed to further spread (Baddon et al., 1987). In the last three years, the government has embarked upon an extensive programme of privatisation, involving the selling off of sectors under public ownership, with a considerable emphasis on share ownership across a much wider span of the population. A measure of this is given by the National Opinion Poll survey for the Treasury, which reported that 14 per cent of adults in the United Kingdom owned shares, double the figure in a 1979 survey (HM Treasury, 1986a). To the extent that this has provided a broader base for a 'capital-owning democracy', it may yet have an effect on the willingness of employees to participate in share ownership within their own employing organisations.

A second string to the government's bow has been a willingness to contemplate a more general form of profit-related pay, based on the Weitzman analysis (1984) that if a high proportion of pay were to be related to performance it would both reward the productive worker and provide much-needed wage flexibility, as well as acting positively on unemployment (HM Treasury, 1986b). The government's view is that if pay can be partly related to changing market conditions, employers will be more willing to keep workers on when times are bad. When markets improve, employers can have greater confidence about their ability to sustain extra jobs. Thus profit-related pay is seen to contribute to a solution of the long-standing unemployment problem. Reaction from union and employer quarters has been uniformly sceptical, but despite this the 1987 budget announced a new tax relief for people in schemes providing profit-related pay.[6] Early indications are that take-up of such schemes is slow.

This is an area in which judgement of the longer-term significance should be deferred. The government's general strategy remains focused on the problems of reducing employment costs per unit of output as a means of reducing unemployment, and its efforts to weaken trade union bargaining power by legislative and other means have yet to prove themselves in terms of a substantial lowering of wage claims and settlements relative to prices. In these circumstances, the new emphasis on profit-related pay is understandable, and this, plus the effects of privatisation and the introduction of personal equity plans with tax benefits, could yet produce a tangible increase in share ownership and profit-related components in household income. Though trade unions have in the past been unconvinced, though only occasionally hostile to employee share ownership, there are signs that some unions may be taking more interest in negotiating improvements in the terms of share schemes available to their members.

A further qualification is required in view of the stock market collapse towards the end of 1987. Capital gains made by employee shareholders must have been largely wiped out and the view that share acquisition was riskless must have been severely shaken. The long-term consequences of this development will no doubt be carefully assessed right across the political spectrum.

### The state and government–union–employer relations

The Conservative government since 1979 has materially changed the complexion of British industrial relations and the tenor of relations between government, the trade union movement and employer organisations. The government's policies reflected a view of the world fundamentally different from that of the Labour governments of 1974–79 in which tripartism was strong and the social contract between the government and the trade union movement provided a mutual accommodation of interests in a difficult economic context. That approach had strong elements of corporatism, but any dangers in that for trade unions were outweighed by the easy access to the ears of government and a heightened ability to influence policy. The new Conservative view is one in which tripartism, consensus and compromise are unacceptable constraints on the determination of government to pursue a clear political and economic strategy. Within that strategy, the reduction of trade union strength and greater flexibility in the labour market are seen as important means of improving the long-term performance of the economy as a whole.

We have already noted the legislative programme that has unfolded steadily since 1980, and in December 1988 further proposals were unveiled, pushing further along this path, with more restrictions on the post-entry closed shop, additional protection for the rights of individual union members in dispute with their union and greater accountability of union leaders to the rank and file (Green Paper, 1987). But quite apart from the legislative curbs, government has diminished the access of the labour movement to policy makers. Some important institutions of tripartism still remain. The National Economic Development Council, a forum for the discussion of economic policy with top level representation from government, unions and employers, remains in existence after twenty-five years, but the unions have expressed concern that the council's influence on government has become more limited in recent years, and Labour's preference would be for a National Economic Development Council to act 'as a permanent forum in which the development of economic, industrial and regional strategies can be planned', and for the industry Economic Development Councils to be strengthened (cf., *New Industrial Strength for Britain: Labour Programme for National Renewal*). On two occasions between 1979 and 1982, arguments were made for TUC withdrawal from the council in protest against the government's economic and industrial relations policy, but anxiety to maintain the council as a long-term symbol of tripartism won the day on both occasions. However, the government's ban on trade union membership at the Government's Communications Headquarters (GCHQ), which is central to intelligence gathering, introduced in 1985 on the grounds of national security, soured relations so much that for most of that year the TUC withdrew from participation in the National Economic Development Council, though not its industry-level councils and working parties. The Advisory, Conciliation and Arbitration Service, governed by a council drawn from the Confederation of British Industry and the TUC, plus an independent element, likewise survived, though not without some criticism from the right about its statutory duty to promote collective bargaining. The Manpower Services Commission blossomed as it became the primary vehicle for a range of special measures to tackle aspects of the unemployment problem.[7]

Elsewhere, the tendency was for the government to withdraw from partnership arrangements and to pursue a policy of deregulation. The National Enterprise Board was dissolved; the promise of planning agreements between the state and large companies was stillborn; the structure of Industrial Training Boards was largely dismantled; the Fair Wages Resolution was revoked;[8] the Wages Council system, governing low-paid employment, was threatened with elimination, but has so far survived in a weaker form. These are merely some of the most prominent examples. Trade union opposition to these radical changes was continuous but largely ineffective. The TUC regularly debated the wisdom of strategies of more active opposition and withdrawal of co-operation, but it was not able to muster sufficient all-union support to tackle the government head-on. The reasons for this are not hard to find. Through a series of mainly public sector strikes the government's unwillingness to bend has been unmistakable—the coal-mining strike and the Government's Communications Headquarters affair perhaps being the clearest intimations of this. But in any event, the union movement was itself in the throes of reorganisation to meet the challenges of the future, quite apart from its weak position resulting from the condition of the economy. The structure of the General Council of the TUC was radically altered in 1982 to provide representation of unions in such a way that the changing industrial and commercial structure of the economy would be reflected automatically in council composition, without the need for constant debate about election procedures. Unions with over 100 000 members were guaranteed at least one seat on council, producing some reorientation at the top level of the movement. Union solidarity was weakened by splits on issues such as non-compliance with the law, the wisdom of accepting government funds to pay for the expenses of secret ballots, and the encroachment of some unions on the traditional territory of others with respect to the emergence of single-union agreements. Finally, the government's privatisation programme, although opposed by the trade union movement, rolled on without serious disruption.

The TUC's own initiatives were less successful. The accommodating stance in relation to new technology, as we have seen, had little influence on the ability of unions to become jointly involved with management in the planning of change. The campaign for reduced working time, launched in 1980 with the aim of moving towards a 35-hour basic week, six weeks annual holiday and cuts in overtime working, has made only partial progress. Union worries over the implications of the expanding Youth Training Scheme led to an attempt in 1984 to withdraw support, but this was not carried by congress, and the Youth Training Scheme programme has been further expanded in length and members covered, providing a new, if still imperfect, basis for industrial training of new entrants to the labour force (discussed further below).

Within this stressful period for the trade union movement, there have, nevertheless, been a few positive signs. Although the TUC has undoubtedly been embarrassed by the lack of success—and on occasion the tactics—of member unions embattled directly or indirectly with the government, it has sought to play a constructive role in the settlement of some of the major disputes, such as in coal mining, and both the provincial and national press. It has also recognised the need to re-examine the state of union–member relations, not only because of legislative pressures but also because of its recognition of changes taking place in the structure of collective bargaining, and the increased role of company bargaining. More recently, in 1986, the TUC acknowledged the changes taking place in employer practices with regard to flexibility in labour utilisation and for the first time put its weight behind the case for a statutory national minimum wage, which would provide some protection for some groups in the growing peripheral labour force, although the main reason for the minimum wage is the pursuit of a 'fair wage' policy and a general improvement in the wages of low-paid workers generally.

It may be little consolation for the trade unions that their employer organisation counterparts have, in some respects, fared little better. The Confederation of British Industry has shown concern about government's industrial policy, especially as it has affected manufacturing; the high-point of this unease was the promise, in 1981, from the then director-general, of a 'bare-knuckle' fight with the government, specifically with regard to policy on interest and exchange rates. The Confederation of British Industry, like the TUC, has found it hard to catch the ear of government, though it has, understandably, been broadly supportive of a good deal of the legislation designed to curb union power. The confederation likewise has had its membership problems. Having added the nationalised corporations to its bedrock membership in manufacturing, it experienced membership loss in the 1980s, primarily as a result of the recession. To compensate, it recruited new members, especially in finance, retailing and the professions, but the membership interests are now quite heterogeneous and are by no means easy to cover effectively in lobbying the government. The confederation thus faced the problem that smaller, more specialised, associations may be seen by members as a more effective voice to government, while the generally right-wing views of the Institute of Directors on matters such as deregulation have perhaps enjoyed a more favourable reception than under previous governments, not least because the Institute of Directors speaks for the interests of small business, which the government sees as a basis for economic regeneration. In the last resort, however, the most substantial voice of British employers as a whole is undoubtedly that of the Confederation of British Industry.

## Problem areas in the future

This chapter has portrayed an industrial relations system in the throes of substantial change, but nevertheless managing to preserve a basic stability in its fundamental institutions. The critical question for the future is whether these changes will be consolidated or whether there will be significant reversals in some dimensions. This issue hangs on three factors: political change, economic policy, and management and union membership attitudes.

The significance of the political dimension was heightened by the Conservatives' return to office, with a substantial overall majority, in the general election of June 1987 again influenced by both industrial relations and economic policy. Because of the sharply opposed policies of the parties, and their very different implications for industrial relations processes, it is worth spelling out the main lines of their positions. Both major parties had clear legislative intentions, which in their own ways were addressed to individual rights, but there nearly all resemblance ends. Conservative proposals, enacted in the Employment Act 1988, provided additional rights for union members within their unions (e.g. the right to choose to work or cross picket lines despite a strike call, or to take action to restrain their union from calling a strike without first having conducted a secret ballot). These measures were clearly extensions of the earlier 1979 legislation. In contrast, the Labour Party–TUC proposals envisaged the complete repeal of the post-1979 industrial relations law and a radically different approach to the whole area of employee rights at the workplace, framed in what would effectively be an employees' charter of rights at work and significant strengthening of collective interests (Labour Party, 1986).

The significance of these differences in approach is that they offered very different plans for industrial relations, and posed the choice between further weakening of union strength and a major extension of individual protection and collective organisation. These options were allied to quite different economic strategies, which we cannot develop here except to say that the Labour Party proposals envisaged a much greater emphasis on economic planning and an attempt to reduce unemployment more rapidly than the Conservatives thought feasible. The industrial relations alternatives, however, deserve to be further spelled out.

The continuing Conservative administration is already committed to consolidation of the reforms it has implemented, and re-election to a third consecutive term of office confirmed its view that it is pursuing generally popular policies. The government's priority programme will, however, lie elsewhere, especially in the gradual reduction of unemployment without markedly reintroducing high inflation. For many observers, this strategy is expected to be pursued in a spirit that will do nothing to restore the position of a weakened trade union movement. And if economic improvement heightens union bargaining power, the means to counteracting that may be further legal restraint. Scope for such measures undoubtedly exists (in addition to the measures foreshadowed in the 1987 green paper): the pre-entry closed shop persists; collective bargaining could be made legally binding; and there is a continuing debate about banning strikes in essential services. Again, as we have seen, there has so far been little effort to dismantle existing collective bargaining and other institutions that are part of the British tradition, but there have been ministerial calls for an end to national pay bargaining and a ban on the annual pay round, 'the going rate', comparability, and job evaluation, with more emphasis being given to ability to pay and rewards for merit and performance. According to Mr Kenneth Clarke, when he was at the employment ministry, there was no reason why 'bank clerks, civil servants and teachers are paid the same, irrespective of whom they work for and in which part of the country they live. The costs which employees face differ. An efficient and effective labour market would respond with differential rates of pay for companies, industries and geographical areas' (cited in *Employment Gazette*, March 1987:115). What lies behind this is, once more, the government's anxiety over pay inflexibility in the downward direction,[9] and its desire to encourage more geographical and enterprise-level differentiation in pay, related to differential circumstances. Perhaps the biggest challenge in this connection lies in the public sector itself, where centralised bargaining tends to be the norm. According to Mr Clarke, 'Where the government is the employer we will seek to gain acceptance of a wider geographical variation in pay rates' (*Employment Gazette*, March 1987:115).

The scenario under a Labour government would have been quite different. The repeal of the Conservative's post-1979 legislation would have been accompanied by the use of new laws 'to enlarge, not diminish, the freedom of workers to control their environment'. This strategy has been much more fully spelled out in a revised Labour Party Policy Review (Labour Party, 1989), which seeks to build on a reshaped training framework and to bring British employees into line with standards in most other European countries. Greater protection is envisaged for part-time workers, an Employees' Charter would ensure a full range of basic employment rights and reduce discrimination, and collective rights of people at work, based on trade unionism, would be increased. A National Statutory Minimum Wage would be introduced, rising over time to secure for the lowest paid worker an hourly rate no less than two-thirds of that of the male median full-time worker. The Employees' Charter would guarantee the right of individual workers to be represented by a trade union and offer protection on a range of individual grievances. A statutory procedure for union recognition would be reintroduced and the development of collective bargaining embraced as an act of public policy. A considerable extension of employee participation is envisaged, with greater rights to information, consultation and access to key decisions affecting employment and other matters such as pensions.

The long-term significance of this set of proposals was more than that of a simple pendulum effect, reversing the most recent changes and effectively restoring the situation of the late 1970s. It would in effect have provided a new basis for individual rights and collective relationships, rooted in law, in many respects bringing Britain more into line with other western European countries. And there is little doubt that the legislative package would require some rethinking of policies among both employers and unions. In addition, a Labour government would have repaired the routes of access from the trade unions to the government itself, not least because a more expansionist economic policy would require some self-restraint from unions if the programme to

reduce unemployment were not to generate a resumption of high inflation and the reintroduction of emergency measures.

In attitudes, the problems for a government of either complexion are
equally formidable. On the one hand, a Labour government seeking to
turn back the pages of recent history might have found that one of the
main characters—the union membership—was not wholeheartedly sympathetic to losing its increased voice in union government and tactics,
while the new pattern of employment in both industrial and functional
terms, which is not likely to be reversed, has changed the background
against which the action is played out. For the Conservative government, on the other hand, if it accepts some of the suggestions advocated
by pressure groups, the difficulty may lie more in persuading employers
that more legislation is needed and that, in the last resort, they should
actively seek to dismantle existing mechanisms for the orderly conduct
of collective relations (such as national bargaining). Even now, there is
some anxiety among employers that further weakening of trade unionism may undermine the constructive role played by the more responsible union leaderships and, in the final analysis, establish a rallying
point for the forces of the hard left, producing a much more confron-
tational atmosphere than has been experienced even since 1979. To
pursue that strategy, also, would imply the abandonment of a known and
tried set of institutions for a much more uncertain structure within
which behaviour would be more unpredictable. Nor is it certain that
this would produce the desired effect in terms of wage flexibility, for
recent evidence indicates that the fastest rate of growth of earnings in
recent years has been in areas of manufacturing where pay is determined
not by collective bargaining but by management award (Gregory, Lobban & Thomson, 1985, 1986).

Quite apart from politics, other problems will need to be addressed by
trade unions and employers. One of these is the behaviour of pay which,
even in a depressed economy, has still persistently outrun productivity
and prices, despite the considerable changes in the structure of bargaining. With a growing responsibility for pay bargaining at company level
within the private enterprise sector, it might have been expected that
managements would have sought to relate pay increases more strictly to
the productivity of their own organisations, thereby controlling unit
costs and relieving some of the familiar pressure on wage inflation. That
wage inflation has continued in these circumstances is one of the
puzzles of the British economy, and one that has increasingly worried
the government, which has expressed its desire to see more downward
flexibility in pay, when product demand is weak and competition strong.
One explanation may be that employers have pursued a policy of adjusting wage costs by reducing labour, substituting part-time and temporary labour for full-time workers, and increasing flexibility in the way
labour is used. That is to say, it may have been easier for employers

facing the uncertainties of a severe recession to take direct action on employment levels and the development of more flexible work organisation structures than to try to secure a change in the conventional criteria of collective bargaining, including pay-comparability. On the trade union side, the persistence of wage claims well above inflation levels reflects a greater practical concern for the employed than for the unemployed, and tendencies in this direction may have been aided by the transfer of such bargaining from the macro (industry) to the micro (company or establishment) level.[10] The interest of negotiators at company or plant level is likely to be more heavily influenced by the immediate pressures from company employees, and the differences in interest between 'insiders' and 'outsiders' may well have a part to play in explaining this phenomenon.

Not the least of the problems on the pay front is that of public sector pay, especially in the non-trading sector, where a series of difficulties have developed in the absence of a set of clear guiding principles in the approach of government, and indeed the abandonment of existing machinery, such as the pay research procedure for the civil service and the Burnham collective bargaining machinery for teachers in England and Wales. This area is surely one that the government must address.

A second area of widespread concern is that of training. The dominance of a craft-based skill training attached to a relatively narrow industrial or occupational base would now seem to have passed away, and with it the reliance on straightforward time-serving as a condition of skill status. Traditional apprenticeship still exists, but on a vastly reduced scale, and increasingly it has been bound up with the use of Youth Training Scheme provisions, involving modular off-the-job training as well as work experience. Not only has manufacturing employment shrunk dramatically, but its structure has also changed, increasing the demand for more company-specific training: that is, the emphasis has swung from dependence on a general skill to be traded in the external market to reliance on skill acquisition in line with the technology and work organisation structure of the specific employer. Modular training, particularly when associated with skill testing at the end of the training period rather than time-serving, is an ideal context in which to allow companies to develop the particular blend of skills and on-the-job experience they require. Thus the experimentation that has occurred with flexible job organisation has combined with one of the main responses to youth unemployment to create a basis for a major transition in British training. Microtechnology, by cutting across conventional job boundaries, not least between manual and non-manual activities, has added to the impetus of change.

It is doubtful if a fully coherent pattern for the future is yet discernible. School curricula and qualifications are undergoing substantial revision, work is now progressing on greater standardisation of vocational qualifications, and employers are still experimenting with alternative methods of bridging the school–labour market transition (see, for example, Sako & Dore, 1986; Leese, 1986; Tenne, 1986). The outcome may depend in part on how far employers push the 'core–periphery' division of the labour force. It is quite conceivable that in future a core labour force will emerge in many organisations, with harmonised conditions, a strong internal labour market and appropriate provision of training and personnel development, alongside which will exist a low-skill, low-paid, easily replaceable periphery that has to rely much more on finding a succession of employments in the external labour market (cf. Brown, 1986:162–3).

Much may depend here on the attitude of trade unions, which have in general been supportive of internal labour market arrangements. To the extent that unions have adjusted to single-employer bargaining, it becomes easier for them to safeguard members' interests within the internal labour market, but at least two problems then have to be faced. First, collective bargaining in the internal market cannot be as fully serviced by full-time union officials as industry-wide negotiations, especially as most manual unions have been forced to reduce their complement of officials in the face of declining membership and revenue. More advanced training of enterprise-level representatives is a prerequisite if this challenge is to be accepted. Second, unions cannot lightly disregard the interests of the periphery who are, by definition, much more difficult to recruit and organise. Again, the unions' approach to training may be critical for the minimisation of this problem: co-operation in adjustment of training institutions but seeking to embrace a wider labour force would seem to be the best strategy to retain future membership and a share in job regulation within the enterprise.

*Unions*

Union membership is unlikely to fall much further unless there is a determined effort to dismantle the institutions of national collective bargaining, and union density will probably continue around 40 to 50 per cent. However, a continued redistribution of membership will take place, bringing with it further issues of internal reorganisation, and merger activity, which may eventually lead to a structure of no more than about 30 substantial TUC-affiliated unions. Such a structure may provide a better basis for the development of a more cohesive union movement than we have witnessed in recent years, but achieving such a cohesion still presents a major challenge. More worrying even than the drop in membership and income may be the narrowing confines into which the unions are admitted, both by government and by employers. At national level it is difficult to see what the unions can do to improve access to a government that is less open to a labour lobby than any in postwar British history, except that the unions must seek to improve their general public image and increase their credibility as legitimate representatives of employees. In this respect, increased use of pre-strike ballots and greater openness with regard to union elections may actually be helpful, while some unions are already taking a more positive approach to securing improvements in conditions for 'peripheral' workers. At the micro-level, where change seems to be introduced increasingly without negotiation and where, if consultation takes place, it often occurs late in the process and is concerned more with implementation and its consequences than with planning, the unions may have to rethink their traditional philosophy of seeking to regulate change by negotiation. The alternatives would seem to be either more open resistance or a more co-operative approach, which would trade off the (diminished) right to negotiate for an enhanced right to consultation over planning. The TUC at present does not appear to have the authority over its members to resolve the major differences of philosophy exemplified by the National Union of Mineworkers, and the Transport and General Workers Union on the one hand, and by the Amalgamated Engineering Union and the (now expelled) Electricians Union on the other.

## Management

Although employer associations and management interests have suffered considerable shocks and operating problems in the last few years, often because of the very same factors that have affected the unions, the extent of the damage has been less, and adjustment has been relatively rapid. At the national level, the Confederation of British Industry has put behind it the crisis of the early 1980s and may well be anxious to achieve a state of greater stability in industrial relations and its legal framework. Employer organisations and management alike need time to absorb the lessons of the recession, the new legal framework, and the implications of new technology for work and labour force organisation. Some anxiety is quietly being expressed in certain quarters at the prospect of further weakening of established institutions, because of either economic or political–legislative factors, lest the unions get pushed into more militant resistance to change. Many managements wish to encourage a more co-operative approach from responsible and representative unions, and if they are to do so they must ensure that adequate mechanisms for consultation and for providing information are available to allow employees, through their representatives, to contribute constructively to the adjustment process. Given the continuation of Conservative economic policy, there may also be a heightened need for management to develop a more proactive stance in the development of the kind of industrial relations they would wish to have. Despite the advantage management has enjoyed in recent years, there has been comparatively little evidence of new and innovative thinking, such as has characterised at least some parts of the management scene in the United States.[11] There is clearly an implicit opportunity here for management, and perhaps a major role for the Confederation of British Industry.

We may reasonably conclude that the British industrial relations system is continuing to undergo transition, but has not yet reached a new plateau of stability. It is a system in which the law plays an increasing role but has not yet ousted the traditional voluntarist philosophy. It is a system in which the problems have shifted to a large extent from the private to the public sector. Above all, it is a system operating against a background of sustained mass unemployment, which perhaps subdues for the time being some of the underlying social divisions. It continues to give rise to anxiety about its inability to match pay increases to productivity, and in that respect at least reminds us of the long-term concern that the industrial relations system is an inhibiting factor in Britain's economic performance. But it has shown considerable flexibility in the face of enforced changes arising from economic and technological forces, in recent years. Whether the efficiency achieved by that flexibility can be matched in the longer term by greater equity, such as the unions feel to be missing at present, must remain a matter of speculation.

## Notes

1 These distinctions are due to Atkinson (1984a, 1984b).

2 Figures in this paragraph are from the *Employment Gazette* (Department of Employment). For a summary of the basis of these figures, see *Employment Gazette*, February 1987, pp 84–5). Some of the organisations included may not be conventional trade unions engaged in the full range of collective bargaining activity, but they will mostly be small in membership. Thus the *trend* figures reported below are likely to give an accurate reflection of change.

3 According to the 1980 Workplace Industrial Relations Survey, nearly half of all establishments recognising trade unions had more than one manual union, and a quarter had more than one bargaining unit. In the largest establishments, three-quarters had three or more recognised unions.

4 For a fuller description, see Millward and Stevens (1986: ch. 9), which compares findings of two major surveys of workplace industrial relations in 1980 and 1984. These surveys exclude establishments with fewer than 25 employees.

5 A particularly useful summary of evidence under this heading is given by Willman (1986).

6 In the 1987 proposals, half of the profit-related pay element will be free of

income tax up to the point where it is 20 per cent of the employee's total pay, or 3000 pounds a year, whichever is lower. The profit-related pay schemes will have to be registered with Inland Revenue.

7 This responsibility continues, although responsibility for the employment service is being transferred to the Department of Employment, while the Manpower Services Commission has been renamed the Training Commission, with emphasis on programmes for training and retraining.

8 The 1946 Fair Wages Resolution was set aside in 1983. The purpose of the resolution was to ensure that government contractors and subcontractors observed standards of pay and conditions not less favourable than those established for the trade or industry in the district by collective bargaining, or in the absence of bargaining not less favourable than the general levy of comparable employers. It also required contractors working for a government department to recognise the freedom of employees to be union members.

9 References to pay inflexibility in this paper are essentially related to the government's wish to see downward adjustments in real wage costs when there is a fall in demand. In part this may reflect a view that pay generally is too high and that this militates against employment recovery. But it is primarily a concern that productivity and pay should be better related if the economy is to remain competitive in a changing world market.

10 For a related argument, see Oswald (1986, 1984).

11 cf., chapter 2 in this book. The United Kingdom has, however, witnessed the beginnings of a move from traditional personnel management to strategic human resource management, in which personnel control is linked closely to overall corporate strategy.

# 6

# AUSTRALIA

## JOHN NILAND
## and
## KERI SPOONER

In common with most industrialised countries, Australia has experienced in recent years tremendous economic pressures, resulting in significant changes to traditional structures, policies and practices. Emphasis in this chapter[1] is on the industrial relations consequences of these forces for restructuring and, in particular, the responses of the various players. The key theme of the chapter is that Australia presents a clear instance of adjustment to change by an industrial relations system in transition, and that trade unions have been pivotal in generating the reforms. A modified version of Dunlop's Industrial Relations System Framework, developed by Kochan, Katz and McKersie (1986) provides the guiding framework for analysis.

First, the pressures for reform toward greater flexibility in Australia's industrial relations are outlined. The responses of the players to these pressures are considered within a framework consisting of four tiers. The activities of the top tier, consisting of peak employer and union bodies as well as government and central government authorities, are discussed as well as the impact of each of their strategies upon the others. The activities of the upper middle tier, consisting of corporate and union leadership, are examined, with attention directed to investment, business, organisational and other policies. The lower middle tier, consisting of management and union officials, is examined and policies and activities regarding personnel and industrial relations are considered. The bottom tier, concerned with the workplace and its relationships, is also examined. Finally, conclusions are drawn concerning the nature of Australia's industrial relations transformation.

## Pressures for reform toward greater flexibility

Since the mid-1970s, economic difficulties and a desire to be more competitive in international markets have led many countries to alter their labour market and industrial relations policies and practices. Sources of both wage and non-wage inflexibility have been targeted.

In Australia, pressures for reform in industry came from these international developments. Few individuals in Australia today are unaware of the need for reform to achieve greater efficiency in work. Indeed, something of a national consensus emerged in the 1980s that economic viability is at stake. But while the cultural change has been remarkable, it is not universal. There are also conflicting views about how change should be effected, but by and large the goals for restructuring and efficiency to prosper as an industrialised country are widely accepted throughout Australia. The strategic responses of the various parties at the different tiers of the Australian system will be discussed and analysed in this chapter.

Pressures promoting the search for reform in labour market and industrial relations policies and practices come from several sources. Some are common to other countries, such as the impact of multinational companies, with their ability to move house if a particular environment is not suitable to their needs. Other pressures, such as the decline in export earnings from primary products, may have had greater impact in Australia, where 85 per cent of income from goods exported is derived from minerals and primary products.

High levels of unemployment, inflation and interest rates during the first half of the 1980s in Australia acted as pressures for industrial relations reform. Protectionist policies have been reversed over about the last fifteen years in Australia, as successive governments perceived a need to internationalise the economy. Tariffs are progressively being reduced and this has severely affected employment in the manufacturing industry, where employment shrank from 27 per cent of the workforce in 1975 to only 18 per cent in the mid-1980s. In the context of declining tariff protection but continuing comparatively high wage rates, a number of Australian firms either closed down or moved offshore.

While Australian manufacturing has experienced a reduction in its tariff protection, Third World manufacturing has continued to develop. Over the past few decades businesses in developing countries have been generally more willing than their Australian counterparts to invest in new technology and training, as well as research and development. And countries such as Sweden have been more prepared to experiment with innovative management systems and work organisation techniques, while in other cases, such as Korea, labour costs remain low compared with Australia's. As a result, many Australian businesses have experienced a squeeze on profits and have had to search for survival techniques.

A further source of change in industrial relations policies and practices has flowed from government efforts to reduce their expenditure and budget deficit by effecting reforms both in the public sector proper and in statutory authorities. The commercialisation of a number of public enterprises has already begun at both federal and state levels and appears certain to continue. Some state-owned bodies will undoubtedly experience privatisation in one form or another in the near future, while government departments generally are under increasing pressure to become efficient. The quest for greater efficiency dominates public employer industrial relations policies and provides a role model for the private sector.

Changes in the nature of corporate shareholding have also created pressures for industrial relations change. The emergence of managed funds and the growth in pension provisions over the past few decades has meant that significantly greater proportions of shareholding are now in the hands of professional fund managers whose performance is closely monitored. Such funds are more likely to quickly offload shares of companies judged not to be performing, and the net result is that corporate performance is evaluated within a much shorter time frame. This pressures management to improve its company's efficiency or run the risk of falling share prices and possible subsequent company take-over.

During the past few years in Australia the most important factor bringing pressure for increased economic efficiency has been the nation's current account deficit and chronic foreign debt. A serious decline in the terms of trade from 1985 acted as an added catalyst to reform throughout the economy. The fall in both sales and prices of primary exports highlighted the vulnerability of Australian living standards to fluctuations in international commodity prices. Developments on this front were sufficiently serious for the Treasurer to warn that, unless trends were reversed, Australia would become a 'banana republic'.

Arising out of these pressures has been a quest for greater labour market flexibility. The Australian experience of seeking greater efficiency in industry through the removal of restrictive practices, more effective staffing and wage restraint, while also attempting to handle such problems as redundancy and unemployment, is not unique. What distinguishes the Australian experience is that reform has been largely directed by leaders of the labour movement and has taken place within the established tribunal system.

## Activities of the top tier

In considering the activities of the top tier of the industrial relations system in Australia, the role of peak employer and union bodies, as well as government and central government authorities, and their impact on each other are considered.

### The traditional state of play

The top tier in Australian industrial relations has throughout this century been strongly influenced by centralised systems of conciliation and arbitration. Arbitration systems exist at the federal level and in all six states of the Commonwealth. Respective federal and state acts of Parliament provide for the establishment of conciliation and arbitration tribunals, the registration and legal recognition of employer and employee associations, and detail the rights and obligations of the parties. The tribunals are empowered to handle industrial disputes and to set wages and conditions of employment embodied in awards of the tribunals, power to deal with which generally is denied the federal government by virtue of constitutional limitation. Although not strictly or legally required to do so, the federal tribunal does in effect implement the wages policy of the government of the day. Similarly, state tribunals are not legally required to follow the major wage case decisions made by the federal tribunal, but they generally do.

About 50 per cent of the workforce is unionised; employer and employee associations, together with the industrial tribunals, have dominated the wage setting and dispute-resolution processes. Workplace relationships involving the non-unionised have also been dominated by the centralised system, as awards of the state tribunals have a common rule application, meaning that individuals performing the category of work specified in an award are covered by the provisions contained therein.

Australia's centralised system of dispute resolution and wage fixation has traditionally been a source of labour market inflexibility and inefficiencies. Unions, predominantly, are occupationally based, and the awards of the tribunals therefore cover particular occupational groups in specified industries. The typical manufacturing establishment would host five to ten trade unions, each with bargaining rights. As demarcation lines separate one occupational job from another, work must generally be organised according to union and award coverage, with restrictive work practices proliferating. The system of training, particularly in the area of skilled trades, further institutionalised occupational segregation by restricting entry to the trades and by producing people trained only for one trade skill.

The centralised system has also had the effect of retarding any quest for flexibility. The parties to industrial relations developed a reliance on the formal third-party system and have been traditionally ill-equipped and unwilling to resolve major differences through negotiations. Those wanting to resist pressures for change turned to the formal system for assistance. In many cases, the industrial tribunals supported those seeking protection from change, even where restrictive work practices were concerned. 'Custom and practice' was frequently afforded legal standing and therefore unassailable protection. With so much of industrial relations being determined far from the workplace, not surprisingly, personnel practices in most Australian organisations have been virtually non-existent, with mature recruitment, induction, training and even record-keeping systems the rare exception to the norm.

### Change in the early 1980s

The centralised system of conciliation and arbitration in Australia, together with the protectionist policies of former governments, gave haven from change for both unions and employers. The pressures outlined earlier have caused restrictive work practices and relative wage flexibility to assume prominence on the public policy agenda in Australia. The approach to labour market flexibility adopted accommodates the distinctive features of Australia's unique institutional framework.

Majority support in the top tier in Australia during the first half of the 1980s was for restraint through centralism over flexibility through decentralism, a preference summed up by the Australian Department of Employment and Industrial Relations: 'restraint in prices and incomes is a fundamental prerequisite to transition to sustained economic growth ... The necessary process of sustained economic growth requires a commitment by all groups to a fair sharing of the burdens of restraint' (DEIR, 1985:239).

A system of wage indexation had been introduced in Australia in 1975 in an effort to halt spiralling wages (Niland, 1986:243). During the indexation era, 1975–81, the Arbitration Commission awarded full consumer price index adjustment on seven occasions out of nineteen (Dabscheck & Niland, 1985:57). In the end, union pursuit of full indexation free of restraining guidelines led to the abandonment of indexation in July 1981.

Immediately before the March 1983 federal government elections, a document known as the Accord was agreed to between the Australian Council of Trades Unions (ACTU) and the Australian Labor Party (ALP) (Niland, 1987:11–14). The agreement essentially sought to implement an economic policy to simultaneously redress inflation and unemployment. The government planned to increase expenditure to alleviate unemployment without inflation, and in return the unions agreed to exercise wage moderation, but with full wage indexation. Under the Accord, the ACTU was afforded, and still exercises, consultative rights in a range of matters affecting unions, including immigration, economic planning, social policy and industrial development.

As the result of the government–ACTU overtures to the commission, it agreed to reintroduce wage indexation in September 1983. Each union seeking the benefits of indexation was required to undertake that it would abide by the restrictions of the guidelines. The commission opted for a centralised rather than decentralised approach to wage determination, because in its view that approach provided 'the best prospects for maximum labour cost restraint together with reasonable

industrial stability, both essential ingredients for economic recovery'
(ACAC, 1986).

Although the implementation of centralised methods of ensuring a
'fair sharing of the burdens of restraint' has not been problem-free, by
both economic and industrial relations criteria it was remarkably successful. Between 1983 and June 1986, the number of working days lost
in strike action was only 40 per cent of the average for the preceding ten
years. This commitment was the more remarkable in the light of economic and employment growth. Between July 1983 and April 1986,
full-time employment grew by 8 per cent, while total employment grew
by 10 per cent. Unemployment fell over the period from 10.3 per cent
to 7.9 per cent, and would have fallen to 5.2 per cent but for a substantial increase in the labour force participation rate.

Even so, pressures so built up within the system that the Accord
partners moved to abandon indexation, but in an orderly manner aimed
at minimising wage restraint and any political fall-out. Deficits on both
the domestic budgeting front and on the external balance of payments
played key roles in forcing this shift. Concern with reducing the budget
deficit had reduced the government's capacity and willingness to trade
for wage restraint with unions. Further, developments on the international front made it difficult for the government to honour its com-
mitments regarding superannuation and reduced taxation, which had
been agreed to under the Accord Mark II in 1985. The government had
inherited a deficit of $A6.7 thousand million in 1983. By the end of
April 1986, this deficit had nearly doubled, partly as the result of
increased value of imports.

### Change in the late 1980s

While the centralised approach to ensuring restraint attracted mainstream support during the first half of the 1980s, an alternative philosophy was provided by the emergence of the New Right. The New Right
argued, and still does, for deregulation of the Australian economy, even
the destruction of the arbitration system itself in the interests of a more
*laissez-faire* labour sector. It has sought to institute negotiated labour
contracts, even with just individual employees, and to remove the centralised industrial relations system. Its philosophies have been supported
by industrial actions that have seen unions prosecuted in common law.
While the New Right have not managed to dominate mainstream employer associations, they have in effect pressured employer associations
to maintain their quest for labour market flexibility.

Under pressure from the government and the New Right, the unions
accepted the abandonment of wage indexation. In a speech to the
Federal Unions Conference in 1986, the secretary of the New South
Wales Labor Council advocated a two-tier wages system, arguing that 'if

unions failed to unite around the ACTU's proposal they would leave the movement less able to defend itself from attacks by the New Right employers' (Davis, 1987:12).

Following a lengthy national wage case in March 1987, the commission promulgated a new set of wage determination guidelines which removed the indexation system. The new guidelines, in the commission's view, were developed,

> in the context of general agreement as to the need for restraint and sustained efforts on the part of all concerned . . . to address the serious economic problems facing Australia. In particular, the package has been introduced to ensure . . . that changes in labour costs are closely monitored; opportunities are provided to increase efficiency and productivity at the industry and enterprise level; and protection is accorded to lower paid workers. (ACAC, 1987)

The decision introduced a two tier wages system. The first tier provided for a $10 wage increase to all affected workers and the possibility of a further 1.5 per cent increase in October 1987. The second tier, with an increase of up to 4 per cent, was conditional on offsetting improvements in work practices to achieve greater efficiency and productivity.

These principles, while retaining the regulatory flavour that has characterised Australian wage determination, broke new ground in seeking to promote flexibility within a centralised system, through productivity bargaining within limits. Centralism and uniformity were promoted through the operation of the first wage tier, the ceilings placed on second wage tier adjustments and superannuation contributions, the floor on standard hours reductions, and the standards designed to govern anomalies, inequities, work value and new awards. Uniformity was also promoted by the capacity of weaker unions to resort to arbitration in those situations where they are not able to negotiate changes.

The productivity bargaining element represents the first instance, at least since the Great Depression, in which the commission placed caveats upon national wage increases. Whereas historically such increases have been granted as a matter of right, in this instance the 4 per cent second tier was conditional upon unions and individual managements agreeing to minimise costs through the removal of inefficient and restrictive work practices. An important component of the decision was the understanding that such efficiency must be sought at a decentralised industry and enterprise level.

Employers generally welcomed the new system, with its encouragement for negotiations to remove inefficient and unproductive practices. David Nolan, director of the Confederation of Australian Industry, stated that:

> The catch-cry of so many observers of the industrial relations system, for months if not years, has been that the system is too inflexible, that

it interferes with relations at the work place and that it stops employers from coming together with their employees and making their own arrangements.

Now the second tier answers all those criticisms. It leaves the discretion totally with employers and their employees. It provides a framework where they can look at their own work practices, at the way they do business internally, and the circumstances that confront their enterprise, like profitability, efficiency, productivity and competitiveness in the market place. (Cited by Lucato, 1987:23)

The two tier wages system did result in genuine productivity bargaining, with various forms of increased flexibility resulting. A study conducted by the Committee for Economic Development (CEDA) late in 1987 found that a majority of the 480 respondents from private and public sector businesses had or expected to achieve some real offsets to second the wage increases, and over one-third believed their offsets to be worth more than 4 per cent (CEDA, 1988). Of those that expected or had achieved productivity or efficiency gains, only two respondents expected these offsets not to be permanent.

Many of the offsets agreed to in negotiations were difficult to quantify in money terms, such as agreed grievance procedures. A large number of second tier agreements identified the payment of wages directly into the person's bank account, which in other areas of employment was already a well-established practice. Perhaps more fundamentally significant results were achieved in negotiations such as those that occurred in the metal industry and in Australia Post.

Both unions and employers in the metal industry have played a pace-setting role in Australian industrial relations throughout the 1980s and some of the most positive outcomes of the second tier system occurred in this industry. The parties have to some degree been united by the serious downturn in the metal industry, resulting in a net loss of 152 000 jobs between 1974 and 1983. Some of the significant changes resulting from second tier negotiations in this industry were in the area of 'increased numerical flexibility', meaning a firm's ability to make flexible arrangements regarding hours of work, annual leave, rostered days off, overtime and number of part-timers employed and so on to meet production needs (Rimmer & Zappala, 1988:5). The most important fact to emerge from the negotiations, however, was a greater union–management commitment to industry restructuring for the long term.

The results of the second tier for Australia Post were primarily in the area of functional flexibility of the enterprise, that is, 'the employer's capacity to move labour to different tasks within the workplace ... Functional flexibility depends heavily upon reduced demarcation barriers and improved training facilities' (Rimmer & Zappala, 1988:5). In Australia Post, changes negotiated included reduced demarcation, multi-skilling, rewritten duty statements and the implementation of a three year restructuring programme. Other changes included improved recruitment, for instance allowing adjustments to labour inputs to meet changes in demand, and more flexible work practices, such as in the areas of overtime and shift working, to meet the functional demands of the operation (Rimmer & Zappala, 1988:22).

The experiences of both employers and unions under the two tier system were very mixed. Differences between the parties in negotiating experience, the effectiveness of managements' own ability to be pro-active and variations in shopfloor relations were some of the factors (to be discussed later in this chapter) causing heterogeneous experiences under the second tier. Such factors help to explain why some unions gained the 4 per cent second tier increase relatively speedily while others faced considerable delays. They also account for why some employers achieved real offsets while others either did not, or were at least unable to implement them.

The reasons for the second tier system failing in some ways, however, and for it being replaced by a modified system in August 1988 rest with the power relationships between the parties. To a certain extent, the second tier rewarded the previously inefficient and industrially powerful. Those workplaces where restrictive practices proliferated found it much easier to identify trade-offs than those lacking in such obvious inefficiencies. In areas lacking strong union activity, the employer frequently did not feel compelled to 'pay for' correcting inefficiencies or for changes in work practices that could be introduced unilaterally. Workers in the public sector and those in female-dominated industries found it hardest to negotiate.

While the two tier system had delivered some increased flexibility and efficiency gains, pressure had been mounting from unions whose members had missed out on wage increases, from those who believed that they had paid too much for their 4 per cent increase, and, very significantly, from those union officials facing increasing opposition and resistance from their members to further trade-offs. The signs were clear that if the commission were to pass another decision requiring offsets for wage increases, union support for the system would probably not be forthcoming.

The commission's response to these pressures was to hand down a decision in August 1988 that enshrined 'restructuring and efficiency' while guaranteeing wage increases. The decision provided for a 3 per cent wage increase to be paid not earlier than 1 September and a further $10 a week no earlier than six months after receipt of the 3 per cent. The granting of these increases was made conditional upon unions making a commitment to formal reviews of awards with a view to achieving greater structural efficiency and a further commitment not to seek further increases before 1 July 1989.

The extent to which agreements for genuine restructuring and greater efficiency will be forthcoming remains to be seen. Certainly, unions have only to give a commitment to negotiate, not to actually agree to particular changes, in order to achieve the increases for their members. There will undoubtedly be many cases of employers and unions who find the challenge too difficult or inappropriate to their perceived needs. Indications are, however, that major changes will take place throughout most of the Australian economy. Negotiations have already commenced in a number of major industries.

The two tier wage fixing system laid the foundations for future industrial relations policies and practices. Many employers have become proactive and have or are developing sophisticated logs of claims. On the unions' part, some are resisting the pressures for change while others are being dragged into the play, recognising the opportunity to improve their members' job security and wages through changes in areas concerned with training, multi-skilling and the broad-banding of separate award classifications. For a particular group within the union hierarchy, however, they are merely continuing to live within a changing industrial relations environment, significantly shaped and directed by their strategies.

## Activities of the upper middle tier

The activities of the upper middle tier, consisting of corporate and union leadership outside the top tier, has played a significant role in shaping industrial relations policies in Australia during the past decade, both directly as well as indirectly through investment, business, organisational and other policies. Australia today has a highly centralised wage fixing system, which, while retaining its centralised flavour, is strongly directing and encouraging decentralised bargaining and facilitating labour market flexibility. 'Restructuring and efficiency' describes the guiding principle of Australian industrial relations today.

Australia has witnessed a remarkable transformation in its industrial relations policies and practices over the past few years. This change in direction is made all the more remarkable because although it has been imposed upon some unions (and indeed employers), the shape it has taken has been mainly instigated and directed by several key union members of the top and upper middle tiers. While it is the employer members of this tier that have predominantly, and over a long period, pressured for reform and for greater labour flexibility, it is union leadership under a Labor government that has facilitated and shaped the change.

The policies of the upper middle tier, both corporate and union, share a common impact in that each of their policies has acted to shift the locus of industrial relations activity to the enterprise level and expanded enormously the traditional range of deemed 'industrial relations matters'.

*The corporate leadership*

Corporate leaders in Australia have generally played a far more active role in industrial relations during the 1980s than they did in the past. The formation of the Business Council of Australia (BCA) in 1983 provided a direct avenue for corporate leaders to affect the development of strategy and policy within the top tier. While much of the direction taken in overall industrial relations policy in Australia has been primarily an outcome of negotiations between the Hawke ALP government and the ACTU, corporate leaders have influenced that process tremendously.

Many of the same forces that caused the upper tier to change its policies and practices also led corporate leaders to recognise the importance of the organisation's industrial relations for the well-being of the company. Corporate leaders in Australia have been as much involved in the creation of the pressures on the Australian economy as they have been in attempting to handle them. Large corporations, like those elsewhere in the world, have been vigorously engaged in activity such as takeovers and going offshore to do business, particularly in countries offering a less-regulated environment. They have also had to grapple with international economic and business pressures.

Shifts in the nature of corporate shareholding, the squeeze on profits from Third World manufacturing activity, microtechnology developments and the side effects of a more highly interdependent world economy have caused corporations to adopt investment and business policies that have led to or were accompanied by tougher industrial relations policies. Corporate performance is now evaluated within a much shorter time frame than ever before, and this has contributed significantly to more aggressive management focused at the enterprise rather than the industry or national level. Another force for further decentralisation is the effect of Third World manufacturing activity, which has put pressure on profits in local manufacturing. Competitive pressures have intensified the search for survival techniques and industrial relations have come under particularly close scrutiny. Tightened operations, the design of products more responsive to consumer preferences, greater quality assurance, new wave technology and new management systems emphasising devolution have all affected industrial relations.

One way in which the activities of corporate leaders have affected the top tier in Australia is in assisting the emergence of an industrial relations system emphasising restructuring, efficiency and flexibility. Their activities have also affected the lower middle tier and helped to produce a more proactive management that pays greater attention to enterprise-level practices and relationships.

*The union leadership*

The union leadership in Australia since 1983 has been directly and deeply involved in the formulation of policy guiding Australia's industrial relations. While the pressures for reform can be seen as flowing from the international economy and from corporate leaders, key union leaders have been profoundly important in shaping the nature of Australia's response.

Through the Accord, union leaders were able to influence significantly the nature of government policies developed to address the problems of the Australian economy. Union leaders, with the Labor government, formulated policies aimed at restraining wage increases and at ensuring adequate creation of jobs and a fair sharing of the burden of adjustment. In return for their restraint, union leaders were able to influence a wide range of government policies, especially those relating to industry restructuring, training and taxation.

Perhaps the most remarkable aspect of union activity within the upper middle tier has been the extent to which union leaders at this level have sought to shape government policy in favour of adaptation and change—a great contrast to the traditional union role. A significant policy document was released in June 1987, entitled *Australia Reconstructed* (ACTU–TDC, 1987). The report of a mission by members of the ACTU and the Trade Development Council (TDC) to western Europe in 1986, it was prepared by the TDC secretariat under the direction of the trade union leaders who made up the mission. The mission was funded by the TDC and the report was published by the Australian Government Publishing Service. The mission comprised only union and government, not business, representatives.

The mission had set out to examine how other countries have dealt with trade and other economic problems similar to those currently confronting Australia. The mission visited Sweden, Norway, Austria, West Germany and Britain. The mission was particularly impressed by the 'Swedish Third Way' and 'Austro-Keynesianism'. While a number of employer bodies were extremely critical of the report for its corporatist recommendations, the document displays an intense commitment to economic growth and co-operation to achieve prosperity. Many of the recommendations contained within the report have already been adopted by government, if only in a modified form, while the thrust of the report's recommendations is certain to influence government and union policy formulation for some time to come.

The report focuses upon a large number of issues on the national policy agenda, including macroeconomic policies; wages; trade and industry policy; labour market and training policies; industrial democracy and strategic unionism. The 72 recommendations of the report are similarly wide-ranging. Many of the attitudes expressed represent a

major breakthrough from attitudes of the past and signal a new approach
to such issues as education and training, where unions have been a
predominant source of restrictive practices. The report also espouses a
consensus approach to decision making, which many employer organisations saw as simply an attempt by unions to achieve more power.

*Australia Reconstructed* is a landmark document. The report displays
a clear recognition of the structural adjustment process facing Australia.
It states that 'The central issues are no longer whether to internationalise but how, and how rapidly', and that moderation in wage claims is a
critical component of such strategies. The report recommends that
Australia retain a centralised system of wage determination but with
room for adjustments that are predicated on improvements in productivity, efficiency and skill enhancement at the micro or enterprise
level. Outside national adjustments, such enterprise-level negotiations,
would 'pay due regard to price and productivity movements in the
internationally traded goods and services sector'.

The report proposes linking wage adjustment to the investment decision. It calls for a National Development Fund, which would provide
equity, capital and soft loans for investment in new industry and housing
and would be administered by the Australian Industry Development
Corporation (AIDC). In order to obtain equity or loans, a number of
preconditions would need to be met, including that business and unions
would be required to agree on such matters as superannuation, dispute
settlement procedures and reduction in labour market segmentation.

In some aspects *Australia Reconstructed* simply affirms, while continuing to shape, government policy. The report calls for labour market
policies developed on a tripartite basis to help create a more skilled
workforce, a more flexible labour market and reduced labour market
segmentation. In *Skills for Australia*, published in conjunction with the
1987 budget, John Dawkins, Minister for Employment Education and
Training, and Clyde Holding, Minister for Aboriginal Affairs, made a
major statement on the importance of skills formation and the directions
of future reform. The document emphasises that the objectives for
reform are to increase participation in education and training; to enhance the quality and appropriateness of the skills acquired; to improve
efficiency and flexibility; to ensure equity; and to increase industry's
commitment to training. *Australia Reconstructed* proposes the establishment of a National Employment and Training Fund financed by an
enterprise levy. Firms that meet certain criteria would be able to withdraw up to 80 per cent of their own contributions to finance training
activities. The remaining 20 per cent would be available for firms undertaking additional training specifically related to industry restructuring.

While union members of the upper middle tier have been active in
shaping national policies, a good deal of attention has been paid not
only to the role of unions but also to their structure. At the March 1987

ACTU executive, it was suggested that the union movement plan as a first step the establishment of about 20 union groupings to act as a catalyst for union amalgamation and co-operation. *Australia Reconstructed* also proposed a number of structural and policy changes impinging upon unions, including amalgamation. 'Strategic unionism' was proposed, involving a more sophisticated form of labour organisation, embodying a strong commitment to wealth and income creation, rather than just distribution. In September 1987, the ACTU released its document *Future Strategies for the Trade Union Movement*, in which a programme for amalgamation and a broadened role for unions within the economy were detailed.

An important lesson in Australia is that the sheer complexity of the organisational framework within which trade unions exist and derive legal entity can provide significant protection from management militancy, or at least ameliorate its effects (Niland, 1987). The increased quest for flexibility pursued by both management and governments in Australia, together with changes in workforce composition and distribution put unions under considerable pressure. The institutional framework, however, provided unions with the breathing space necessary for developing survival strategies. These strategies have been developed in a very sophisticated form, enabling union leaders, rather than managers, to lead the push for innovation in work practices and flexibility.

## Activities of the lower middle tier

The lower middle tier, consisting of management and union officials, has been placed under considerable pressure by the policies developed by those above. This level of the system has borne the burden of implementing restructuring and efficiency principles.

For management, changes in investment, business and macro industrial relations policies have placed them under considerable pressure to improve efficiency within the organisation. Inevitably this has required changes to traditional management practices and the devolution of many management functions. Industrial relations activity has traditionally been viewed as the responsibility of specialists in the field and the resolution of conflicts has frequently occurred at a centralised level. The growing importance of improving efficiency and industrial relations generally has necessitated management acquiring new skills, particularly in the area of human relations.

While management experiences of the two tier wages system and the efficiency and restructuring principle have varied significantly, most have sought to cope with the changes by increasing the training given to management and through devolving increasing responsibility for industrial relations to the workplace. These initiatives have been accompanied by the introduction of policies and procedures aimed at shifting power, and in some cases resources, to the shopfloor.

Management policies have turned sharply in favour of stronger bonding between the enterprise and its employees, which inevitably entails decentralism in the system at large. Management is also increasingly adopting a tough stance in pursuing its industrial relations goals. Management strategy has become a more important factor in shaping industrial relations, increasingly embracing techniques to build stronger links between individual employees and their enterprise, which facilitates the use of such production control techniques as total quality control (TQC) and just in time (JIT).

Overall the strategy adopted by management in the lower middle tier has been to shift the focus of industrial relations responsibility to the workplace and to develop improved human relations in their organisation. The major resistance to this strategy has come from line managers, whose role will be examined under the bottom tier.

The major strategy adopted by union officials to handle the pressures exerted upon them, both from the top and upper middle tiers, has been to identify trade-offs for the workforce in accepting change and also to upgrade the role played by union members in negotiating change. While some union officials have persisted in encouraging their members to resist negotiations, most have accepted the need to be proactive and to attempt to shape the nature of industrial relations outcomes. Frequently trade-offs have been identified in the area of devolution. By ensuring a more meaningful role for their members, and particularly for union delegates, officials have sought with some success to build their members into the process of change. A further pressure for such devolution has come from the sheer quantity of work now demanded of union officials. Under a centralised system, conditions covering workers in a variety of enterprises can be handled at a centralised level. The increasing emphasis on restructuring and efficiency has required activity at the enterprise level, necessitating improved shopfloor organisation.

Many union officials have, however, faced increasing hostility from their membership regarding abandonment of some traditional practices that were regarded as hard-won conditions of employment. Wage restraint over the past few years has also resulted in a lower standard of living for many unionists, which has also put considerable pressure upon union officials. The pressure on this level of the union hierarchy was particularly severe during the period of the second tier wage negotiations and contributed greatly to the modifications to the wages system in August 1988. The leadership and structural challenge is to both *decentralise* the power and authority needed to bargain at enterprise levels, but also to *centralise* the provisions of staff expertise and other resources needed to develop long-run strategies and advise local union entities on the increasingly complex array of technical, economic and organisational issues that confront labour today.

Both management and union members of the lower middle tier in Australia have experienced pressure for reform from above and resistance from below. They have been the colloquial 'ham in the sandwich'. Both sides were ill-prepared for the changed role thrust upon them. Neither group possesses the training or experience necessary to equip it for its current role, although in many instances it is the union officials who have been best placed. While there are many instances in which members of this tier have adopted a strategy of resistance to change, as the pressure for restructuring and efficiency has increased, such a strategy of resistance has become more and more impossible to maintain. The dominant strategy adopted by both management and union officials to cope with the pressure exerted on them has been to establish negotiating relationships aimed at protecting their respective interests during the change process and to develop the role played by those at the workplace.

**Activities of the bottom tier**

It is at the level of the bottom tier, concerned with the workplace and its relationships, that the full effect of changes at the top tier is being felt. Policies aimed at improving Australia's industrial relations and facilitating greater flexibility have shifted attention and activity to the shopfloor.

Until the past few years in Australia, relatively little attention was paid to developing industrial relations expertise at the workplace. This is particularly true of line managers, who were most commonly bypassed by both union officials and senior management in the handling of industrial relations. While union delegates have tended to perform a more direct and substantial role in the resolution of workplace grievances, they have not generally been required to accommodate change; rather they have played a role of resistance.

At the workplace, line managers are now commonly being required to play a more direct and positive role in handling workplace matters. Responsibilities for both technical and non-technical matters are increasingly being devolved to lower-level management. In many cases this is a major change from a past in which their organisations did not actually accept or treat them as part of management. Experiences of the past have caused many supervisors not to view themselves as part of management. It is common to find that their conflict with the workforce is only exceeded by their hostility toward senior management. Consequently, a major barrier to the implementation of changes, including those agreed to in second tier negotiations, has come from line managers.

Similarly, union delegates at the workplace have traditionally performed a fairly restricted role in industrial relations, being concerned mainly with the protection and betterment of their members' conditions. The notion of structured bargaining, problem solving and trade-offs is still fairly foreign to them, and the commitment to such principles as restructuring and efficiency espoused at the higher levels of union organisation have not yet been truly accepted by the bulk of unionists at the shopfloor. Like union organisers, elected delegates have come under considerable pressure from their members to protect traditional standards.

Many changes have already occurred in workplace practices as a result of negotiations, including electronic funds transfer of wages, disputes procedures, flexibility in manning levels, reduction in demarcation lines, co-operation in eliminating waste, restructuring of job classifications, increased spread of working hours, removal of restrictions on overtime and provision for foremen/supervisors to perform subordinates' duties (CEDA, 1988). These changes, despite some opposition at the shopfloor, are happening and, in the process, the industrial relations role of those in the bottom tier is being enhanced.

Training in both technical and non-technical areas has assumed major importance. The next few years in Australia will see the focus of attention directed to equipping those at the workplace with the knowledge and skills required to achieve restructuring and efficiency goals.

## Conclusions

The prevailing theme of Australia's industrial relations transformation over the past few years has been the quest for survival through flexibility. While it is the employer members of the top and upper middle tiers who have been the major source of pressure for labour flexibility, it is the key union leaders who have developed the strategy determining the nature of Australia's response.

Australia has sought to cope with the variety of economic and other pressures by encouraging workplace flexibility within a centralised system. The result of both employer and union responses to the needs of the 1980s has been to devolve the responsibility for industrial relations increasingly to the shopfloor and to develop the procedural and training resources necessary for this to succeed.

## Note

1 This chapter is based on a paper first prepared for the Labour and Economic Development Conference, Chung-Hua Institution for Economic Research, Taiwan, 21–23 December 1988. In an updated and modified form it was subsequently presented to the Eighth World Congress of the International Industrial Relations Association, Brussels, 4–7 September 1989.

# 7
# The dynamics and dimensions of change
## OLIVER CLARKE and JOHN NILAND

The objective of this book has been to throw light on the nature, extent and dynamics of change in industrial relations, mainly by reference to the experience of major industrialised market economies. Having set out the general background and analysed the recent experience of five of the countries, an overall assessment can now be attempted. For this purpose it is useful to consider a series of questions, namely:

- What is the experience of change?
- What is the rationale for change?
- Who are the agents of change?
- What are the levers for securing change?
- What are the barriers to change?

## The experience of change

Looking back over, say, 60 years, it is surprising how few radical changes there have been in industrial relations. Leaving aside the installation of Nazi and Fascist systems in the early 1930s, that decade saw no more than three or four substantial changes in the countries discussed here. In the United States the spur of the Depression prompted a New Deal, in which the strengthening of trade unions (with which the rapid growth of industrial unions was associated) and the establishment of a nationally applicable base for collective bargaining played a major part. In Sweden, there had been long years of industrial strife when the accession of a social democratic government, fear of government intervention, a change in leadership for both the employers and the unions, and a deep dissatisfaction with the existing conflictual situation among employers and workers set off the talks that culminated in the Saltsjö-baden agreement of 1938, thus laying the basis for the much-praised 'Swedish model'. In Switzerland, too, fear of government intervention and distaste for prevalent conflict led to the first industrial peace agreement of 1937. A fourth change, part of the *expérience Blum* in France in 1936, proved to be mainly transient. Having foundered on economic crisis, the opposition of employers, and political dissension among the trade unions, it left behind it little more than the establishment of paid holidays and a notional 40-hour week.

The 1940s showed another, if expensive, way of changing an industrial relations system—war. In chapter 1 we noted how the war-damaged countries of continental Europe, together with Japan, reconstructed their industrial relations systems. In the liberated countries there was usually some infrastructure that had not entirely disappeared under occupation and could be revived, but the new systems differed significantly from the old. In Germany, Austria and Japan completely new systems had to be devised, while in the case of Japan, key new elements were introduced by the occupying powers (Gould, 1984).

From 1950 on, however, radical systemic changes were few, the most substantial being those wrought as a result of political change in Spain, Portugal, Greece and Turkey. Elsewhere institutional changes in numerous countries contributed to a greater industrial democracy. Changes that need consideration, however, are those that have taken place in the 1980s in France, Britain, Sweden and Australia, in contrast to the United States and Japan where there have been few systemic changes.

As Delamotte explains in chapter 5, the Socialist government that came to power in France in 1981, after decades of government by right-of-centre parties, sought to curb unstable employment, to encourage employment by reductions in working hours, and to promote workers' rights in the enterprise. But the four substantial laws passed in 1982, the 'Auroux' laws, which the centre-right government of 1986–88 did not seek to change, seem to have made remarkably little difference to French industrial relations (Moss, 1988). And, considering that the rate of unionisation in France is now probably no more than 15 per cent, and less in the private sector, a great many formal aspects of industrial relations are not applied in practice.

In the aftermath of the war, British industrial relations were considered to be among the best in the world. The British saw a key element as being the voluntarism of the system. As Kahn-Freund described it: 'there is, perhaps, no major country in the world in which the law has played a less significant role in the shaping of [labour–management] relations than in Great Britain, and in which today the legal profession have less to do with labour relations' (Kahn-Freund, 1954:44).

Voluntarism was upheld by the Donovan Commission on Trade Unions and Employers Associations, reporting in 1968, but already in 1969 the Labour government, while accepting much of Donovan's analysis, were moved by the nature and amount of industrial conflict at the time to propose greater intervention by the law in strikes. Then in

1971 the succeeding Conservative government passed an Industrial Relations Act that considerably augmented the extent of legal involvement in industrial relations. The Act was an embarrassing failure, but any possible further change was cut short when the government left office in 1974—incidentally, effectively as a consequence of a major coal strike. The subsequent Labour government (1974-79) put an end to almost all of the 1971 Act and substituted its own framework, which more or less restored the legal position to what it had been before 1971 and, in addition, strengthened the position of both workers and unions. This legislation in turn had to give way to the series of very different Acts introduced by the Conservatives between 1980 and 1988 (with further legislation envisaged). There is no doubt that in the event of Labour again attaining office, there will be a further reconstruction of labour law.

Apart from the general legal framework, the British government forced a substantial shift in public sector industrial relations, as evidenced in its tough stance in imposing cash limits to contain labour costs in the public service in the early 1980s; its refusal to subsidise large wage increases in nationalised industries; its termination of the Civil Service Pay Research Unit; and its replacement of the traditional negotiating arrangements for schoolteachers.

In effect, what had been a consensus in Britain concerning industrial relations has increasingly, since the 1960s, become a political football, and there seems little prospect of the major political parties, whose beliefs concerning industrial relations mirror their strong disagreement over a wide range of policy issues, agreeing on what constitutes a good industrial relations system. The most that one can say is that a return to a system as free of legalism as British industrial relations were up to the 1960s is extremely unlikely. The present choice appears to be between a further weakening of the trade unions and a new legal framework that strengthens them. As Hunter points out in chapter 5, British industrial relations have not yet reached a new plateau of stability.

A formidable body of legislation concerning trade unions and industrial relations has, then, been placed on the statute book—five major Acts in nine years. But what has been its effect on the actual conduct of industrial relations in Britain? It has had little effect on the shape of trade unions and employer associations. It has not changed the levels at which collective bargaining is conducted, or the nature of the formal bargaining machinery. It has left untouched public assistance rendered by the Advisory, Conciliation and Arbitration Service (ACAS). Though it has, together with the changed economic environment, weakened the bargaining power of the trade unions, wage increases for workers generally have consistently been running at levels appreciably above what can be afforded without adding to inflation. British labour productivity, despite some gains, is still considerably lower than productivity in comparable countries. It would be wrong, however, to assume that the new laws have had no effect. They have inhibited indiscriminate union-backed use of the strike weapon; they have reduced the extent of the closed shop; and they have made union leadership more accountable to the members. But if they have persuaded militants to be circumspect and encouraged management to be more assertive they have done little to change the attitudes that underlie British industrial relations.

The Swedish industrial relations system has for long been considered a shining example to other countries. But the 'Swedish model', though still among the most effective, is hardly what it was (Ahlén, 1988 and 1989; Lash, 1985; Lundberg, 1985; Myrdal, 1980). Briefly, at the end of the 1960s the unions were concerned with the increasing concentration of Swedish industry and were anxious to achieve gains for their members beyond simple wage increases. Though one of the bases of the Swedish model was that unions and employers should resolve their differences between them, and keep the government out, the unions now turned to government (on the grounds that the employers were unwilling to satisfy their demands and that some of those demands could only be fulfilled by legislation). The result was a series of Acts, notably the Board Representation Act 1972, strengthened in 1976 and 1987; the Shop Stewards Act 1974; the Codetermination at Work Act 1976, which ended the understanding dating from 1906 recognising the employers' prerogative in respect of employment and the distribution of work; the Job Security Act 1974; the Work Environment Act 1978; and, finally, the most divisive measure, the Wage Earner Funds Act 1983.

Beyond these legislation-driven changes, Sweden's highly centralised collective bargaining system weakened in the 1980s. There was increasing bidding up between the three central bargaining units—the blue-collar private sector, the white-collar private sector, and the public sector. For most bargaining rounds in the 1980s, in the key private blue-collar sector it was not possible to arrive at a generally applicable central agreement. But if there were now, in the 1980s, some substantial conflicts, relations in industry were still good, and the efficiency of Swedish industry remained a shared goal for employers and unions alike and the necessary structural change was carried out speedily, effectively and humanely, as exemplified by the closure of shipyards (Stråth, 1987).

Australia, as Niland and Spooner point out in chapter 6, has experienced significant changes in its traditional industrial relations structures, policies and practices, though these have not, either for the Commonwealth or the states, signalled departure from the system of compulsory conciliation and arbitration that has been the centrepiece of industrial relations since the beginning of the century. The significant changes have come about as a result of increased economic pressures, flowing from setbacks in the value of Australia's primary products in the export market, the uncompetitiveness of Australian manufacturing industry, and the more difficult world economy. Equally significant, however, have been shifts in political judgement about the rationality and viability of the traditional application of a firmly centralised approach to wages regulation and the newfound interest of the national Industrial Relations Commission in a policy stance giving a greater role to productivity and efficiency concerns.

After considerable difficulties in accommodating wage pressures, the last Liberal–National (i.e. conservative) government brought about a wage freeze at the end of 1982, a time when unemployment and inflation were each running at around 10 per cent. Before the freeze had run out the Hawke Labor government had come to power, with an agreement (the 'Accord') with the trade unions, undertaking wage moderation on the basis of government assurances covering a wide range of economic, industrial, and social policies. The Accord was, in effect, immediately ratified by a spectacularly successful national economic summit meeting between Commonwealth and state ministers, employer association representatives and individual employers, and trade union representatives in April 1983.

Consensus-based incomes policies have a very poor track record in most countries. The Australian Accord has endured and given results. Real wages have fallen (though the 'social wage' has risen). Employment and profits have increased. Inflation, though still high, has decreased. Days lost in strikes have fallen, though they are still high by international standards.

The durability of the Accord, and its continued constructive role, have been made possible by the flexibility that government and unions have shown in negotiations, and the fact that there is no attractive alternative for them. What is significant for this chapter is that it has been possible, through government–union agreement, employer acquiescence, and the aid of the Industrial Relations Commission, both to respond to changing needs and steadily to move towards enhancing productive efficiency. Tax concessions, superannuation, health care costs, and post-dating of wage increases have been elements in the successive agreements reached. As regards efficiency, in 1987 growing strains in the Accord were eased by an unprecedented two tier award providing a general increase together with a second adjustment dependent on productivity improvements to be gained through 'restructuring and efficiency negotiations', not at the traditional centralised level, but through negotiations at an industry or enterprise level. The August 1988 decision of the commission again in effect provided a two tier wage increase, laying stress on a new structural efficiency principle, aimed at enhancing flexibility and competitiveness.

Other countries experienced less systemic change. In the United States the only significant attempts to strengthen the New Deal model fell by the wayside. The Common Situs Picketing Bill was vetoed by

President Ford in 1976 and the Labor Law Reform Bill was lost in the Senate in 1978. But there was substantial non-structural change. As Kochan and Wever describe in chapter 2, the onset of recession brought concession bargaining and, to a lesser extent, two tier bargaining (which, with its provision for differential wage levels within a single workplace is different from Australian two tier bargaining where the effect is to produce variability between workplaces). With the change in personnel in the National Labor Relations Board under the Reagan administration unions had less and less success in gaining negotiating rights. And unionisation declined steadily from 35 per cent in 1955 to 17 per cent in 1988.

In Japan, the inevitability, and to a large extent desirability, of change is readily accepted. The planning of change, including securing a consensus for it, is evident at all levels, from the shop floor quality control circles, through the *ringi* processes of decision making to the evolution of national 'visions' by trade unions or government sponsored committees, is part of the way of life. 'How can we do it better' is a shared outlook in that productivity-orientated culture: there are few barriers to necessary industrial change in Japan.

Japan being a country where relations between people are viewed as being more important than legislative interpretations, there have been few significant legislative changes in the 1980s. But there has been one structural change of note, namely the coming together of the four trade union centres to form Rengo in November 1987 as a single peak organisation for the trade unions of the private sector, and Shin Rengo, including the public sector, in November 1989. This move, prompted by desire for greater unity *vis-à-vis* the government and in the annual wage round, and facilitated by containing political differences, does not, however, seem likely to bring about any fundamental change in Japanese industrial relations.

The successful and stable industrial relations system created in Germany after the war has not undergone any substantial alteration other than the strengthening of the organs of codetermination, notably the Works Councils Act 1972, the Codetermination Act 1976, and the relevant minor amendments of 1988. Though the parties are not without their differences, as Streeck highlights in chapter 3, those differences have not hitherto proved insurmountable. Collective bargaining, the German legislature, the Labour Courts, and the arbitration provisions to deal with intra-enterprise disputes have worked effectively to ensure that the system takes changing needs in its stride.

Looking briefly at other industrialised market economy countries, there have been no major reconstructions of industrial relations systems. Canada, whose practices have much in common with those of the United States, continues to have a decentralised and conflictual industrial relations system. Notably few Canadian employers have sought concession bargaining or two tier bargaining (Thompson, 1989). Italian industrial relations remain conflictual and attempts at reform have met with little success. The Spanish and Portuguese industrial relations systems installed after the Fascist era have proved viable, but have been somewhat unsuccessful in facilitating greater flexibility and in avoiding conflict between collective bargaining outcomes and the needs of economic policy; Spain, in particular, suffers high unemployment and very high strike levels. There have been no sweeping changes in Denmark, Norway or Finland, but periodic difficulties in containing wages continue. There have been no fundamental changes in Austria, Belgium or the Netherlands. Ireland has been engaged in a review of labour laws, but this has not produced any fundamental changes, and Swiss industrial relations have continued on their peaceful way.

As to the international scene, no substantial changes in the organisation of employers or unions during the 1980s are evident, nor has there been any significant development of internationally agreed guidelines for multinational enterprises since they were introduced in the seventies. There has, however, in most recent years, been some small movement in the direction of cross-national consultation in a handful of multinational enterprises (Northrop et al., 1988). The development of international industrial relations in the European Economic Community has already been discussed in chapter 1.

From one perspective it is surprising how well industrial relations systems have withstood the tests of structural change and the need to achieve labour market flexibility and hence improve competitiveness that the 1980s have imposed on them. By meeting the challenge they have forestalled the need for fundamental change, although the significance of the adjustments to processes and strategies in some areas are noteworthy, if mixed. A review of the countries discussed here shows that, if trade unions have lost members overall and if in others they have lost heavily, in some countries they have actually increased their membership. Some unions have amalgamated, but in general the configuration of unionism has changed little, as is the case with the configuration of employer associations.

In collective bargaining management strategy has played a generally stronger role, and there has been a greater emphasis on decentralisation, with more matters being dealt with at the enterprise or workplace level. But across the board there has been no sweeping change in the way in which wages and working conditions are determined. Most of the countries that experienced inflationary pressures from collective bargaining in the 1970s have continued to experience such pressures, albeit less severely, in the 1980s. Industrial conflict as measured by strike statistics has shown a substantial reduction fairly generally but in no case has a country moved from being a high-strike country in the 1970s to being a low-strike country in the 1980s, or vice versa. Neither has the role of the state changed substantially across the 1980s, except, perhaps, in Britain and to a degree in Australia.

So there has been no major change to speak of in industrial relations structures and institutions in the 1980s, which could lead some observers, mistakenly, to believe that industrial relations systems are a bulwark against those adjustments made vital by economic crisis. This would be to ignore the substantial shifts in the focus and style of collective bargaining, with stronger emphasis on strategy and workplace bargaining and consultation arrangements. To sum up, it would appear that there has been relatively little change in industrial relations *systems* but significant change within industrial relations as such.

### The rationale for change

The previous section demonstrated the wide variety of change and how it came about. Clearly, some of the most effective reconstruction has taken place as a result of cataclysmic defeat in war—hardly a recommendable means to change! Some has eventuated from political upheaval, like the Spanish and Portuguese, or more modest political change, as in the case of the French Auroux reforms. Other improvements, like the Swedish and the Swiss in the 1930s, have come about through a desire to avoid governmental intervention and reaction to a period of strife. Yet others have evolved, directly or indirectly, as a reaction to economic pressures. The American New Deal and the Australian Accord are examples.

Of these changes the Swedish case deserves particular note. Apart from coming about peacefully, the model that was agreed at Saltsjö-baden in 1938 was the fruit of very careful preparation, and both sides have continued to take a far-sighted view, formulated through intensive consultation with their constituents and strengthened to become the highly successful model of the 1950s and 1960s, accomplished with scarcely any legislative aid. The way that model developed shows us that employers and unions together *can* reconstruct a new industrial relations system for themselves within the limits laid down by law. (There were, incidentally, no major legislated structural changes in Swedish industrial relations between the Acts of 1928 and 1936, and the substantial wave of legislation in the 1970s.) Such a successful transformation to good industrial relations is unlikely to come from beyond the prime industrial parties. That is, the particular agents, or 'owners', of the change process can strongly influence its form and substance.

### The agents of change

The agents of change, that is, the people or institutions whose intervention can bring about substantial reform of an industrial relations system, are, potentially:

- employers and their associations;
- trade unions;
- governments/legislatures;
- the judiciary, or industrial tribunals, or both; and
- individuals.

In recent years employers have certainly tended to take a more vigorous approach in their relations with their workers and trade unions. Equally certainly, they and their associations have always sought some influence with governments, promoting or countering proposed legislation. In their relations with unions, employers have, in the nature of things, more often sought to block or water down union demands for change than to bring change about, though there are examples of employer-led innovation. For example, the Swedish employers were primarily responsible for setting the levels at which bargaining has been conducted in Sweden and, to take a sectional example from the formative days of industrial relations, after the great engineering dispute of 1897–98 the British engineering employers caused a whole industry-wide framework of negotiation to be embodied in the terms of settlement. More recently, as Kochan and Wever point out in chapter 2, it is the employers who have been setting the agenda for industrial relations in the United States. This has certainly affected the operation of the industrial relations system, though it has not changed the structure of the system itself. But the conclusion must be that it is impossible to find a case where employers, collectively or on their own, have substantially led the reconstruction of an industrial relations system.

Far more change originates with trade unions, as is natural since their objectives imply seeking change in the status quo. The Swedish unions, for example, led the way to the active labour market policy and insisted on the solidaristic wage policy in Sweden. They also set afoot the Swedish industrial democracy legislation of the 1970s and the wage earner funds of 1983. The German trade unions' insistence on co-determination introduced a significant change into German industrial relations—and indeed the whole of that system owed much to the trade unions in its formative stage, immediately following the war. The British unions were largely responsible for the form of Labour's short-lived legislation of the 1970s. The Australian unions, joint originators of the Accord of 1983, have throughout the 1980s been the key agents of change, although it might be argued that their prime concern is to preserve or improve their position in specific ways rather than to seek to reform the system as such. Still, the end result is a transformed system.

The best test of alleged 'change' is whether it significantly affects the relations of management and workers and the terms of employment at the workplace itself. Much legislation would fail this test, but legislation is nevertheless the principal agent to which employers, unions and the general public look for change. Legislation normally sets a framework for the rights and obligations of unions and employer associations, and management and employees, and the relations between them. It may set minimum conditions for employment; it may provide help to resolve industrial disputes. And it is expected to safeguard the public interest. Government as an agent of change also has the opportunity to set an example by the arrangements it makes concerning its own substantial number of employees.

Government may be proactive in legislating reform for ideological reasons or because of an obvious, serious need. Otherwise it is only likely to legislate when persuaded to do so by employers or unions or by public pressure voiced through the media.

The fourth potential agent of change is the courts of law (and quasi-judicial bodies such as the industrial tribunals in Australia). The experience of trade unions with the courts has not always been happy. The legal profession, at least in the English-speaking countries, has been reared on the importance of protecting the interests of the individual, and of trade; it is not always sympathetic to the collective interests associated with organised labour. As Winston Churchill remarked, in 1911: 'It is not good for trade unions that they should be brought in contact with the courts, and it is not good for the courts' (cited in Wedderburn, 1986:272). In Britain, particularly, the history of labour law shows several examples of court decisions adverse to trade unions being followed by legislation to reverse the effect of the decisions. The leading example was the Taff Vale judgment of 1901, making the union liable for the damages caused by an industrial dispute (reversed by the Trade Disputes Act 1906); another was the Osborne judgment of 1910, concerning the right of a union to use membership dues to support a political party (reversed by the Trade Union Act 1913).

In the United States, the early history of industrial relations was much influenced by court decisions, and notably by the use of the injunction. More recently it was the Supreme Court's judgment in the Lincoln Mills case (1957) and the Steelworkers Trilogy (1960) that effectively established the quasi-autonomy of arbitration in grievance procedures in the United States. More recently still, when some American companies rid themselves of their obligations under collective agreements by filing under section 11 of the bankruptcy law, Congress moved rapidly to establish that this was not permissible.

In Germany, the Federal Labour Court 'has become at least as important as the legislator as far as regulations in the field of labour are concerned' (Weiss, 1987:34). The rules concerning strikes, for instance, have largely been evolved by the court. Thus, in a case concerning the formulation of a union claim in the metal industry in Schleswig-Holstein in 1956, the taking of a strike ballot before the existing agreement had expired was held to have violated the peace-keeping obligation and the union was fined heavily. Examples could also be quoted from other countries.

Of all the countries considered here, it is Australia where a judicial-type body outside the normal courts of law has had an important role in respect of industrial relations. Section 51 (xxxv) of the Australian Constitution 1901 empowers the Commonwealth to legislate with respect to 'conciliation and arbitration for the prevention and settlement of industrial disputes extending beyond the limits of any one State'. In accordance with this power the Commonwealth established a tribunal—the Court of Conciliation and Arbitration—charged with the compulsory arbitration of labour disputes. The purely judicial functions that the court had were hived off in 1956, as a result of the High Court decision in the Boilermakers case, ruling that it was unconstitutional for a Commonwealth tribunal to exercise both judicial and non-judicial functions. This tribunal has now become, as a result of the Industrial Relations Act, 1988, the Australian Industrial Relations Commission. As chapter 6 indicates, the role of the commission since 1983 has, in practice, largely been to endorse agreements reached by government and trade unions and more or less reluctantly acquiesced in by employers, but the commission is by no means *required* to follow such agreements, and there have been instances in the 1960s and 1970s when the federal government, which is constitutionally inhibited in legislating directly in industrial relations, and the key industrial tribunal, in whom such powers are vested, have been at loggerheads. The stance of the latter body prevails in such instances.

As agents of change, the courts generally have a limited role. Their interpretations can, and often do, have an effect on the operation of industrial relations, but they are not in any position to carry the burden of any substantial revision of industrial relations. The Australian Industrial Relations Commission is a special case. The 'principles' it has laid down since 1985 have had a marked impact on workplace industrial relations, no doubt largely because they went in a direction already clearly indicated by the government–union agreements. But in a more politically open situation it is doubtful whether the commission could appreciably influence the industrial relations scenario, as distinct from particular terms and conditions of employment.

The fifth and final agent of change is the individual. Evidently, at all times charismatic or powerful individuals put their mark on industrial relations as on other human institutions, leading them in new directions. In Britain in the late 1860s, when trade unions were under attack as a result of the Sheffield outrages, a small group of union leaders (called the Junta by the Webbs), influenced the Royal Commission on Trade Unions, sitting at the time, and turned public opinion to the positive characteristics of unionism, thereby creating a climate for the succession of laws favourable to the trade unions passed in the 1870s. In another example from Britain, Walter (later Lord) Citrine, as General Secretary of the TUC, did much to turn the trade union movement into what came to be known, in the Second World War, as an 'estate of the realm'. In Australia, it is difficult to imagine the 'new look' that the Accord of 1983 gave to industrial relations without the personality of the former ACTU president, Prime Minister Bob Hawke.

Public opinion too, with some assistance from the media, and given time, plays a part in reform. Thus the British 'winter of discontent' of 1978–79 was influential in the election of the Conservative government in 1979, and in creating a climate that assisted the series of legislative changes on which that government embarked. Public distaste for the postwar wave of strikes in the United States facilitated passage of the Taft–Hartley Act of 1947.

### Facilitating change

But if change is desirable and becomes feasible, how can it be facilitated? What are the agencies that can give it legitimacy, smooth out the obstacles, carry it forward, and iron out any problems that arise in its implementation (Niland: 1986:245)?

Probably the greatest, and most desirable, facilitator is consensus. When opinion leaders are supported by a kind of critical mass among the population, change becomes relatively easy. But how can such a consensus for change be achieved, given that most people are naturally suspicious of change unless they are convinced in advance of its value?

Again, the media are likely to be influential, but they in turn are likely to be influenced by opinion-forming individuals and bodies. The process has a certain circularity. Politicians, pressure groups, academic authorities, international organisations, consultative bodies, and specially appointed investigative bodies all play a part in this process. The roles of most of these are obvious enough, but the part played by the last two deserves some comment.

Modern industrial societies contain a mass of standing bodies designed, first, to advise government or to oversee the operation of public agencies; second, simply to act as forums to exchange views and experience; or third, to ensure that different points of view are debated. Pertinent to industrial relations, the Social and Economic Councils of France, Italy and the Netherlands—and on an international level the Economic and Social Committee of the European Economic Community—are prominent examples of the standing consultative body. The typical council has the right, and indeed obligation, to express its views to government and the public on proposed social and economic legislation. But it can also debate questions of its own choosing. It is usually tripartite or multipartite in membership. The commissions associated with the French planning apparatus (see Cooper, 1982) are another example of this kind. The National Labour Consultative Council in Australia is another variant. The British Advisory, Conciliation and Arbitration Service (ACAS) is an example of the second category: it has a council (comprising employers, unions, and a small number of independents) that watches over the work of the service and can express views on relevant issues. The Japan Productivity Council can serve as an example of the third category. Finally, there are bodies which, at least informally, may go beyond consultation, and provide the basis for agreements or understandings between governments, union and employers, like the Norwegian Contact Committee or—except that government sits as an employer rather than as government—the Irish Employer–Labour Conference (Addison, 1979; Cooper, 1982).

The usual role of the public inquiry is to present a weighing up of the different aspects of a complicated subject with much fuller consideration than can be given by, say, a cabinet committee. Most inquiries are appointed to expose the arguments and possible courses of action and then to ascertain the views of the public on them so that mature decisions can be taken, though it has been said that some inquiries are used to relieve government of having to take a decision on a thorny subject by deferring it for what might prove to be three years or more. As the government in effect appoints those who make up the inquiry, and decides its terms of reference, it is possible for a government to set up an inquiry that will probably support an option that the government already favours, but this is not invariably the case and when used it may backfire. As an example, the Bullock Committee of Inquiry on Industrial Democracy, set up in Britain in 1975—for which the terms of reference prejudged the desirability of workers' representatives on boards of directors, and the membership of which could be counted on to split, with the majority making radical proposals—produced a report which met such a frigid reception that the subsequent White Paper was a very much weaker affair. (In the event, the dissolution of Parliament meant that the matter was not proceeded with.) Incidentally, the Bullock Committee considered the private sector. A parallel inquiry in respect of the public service was entrusted to an interministerial committee—yet another option open to governments.

The Royal Commission or Committee of Inquiry is a favourite instrument in Britain, Australia and Canada. The Hancock Committee (1983–85) in Australia, the Donovan Commission (1965–68) in Britain, and the Woods Task Force reporting in Canada in 1968 are examples drawn from industrial relations of this kind of inquiry. In the United States the equivalent tends to be the Hearings conducted by committees of the Senate or the House—the Senate hearings on worker alienation at the beginning of the 1970s are an example. The French, as well as using parliamentary committees, the Social and Economic Council, and bodies like the Sudreau Committee, which reported in 1975, also use inquiries by one or two experts: examples are the Adam Report of 1972 on collective bargaining; the Auroux Report of 1981, covering many aspects of industrial relations; the Taddei Report of 1986, concerning working time; and the Aubry Report of 1988, on the significance for France of the social aspects of the Single Europe programme of the European Economic Community. In an example from Germany the Biedenkopf Committee reported in 1970, with an assessment of co-determination.

The Green Paper and the White Paper, in which government puts forward more or less tentative ideas, represent another way of eliciting the reactions of the public without committing government to a particular course of action.

In short, a wide variety of instruments are available to governments to secure considered views and to test public opinion. Further, all of the instruments mentioned help to create a climate of informed opinion which, if the matter at issue has been well judged, serve to give legitimacy to the course chosen. It is then up to government and the parties to consider what problems are likely to arise in implementation and to find ways to resolve them. Important among these is likely to be winning the support of representative groups and giving publicity to examples of successful adoption of the option chosen.

### The barriers to change

We lack a measure of improvement in industrial relations. And good and fruitful relationships cannot be enforced from the outside. But this is not to say that nothing can be done outside the employing enterprise to help create good industrial relations. Clearly, outside agencies should provide positive support and minimal constraints. The most serious barrier to improvement, however, is probably not constraints or lack of assistance but simple inertia, the seeking of refuge, if change is proposed, in the principle of unripeness of time. That inertia can probably be overcome only by the force of competition acting on the lethargic union, firm or consultative committee and a process of education, in which government and interest groups, not to mention the means discussed in the last section, have a part to play.

So far as workers themselves are concerned, there is no evidence to suggest that more than a small minority resist change once they see the reason for it; find that reason credible; and are assured that their interests will be protected as well as possible. But coming to this point is not necessarily an easy experience.

If good industrial relations cannot be imposed, at least unnecessary barriers can be removed. Such barriers may derive from a country's Constitution, from the body of law, from collective agreements, or from the rules of employer associations or trade unions.

For most countries the Constitution—if there is a written Constitution—has little to say about industrial relations but, equally, little that presents a questionable constraint. Australia is perhaps the one country where the Constitution, by accident of its birth, constrains the Commonwealth government by effectively limiting its powers to the provision of conciliation and arbitration as mentioned above which has been interpreted by the High Court and by most federal and state governments as discouraging alternative forms of industrial relations.

The body of law in respect of industrial relations varies appreciably between countries. Germany, notably, has an extensive legal framework setting out the rights and obligations of the parties and making provision for the resolution of their differences. But it cannot be said that the existence of so much law is felt as burdensome by management and workers at the enterprise. And the legislature—as evidenced by the legislation passed in 1988, and as is clear from chapter 3—is at pains to update the law when the need arises.

At the other extreme, in Japan, where the emphasis is on achieving harmonious relations on a personal basis, there is much less need to seek to ensure that the law covers all eventualities and though there is an adequate body of law, there is relatively little recourse to it for industrial relations purposes.

In the United States, there has been little change over the last 30 years in the framework laid out in the National Labor Relations Act 1935, the Labor Management Relations Act 1947, and the Labor–Management Reporting and Disclosure Act 1959. As is clear from chapter 2, there is criticism that this legislation is failing in its original objective of promoting collective bargaining. It fails to facilitate worker representation, while it is viewed by advocates of a 'union-free society' as burdensome. But this is not a question of too much or too little law, but of the adequacy of existing law. Incidentally, the comparable legislation in Canada does work to promote collective bargaining.

The British case has already been discussed. There the question is how to find a legal framework that meets the divergent views between the political parties. Meanwhile, Labour and the trade unions see the body of legislation created during the 1980s as extremely burdensome, while the Conservatives and employers felt much the same about Labour's legislation of the 1970s.

But it is impossible to analyse here the detail of all the possible barriers that the law—and equally collective agreements and the rules of organisations—impose on good industrial relations in industrialised countries. The present purpose is merely to draw attention to an area that certainly warrants research. In general, if the need for change is sufficiently great and clear, barriers will be swept away. But an industrial relations system can decline without the need for change being readily apparent. People tend to be comfortable with a system to which they are accustomed. But a society that shuns change will be very much at a disadvantage in a competitive world. The prizes will go to societies that overcome the barriers to such change as may be desirable to ensure effective industrial relations. The challenge is to achieve change without being made to do so by war or economic crisis. For that, long-term vision, boldness, and a change of mentality are needed.

## Conclusion

To sum up, a number of significant propositions are clear from the arguments in this book:

- A good many industrial relations systems are clearly less than optimal in terms of the tests suggested in chapter 1. But, as with economic systems or social systems, optimality is both a subjective prescription and a goal; where the parties are in agreement, optimality is not necessarily a forlorn hope.

- Industrial relations are by no means the only variable in creating an economically sound and equitable society, but they are one such variable, and one that can be improved.

- The national responses to the problems common to industrialised market economies are strongly affected by the dynamics of the different national systems, so systems will continue to differ.

- Although countries have tended to respond at much the same time to common problems, there is no evidence to support the hypothesis of convergence and nothing to suggest that convergence will be of value.

- The elements bearing on change are quite extensive. They include the actors in the industrial relations system (government, employers, unions, tribunals); the avenues that can open the way to change (politicians and political processes, the law, collective bargaining, managerial and union initiatives); and the impediments to change (lethargy, suspicion of the unknown, existing laws, agreements and practices).

- It is, no doubt, easier to reform a bad system than a reasonably good one, since the need is more obvious.

That said, what practical steps to improve present industrial relations are suggested by the experiences surveyed in the earlier chapters?

First, it must be said that industrial relations start with managers and workers at the workplace. It is often overlooked that the wider industrial relations system tends only to be invoked when managers and workers disagree—which in most enterprises is not much of the time. The elements making for good workplace relations are reasonably well known, if far from universally practised. They can be summarised as:

- managers and supervisors treating workers with respect, and taking their views into account;
- a reasonably clear-cut managerial structure with line management taking its full share of responsibility for the human resources of the enterprise;
- effective forms of consultation and grievance procedure, together with equitable disciplinary arrangements;
- straightforward and fair wage structures and methods of payment;
- well designed tasks; and
- an ability by both sides to process change.

In recent years the role of management in industrial relations is much discussed; the attitudes that workers bring to work much less so. It is in the nature of things that in most respects workers will react to what they find at the workplace; poor morale commonly indicates bad managements. But the differences between the usual attitudes of British, French, German, Japanese, Swedish and American workers toward their employer and their work, as attested to by many attitude surveys (Barbash, 1984) suggest that workers' attitudes, whatever their cause or origin, do count substantially towards good or bad workplace relations.

The links between what happens in the enterprise and the external industrial relations system must also be taken into account. They too, vary between countries. Germany has customarily established detailed laws to govern what takes place within the enterprise and what takes place outside. Japan has preferred to regulate as little as possible. Australia has given the key role in determining the basis of relations within the enterprise to the centralised industrial tribunals, but as part of the agenda for change there has been a lowering of the centre of gravity to foster more enterprise-focused negotiations. The United States has laid down a framework within which collective bargaining takes place, and grievances are resolved between the employer and the union, acting with the mandate of a public agency. As pointed out chapter 1, after the war most European countries constructed systems which provided for conflictual matters to be discussed outside the enterprise, and consensual matters within the enterprise.

In the governance of the workplace many different combinations of legislation, collective agreements made at various levels, and rules made within the enterprise are possible, and examination of the evidence does not justify a conclusion that one combination is, of itself, better than an-other. One can, however, readily identify versions which are not condu-cive to good relations, such as the fragmentation of bargaining (now, for-tunately, somewhat less marked) which grew up in Britain; the multiple, yet inadequate, workplace representation arrangements in France; and, again, the consequences in Australia of giving responsibility for the re-gulation of the workplace to an outside quasi-judicial body.

Turning to industrial relations beyond the enterprise, again there is a considerable variety in the ways in which law and employer–union arrangements combine to make up the framework, as there is in the laws and arrangements themselves. And one finds some similar legal foun-dations and employer–union practices in 'good' and 'poor' industrial relations systems alike. It seems impossible, examining the industrial-ised market economies considered here, to deduce that any particular legal measure of institutional arrangement is the cause of strength or weakness of an industrial relations system. Indeed, the attitudes—of workers, management, government and the general public—brought to the system seem likely to be more important than the framework itself. But that does not mean that the framework is irrelevant.

It is most certainly important that there should be business-like and equitable laws concerning the rights and responsibilities of trade unions and employer associations; at least a minimal framework for collective bargaining; such law concerning industrial conflict as befits the nature of industrial relations in the particular country; and an equitable law of employment. As to the institutional arrangements, on balance it is clear that an industrial union structure—and a relatively small number of unions—with a single central organisation is a worthwhile objective, even if tidiness is of little importance in itself. Collective bargaining levels are likely to depend on national circumstances, but there is evidence that both centralised (Denmark, Norway) and decentralised (United States, Japan) systems can work at least reasonably well. The law of industrial conflict is often vague, particularly the constitutional provisions found in some countries. Such vagueness should obviously be reduced. Most public agencies for mediating conflict have a good track record, as have the forms of bipartite mediation such as those in Germany.

There is now quite long experience of the different systems of worker participation, or industrial democracy involving worker representations on boards of directors, introduced in Germany beginning in 1951 and 1952 and in several other north-west European countries in the 1970s. That experience, though it has disappointed many who hoped for more from it, has been generally positive, (significantly, such arrangements are found in countries where industrial relations have been more con-sensual than conflictual). There is no substantial current of opinion against the system in those countries where it has been adopted. But participation can take other forms. Collective bargaining is one, and may be said to be the basic form in the United States. Another, notably in western continental Europe, is the statutory or nationally agreed works council or works committee, possessing rights to information, consultation, co-determination, and sometimes unilateral decision-making—but also responsibilities. Such bodies, while not demonstrating spectacularly positive effects on industrial relations, have generally been at least modestly successful. But could they be exported to countries that do not have them? They certainly represent an option but they could not easily be adopted in countries where the adversary principle rules, except in specially tailored cases, such as those found in the United States (Cutchter-Gershenfeld, 1986). Lastly, share distribution and profit-sharing schemes have often shown fairly good results—if, perhaps, less than their more fervent advocates proclaim. But neither participative styles nor schemes based on enterprise performance can be satisfactorily imposed from above. In the latter, national input is usually limited to tax relief, leaving the arrangements to management and workers. Nationally operated schemes, such as the Swedish wage earner funds and compulsory profit-sharing in France, have been disappointing.

The reader of a book entitled *Agenda for change* may be disappointed to find no neat how-to-do-it list of prescriptions. But given the substantial differences between countries, we should not expect industrial relations in any one country to easily accommodate prescriptions from others. Our aim in this book has been to show that industrial relations systems, or at least the way they work, can change and do change. And by understanding those changes—their rationale, form and impact— we build a rich source of ideas about how any one country may consider and handle its own agenda for change.

# Bibliography

Abowd, John (1987) 'The Effects of International Competition on Collective Bargaining Settlements in the US', unpublished paper, Princeton University, New Jersey.

ACAC (1986) Australian Conciliation and Arbitration Commission, *Annual Report 1985*, London.

—— (1987) Australian Conciliation and Arbitration Commission, *National Wage Case Decision March 1987*, AGPS, Canberra.

—— (1988) Australian Conciliation and Arbitration Commission, *National Wage Case Decision August 1988*, AGPS, Canberra.

ACAS (1986) Advisory Conciliation and Arbitration Service, *Annual Report 1985*, London.

Adams, R. J. and C. H. Rummel (1977) 'Workers' Participation in Management in West Germany—Impact on the Worker, the Enterprise and the Trade Union', *Industrial Relations Journal* 8, pp. 4–22

Addison; J. (1979) *Wage Policies and Collective Bargaining Developments in Finland, Ireland and Norway*, OECD, Paris.

AFL-CIO Committee on the Evolution of Work Report (1985) 'The Changing Situation of Workers and Their Unions', Washington, DC. American Federation of Labor and Congress of Industrial Organizations.

Ahlén, K. (1988) *Recent Trends in Swedish Bargaining: Collapse of the Swedish Models*, Swedish Institute, Stockholm.

Ahlén, K. (1989) 'Swedish Collective Bargaining under Pressure', *British Journal of Industrial Relations*, November.

Amadieu, J. F. (1986) 'Les tendances du syndicalisme d'enterprise en France: quelques hypothèses', in *Droit Social* 6, June p. 495.

Atkinson, John and Nigel Meager (1986) 'Is flexibility just a flash in the pan?', *Personnel Management*, September.

Australian Council of Trade Unions (1987) *Future Strategies For The Trade Union Movement*, ACTU, Melbourne, September.

Australian Council of Trade Unions and the Trade Development Council (ACTU–TDC) (1987) *Australia Reconstructed*, AGPS, Canberra.

Australian Department of Employment and Industrial Relations (DEIR) (1985) *Supplementary Submissions to the Committee of Review into Australian Industrial Relations Law and Systems*, AGPS, Canberra.

Baddon, Lesley, Laurie Hunter, Jeff Hyman, John Leopold and Harvie Ramsay

———— (1987), *Developments in Profit Sharing and Employee Share Owner-ship—Survey Report*, Department of Social and Economic Research, University of Glasgow.

———— (1989) *People's Capitalism?* Routledge, London and New York.

Barkin, S. (1987) 'The Flexibility Debate in Western Europe: The Current Drive to Restore Management's Rights over Personnel and Wages', *Relations Industrielles* vol. 42, pp. 12–43.

Bartel, W. and R. Falk (1986) 'Einstieg gelungen: Zur Flexibilisierung der Arbeit in der Metallindustrie', *Gewerkschaftsreport* 1 pp. 27–37.

*Bilan Annuel de la négociation collective* 1984, 1985, 1986, 1987.

Blankenburg, E. and R. Rogowski (1986) 'German Labour Courts and British Industrial Tribunals', *Journal of Law and Society* 13, pp. 67–92.

Block Report (1987) *Report by the Efficiency Scrutiny Unit on Proposed Successor Arrangements to the Public Service Board* (mimeo), Canberra, July, p. 26.

Bluestone, Barry and Bennett Harrison (1982) *The Industrialization of America*, Basic Books, New York.

Brown, William (1986), 'The Changing Role of Trade Unions in the Management of Labour', *British Journal of Industrial Relations*, July.

Bütchtemann, C. and J. Schupp (1986), 'Zur Sozio-Okonomie der Teilzeitbeschaftigung in der Bundesrepublik Deutschland', *Discussion Paper* IMM/LMP pp. 86–115, Wissenschaftszentrum Berlin.

Bughin, E. (1985) 'La négociation salariale de branche en 1984', *Travail et Emploi* 24, June, p. 51.

Bundesminister fur Arbeit and Sozialordnung (1978) *Co-Determination in the Federal Republic of Germany*, Bonn.

Bunn, R. F. (1984) 'Employers Associations in the Federal Republic of Germany', in J. P. Windmuller and A. Gladstone (eds) *Employers Associations and Industrial Relations*, Clarendon Press, Oxford, pp. 169–201.

Bureau of Labor Statistics (1970–87) *Current Wage Developments*, January 1970 to February 1987, BLS, Washington, DC.

Bureau of National Affairs (1987) *Daily Labor Report*, February 27 and 1–18 March 1987, BNA, Washington, DC.

Burton, John (1979) 'The Extent of Collective Bargaining in the Public Sector', in Ben Aaron, Joseph Grodin and James Stein (eds), *Public Sector Bargaining*, Bureau of National Affairs, Washington, DC.

Cadbury, A. (1986) 'The 1980s: A Watershed in British Industrial Relations?' (mimeo), Fourth Hitachi Lecture, University of Sussex, p. 23.

Cappelli, Peter (1986) 'Airline Industrial Relations Under Deregulation', unpublished paper, The Wharton School, University of Pennsylvania, March.

Clarke, O. (1984), 'Collective Bargaining and the Economic Recovery', *The OECD Observer*, July, pp. 19–21.

Committe for Economic Development of Australia (1988) *How Has Business Handled Second Tier Wage Negotiations? Survey Results*, Strategic Issues Forum, CEDA, Sydney, April.

Cooke, William N. (1985) *Union Organizing and Public Policy*, Upjohn Institute, Kalamazoo, Michigan.

Cooper, M. (1982) *In Search of Consensus*, OECD, Paris.

Cox, J. C. and H. Kriegbaum (1980) *Growth, Innovation and Employment: An*

*Anglo-German Comparison*, Anglo-German Foundation for the Study of Industrial Society, London.

Cressey, P. (1987), 'New Technology: An Overview of Regulation', *European Industrial Relations Review*, February, pp. 9–16.

Cullen, Donald E. (1985) *Recent Trends in Collective Bargaining in the United States*, International Labour Organisation, Geneva.

Cutcher-Gershenfeld, Joel (1986) 'The Emergence of Community Labor-Management Cooperation', in Warner Woodworth, Christopher Meek and William Foote Whyte (eds), *Industrial Democracy; Strategies for Community Revitalization*, Sage, Beverly Hills, California.

Czada, R. (1985) 'Wirtschaftlicher Strukturwandel und Arbeitslosigkeit', discussion paper for the conference 'Arbeitsmarkt, Arbeitsbeziehungen und Politik in den 80er Jahren', Berlin, June.

Dabscheck, B. and J. Niland (1985) 'Australian Industrial Relations and the Shift to Centralism', *Industrial Relations in a Decade of Economic Change*, IRRA Series, University of Wisconsin, Madison, pp. 41–72.

Davis, E. M. (1987) 'Unions and Wages: ACTU Federal Unions' Conference November 1986', *Australian Quarterly*, vol. 59, no.1, pp. 4–14.

Dawkins, John and C. Holding (1986) *Skills for Australia*, AGPS, Canberra.

Department of Employment (1987) *Trade Unions and their Members*, Green Paper, HMSO, London.

DGB (1985) Konzeption zur Mitbestimmung am Arbeitsplatz, *Schriftenreihe Mitbestimmung 7*, Deutscher Gewerkschaftsbund, Düsseldorf.

Dickens, William T. (1983) 'The Effect of Company Campaigns on Certification Elections: Law and Reality Once Again', in *Industrial and Labor Relations Review*, vol. 36, no. 4.

Dickens, William T. and Jonathan S. Leonard. (1985) 'Accounting for the Decline in Union Membership', *Industrial and Labor Relations Review*, vol. 38, no. 3.

*Données Sociales*, INSEE, 1984.

Donovan Commission (1968), Report of the Royal Commission on Trade Unions and Employers Associations 1965–68, HMSO, London (Cmnd 3623).

Dundelach, P. and N. Mortensen (1979) 'Denmark, Norway and Sweden', *New Forms of Work Organizations*, I, International Labour Organisation, Geneva.

Erdmann, E. G. (1986) 'Die Flexibilisierung muß fortgesetzt werden', *Der Arbeitgeber* 38, pp. 425–6.

Esser, J., W. Fach and W. Vaeth (1983) *Krisenregulierung*, Suhrkamp, Frankfurt am Main.

ETUI (1986) European Trade Union Institute, 'Collective Bargaining in Western Europe in 1985 and Prospects for 1986', ETUI, Brussels.

Farber, Henry S. (1985) 'The Extent of Unionization in the United States', in Thomas A. Kochan (ed.) *Challenges and Choices Facing American Labor*, MIT Press, Cambridge, Massachusetts.

Flanagan, Robert J., D. W. Soskice, and L. Ulman (1983) *Unionism, Economic Stabilization and Incomes Policies: European Experience*, The Brookings Institution, Washington, DC.

Foster, N., S. G. B. Henry and C. Trinder (1984) 'Public and Private Sector Pay: a Partly Disaggregated Study', *National Instiute Economic Review*, February.

Freedman, Audrey S. and William Fulmer (1982) 'Last Rites for Pattern Bargaining', *Harvard Business Review*, March–April.

Freeman, Richard, and James Medoff (1984) *What Do Unions Do?*, Basic Books, New York.

Freeman, R. B. (1987) 'Changes in Union Density in Western Countries' (mimeo), OECD Seminar, May p. 41.

Fulco, Laurence (1986) 'US Productivity Growth Since 1982: The Post-Recession Experience', *Monthly Labor Review*, December.

Galland, O., (1984) 'Contrats de solidarité de préretraite et stratégies d'entreprises', *Travail et Emploi* 22, December p. 7.

Gaspard, M., J. Loos and D. Welcomme (1985) 'Aménagement et réduction du temps de travail dans les entreprises: au service de l'emploi et de l'efficacité économique', *Travail et emploi*, 23, March p. 21.

Ginsbourger, F. and J. Y. Potel (1986) 'Pratique de la négociation collective de brance de 1981 à 1985', *Travail et Emploi* 29, September p. 43.

Goldberg, Joseph, P., Eileen Ahern, William Harber, and Rudolph A. Oswald, (eds) (1976) *Federal Policies and Worker Status Since the Thirties*, Industrial Relations Research Association, Madison, Wisconsin.

Gould, W. B. (1984) *Japan's Reshaping of American Labor Law*, MIT Press, Cambridge, Massachusetts.

Gourevitch, Peter et al. (1984) *Unions and Economic Crisis: Britain, West Germany, and Sweden*, Allen & Unwin, London and Boston.

Gregory, M., P. Lobban and A. W. J. T. Thomson (1985) 'Wage Settlements in Manufacturing: Evidence from the CBI Databank', *British Journal of Industrial Relations*, November.

—— (1986) 'Bargaining Structure, Pay Settlements and Perceived Pressures in Manufacturing 1979–84: Further Analysis from the CBI Databank', *British Journal of Industrial Relations*, July.

Grills, W. R. (1987), *New Zealand Unions in a Deregulated Economy*, Discussion Paper, Department of Economics, University of Otago.

Guillemard, A. M. (1986) *Le déclin du social*, PUF, Paris.

Hawke, G. R. (1986) *Labour and Flexibility*, Report of the Economic Monitoring Group, Planning Council, Wellington, New Zealand.

Heller, J. L. (1985) 'Emploi et chomage en Mars 1985', in *Economie et Statistique* 183, December p. 21.

Hemmer, Hans O. (1985) 'Vor einer Strukturkrise der Gewerkschaften?' *Gewerkschaftliche Monatshefte* 36, pp. 101–111.

Her Majesty's Treasury (1986a), *Economic Progress Report*, March/April.

—— (1986b), *Economic Progress Report*, May/June.

Hoff, A. (1984) 'Assessing Investment-Related Medium-Term Manpower Needs: A Case Study from the German Automobile Industry', *Discussion Paper* IIM/LMP, pp. 84–3, Wissenschaftszentrum Berlin.

Hohn, H. W. (1983) 'Interne Arbeitsmarkte und betriebliche Mitbestimmung: Tendenzen der sozialen Schließung im dualen System der Interessenvertretung', *Discussion Paper*, IIM/LMP, pp. 83–2, Wissenschaftszentrum Berlin.

Hohn, H. W. and P. Windolf (1985) 'Prozesse sozialer Schließung im Arbeitsmarkt: Eine empirische Skizze betriebsinterner Determinaten von Mobilitatsprozessen', in H. Knepel and R. Hujer (eds) *Mobilitatsprozesse aud dem Arbeitsmarkt*, Campus, Frankfurt am Main, pp. 305–27.

Hotz-Hart, B. (1987) *Modernisierung von Unternehmen und Industrien bei unterschiedlichen industriellen Beziehungen*, Haupt, Bern and Stuttgart.

Industrial Relations Section (1987) 'Institutionalizing and Diffusing Innovations in Industrial Relations', a02139, Report for the US Department of Labor, February 27, Sloan School of Management, Massachusetts Institute of Technology, Cambridge, Massachusetts.

Jacobs, E., S. Orwell, P. Paterson and F. Weltz, (1978) *The Approach to Industrial Changes in Britain and Germany*, Anglo-German Foundation for the Study of Industrial Society, London.

Kahn-Freund, O., in A. Flanders and H. A. Clegg (eds) (1954) *The System of Industrial Relations in Great Britian*, Blackwell, Oxford.

Kane, E. (1987) 'Challenges Facing the Trade Unions' (mimeo), address to the 21st World Congress of the International Federation of Commercial, Clerical, Professional and Technical Employees, Rome, 24–28 August p. 13.

Keller, B. (1978) 'Public Sector Labor Relations in West Germany', *Industrial Relations* 17, pp. 18–31.

———— (1987) 'Arbeitgeber und ihre Verbande im offentlichen Dienst. Zur sozialwissenschaftlichen Analyse einer Forschungslucke', *Zeitschrift fur offentliche und gemeinwirtschaftlichen Unternehmen*

Knevels, P. (1985) 'Atomisierung der Tarifpolitik?', *Der Arbeitgeber* vol. 37, no. 9, p. 316.

Kochan, Thomas A., Harry Katz and Robert McKersie (1986), *The Transformation of American Industrial Relations*, Basic Books, New York.

Kochan, Thomas A., Harry Katz and Nancy Mower (1984) *Worker Participation and American Unions: Threat or Opportunity?*, W.E. Upjohn Institute for Employment Research, Kalamazoo, Michigan.

Kochan, Thomas A., Robert B. McKersie and John Chalykoff (1986) 'The Effects of Corporate Strategy and Workplace Innovations on Union Representation', *Industrial and Labor Relations Review*, vol. 39, no 4.

Koshiro, K. (1987) 'Gain Sharing, Wage Flexibility and Macro-Economic Performance in Japan' (mimeo), paper delivered at the Pacific Rim Labour Conference, Vancouver, BC, p. 36.

Krupp, H. J. (1984) 'Herausforderungen des Strukturwandels fur die Wirtschaftspolitik', *Schriftenreihe uber Arbeit und Arbeitsbeziehungen* pp. 28–38.

Kubicek, H. (1986) 'Federal Republic of Germany', in G. Berta (ed.) *Industrial Relations in Information Society: A European Survey about New Technologies and Processes of Bargaining and Participation*, Adriano Olivetti Foundation, Rome.

Kuda, R. (1986) 'Solidaritat statt Konkurrenz', *Der Gewerkschafter* 10, pp. 4–5.

*Labor Law Report* (1987) 48th Annual Report of the National Labor Relations Board, for fiscal year 1983, NLRB, Washington, DC.

Labour Party (1986), *People at Work: New Rights, New Responsibilities*, Canberra.

Lash, S. (1985) 'The End of Neo-corporatism? The Breakdown of Centralised Bargaining in Sweden', in *British Journal of Industrial Relations*, July.

Lawrence, P. (1980) *Managers and management in West Germany*, Croom Helm, London.

Leese, Jerry (1986) 'TVEI—Versatility in Vocational Training', *Employment Gazette*, August pp. 303–350.

Levitan, Sar A., Peter E. Carlson and Issac Shapiro (1986) *Protecting the American Worker*, Bureau of National Affairs, Washington, DC.

Lovell, Malcolm (1986) 'Economic Adjustment and Worker Dislocation in a Competitive Society', Report of the Secretary of Labor's Task Force in Economic Adjustment and Worker Dislocation, Washington, DC.

Lucato, F. (1987) 'The Advantages of Two Tiers', *Rydges*, July.

Lundberg E. (1985) 'The Rise and Fall of the Swedish Models', *Journal of Economic Literature*, vol. 23, March.

Malcher, W. (1986) 'Widerspruchliches bei den Gewerkschaften', *Der Arbeitgeber* 38, pp. 671–2.

Marchand, O. and E. Martin-le Goff (1986) 'L'emploi en 1985: les signes d'une amélioration', *Economie et Statistique*, 187, April, p. 47.

Markovits, A. S. and C. S. Allen (1984) 'Trade Unions and the Economic Crisis: The West German Case', in P. Gourevitch et al., *Unions and the Economic Crisis: Britain, West Germany, and Sweden*, George Allen & Unwin, London, pp. 89–188.

Marsden, D. (1981) 'Collective Bargaining and Positive Adjustment Policies', Report to the OECD Working Party on Industrial Relations, OECD, Paris.

Maurice, M., A. Sorge, and M. Warner (1980) 'Societal Differences in Organizing Manufacturing Units: A Comparison of France, West Germany and Great Britain', *Organisation Studies* 1, pp. 59–86.

Middlemas, K. (1983) *Industry, Unions and Government*, Macmillan, London.

Millward, M. and M. Stevens (1986) *British Workplace Industrial Relations, The DE/ESRC/PSI/ACAS Surveys*, Gower, Aldershot.

Morris, Charles (ed.) (1987) *American Labor Policy*, Bureau of National Affairs, Washington, DC.

Moss, B. H. (1988) 'Industrial Law Reform in an Era of Retreat: The Auroux Laws in France', in *Work, Employment and Society*, vol. 2. no. 3.

Moye, William T. (1980) 'Presidential Labor-Management Committees: Production Failure', *Industrial and Labor Relations Review*, vol. 34, no. 1, October.

Myrdal, H. G. (1980) 'The Swedish Model—Will It Survive?', *British Journal of Industrial Relations*, March.

Niedenhoff, H. U. and M. Wilke (1986) 'Dilemma mit der Jugend: Wie sich die Gewerkschaften im Streit um die Bundnispolitik erschopfen', *Gewerkschaftsreport* 4, pp. 32–9.

Niland, J. (1986) 'Process and Strategy in Industrial Relations Reform', in J. Blandy and J. Niland, (eds) *Alternatives to Arbitration*, Allen & Unwin, Sydney.

—— (1987) 'Gaining Against The Tide: Australian Unionism in the 1980s', *Bulletin of Comparative Labour Relations* 16.

Northrop, H. R., D. C. Campbell and B. J. Slowinski (1988) 'Multinational Union–Management Consultation in Europe: Resurgence in the 1980s?', *International Labour Review*, vol. 127, no. 5.

OECD (1983) 'Collective Bargaining and Economic Policies' (mimeo), MAS (83)23, pp. 24.

—— (1986a) Paris. 'Wage Moderation and Labour Market Imbalances', OECD Economic Policy Committee, Paris.

—— (1986b) Germany. OECD Economic Surveys 1985–1986, OECD, Paris.

—— (1986c) 'Wage Moderation and Labour Market Imbalances: Tables and Charts', Working Party No.1 of the Economic Policy Committee, Paris.

—— (1986d) 'Technical Report by the Secretariat on Labour Market Flexibility', Manpower and Social Affairs Committee, OECD, Paris.

—— (1987) 'Structural Adjustment and Economic Performance', OECD, Paris.

—— (1987a) Employment Outlook, OECD, Paris, September, p. 220.

Osterman, Paul (1988) Employment Futures, Oxford University Press, New York.

Oswald, Andrew J. (1986) 'Wage Determination and Recession, A Report on Recent Work', British Journal of Industrial Relations, July.

Perlman, Selig (1982) A Theory of the Labor Movement, Kelley, New York.

Raybeck, Joseph G. (1959) A History of American Labor, Macmillan, New York.

Reynaud, J. D. 'Problèmes et perspectives de la négociation collective dans les pays membres de la Communauté Européenne', Commission des Communautés Européennes, Etudes, 40.

Rosner, H. J. (1984a) 'Lehren aus einem langen Arbeitskampf', Wirtschaftsdienst VIII, pp. 386–93.

—— (1984b) 'Mehr Arbeitsmarkteffizienz durch Tarifflexibilisierung?' Wirtschaftsdienst pp. 601–608.

Ross, G. and P. Gourevitch (1984) 'Conclusion', in P. Gourevitch et al., Unions and Economic Crisis: Britain, West Germany, and Sweden, George Allen & Unwin, London.

Sachverstandigenrat zur Begutachtung der gesamtwirtschaftlichen Entwicklung (1985) Auf dem Weg zu mehr Beschäftigung–Jahresgutachten 1985/86, Kohlhammer, Stuttgart and Mainz.

Sako, Mari and Ronald Dore (1986) 'How the Youth Training Scheme Helps Employers', Employment Gazette, June, pp. 195–204.

Schmidt, R. and R. Trinczek (1986) 'Die betriebliche Gestaltung tariflicher Arbeitszeitnormen in der Metallindustrie', WSI-Mitteilungen 39, pp. 641–52.

Sorge, A., G. Hartmann, M. Warner and I. Nicholas (1983) Microelectronics and Manpower in Manufacturing, Gower, Aldershot.

Stråth, Bo (1986) 'Redundancy and Solidarity: Tripartite Politics and the Contraction of the West European Shipbuilding Industry', Cambridge Journal of Economics 10, pp. 147–163.

—— (1987) The Politics of De-Industrialisation: The Contraction of the West European Shipbuilding Industry, Croom Helm, London.

Streeck, W. (1981b) 'Qualitative Demands and the Neo-Corporatist Manageability of Industrial Relations: Trade Unions and Industrial Relations in West Germany at the Beginning of the Eighties', British Journal of Industrial Relations 14, pp. 149–69.

—— (1982) 'Organisational Consequences of Corporatist Co-operation in West German Labor Unions: A Case Study', in G. Lehmbruch and P. C. Schmitter (eds) Patterns of Corporatist Policy-Making, Sage, Beverly Hills and London, pp. 29–81.

—— (1984a) Industrial Relations in West Germany: A Case Study of the Car

*Industry*, Heinemann, London; St. Martin's Press, New York.

—————— (1984b) 'Co-Determination: The Fourth Decade', in B. Wilpert and A. Sorge (eds) *International Perspectives of Organisational Democracy*, vol. II of the International Yearbook of Organisational Democracy, John Wiley & Sons, Chichester.

—————— (1986) 'Industrial Change and Industrial Relations in the Motor Industry: An International View', 1985 Leverhulme Lecture in European Industrial Relations, *British Journal of Industrial Relations* University of Warwick, Coventry; 1987.

—————— (1987a) 'Industrial Relations in the Federal Republic of Germany, 1974–1985: An Overview', in E. Kassalow (ed.) *Unions and Industrial Relations—Recent Trends and Prospects—A Comparative Treatment*, Special Issue of *Bulletin of Comparative Labour Relations* 16, pp. 151–66.

—————— (1987b) 'Industrial Relations and Industrial Change: The Restructuring of the World Automobile Industry in the 1970s and 1980s, *Economic and Industrial Democracy* 8, pp. 437–62.

—————— (1987c) 'The Territorial Organization of Interests and the Logics of Associative Action: The Case of *Handwerk* Organization in West Germany', in W. Coleman and H. Jacek, *Regionalism, Public Policy and Business Interests*, Sage, London, pp. 59–94.

Streeck, W., J. Hilbert, K. H. van Kevelaer, F. Maier and H. Weber (1987) *The Role of the Social Partners in Vocational Training and Further Training in the Federal Republic of Germany*, European Centre for the Development of Vocational Training (CEDEFOP), Berlin.

—————— (forthcoming) *The Role of the Social Partners in the West German Industrial Training System*, Report to the European Centre for the Promotion of Industrial Training, Wissenschaftszentrum. Berlin.

Tallard, M. (1987) 'La négociation des nouvelles technologies: éléments pour une comparaison de la France et de la RFA', in *Droit Social* 2, February, p. 124.

Tenne, Ruth (1986) 'TVEI Students and Subjects Studied: The First Two Years', *Employment Gazette*, August, pp. 306–310.

Terry, Michael (1986) 'How do we know if shop stewards are really getting weaker?', *British Journal of Industrial Relations*, July.

Thompson, M. (forthcoming) 'Le plus ça Change', in S. Frenkel and O. Clarke (eds), *Economic Restructuring and Industrial Relations*, Bulletin 18, Institute for Labour Relations, Leuven.

Tilly, Chris, Barry Bluestone and Bennett Harrison (1986) 'What is Making American Wages More Unequal?', *Proceedings of the Meetings of the Industrial Relations Research Association, December 28–30, 1986*, New Orleans, Louisiana.

Treu, T. (1987) 'Social Concertation Macro and Micro: A Comparative Outlook' (mimeo), paper delivered at the Second European Regional Congress of the International Industrial Relations Association, Tel Aviv, 13–17 December, p. 15.

TUC (1979) *Employment and Technology*, Congress House, London.

TURU (1984) Trade Union Research Unit, *The Control of Frontiers, Workers and New Technology*, TURU.

United States Government (1987) *1986 Economic Report of the President of the*

*United States*, US Government Printing Office, Washington, DC.

Visser, J. (1985) 'European Trade Unions in Retreat', paper prepared for the Conference on 'Europa im Wandel', Mannheim, October.

—— (1987) 'Trade Unionism in Western Europe: Present Situation and Prospects' (mimeo), paper delivered to the ILO Symposium on the Future of Trade Unionism in Industrialised Market Economies, Turin, 9–11 December, p. 77.

Weber, H. (1985) *Konkurrenz und Solidaritat: Zur Arbeitskampfstrategie der metallindustriellen Arbeitgeber im Tarifkonflikt 1984*, typescript, Bielefeld.

—— (1986) 'Desynchronisation, Dezentralisierung—und Dekomposition? Die Wirkungsdynamik des Tarifkonflikts '84 und ihre Effekte auf das System industrieller Beziehungen', *Arbeitsberichte und Forschungsmaterialien* 19, Forschungsschwerpunkt 'Zukunft der Arbheit', Universitat Bielefeld.

Wedderburn, K. W. (Lord) (1986) *The Worker and the Law*, 3rd edn, Penguin, Harmondsworth.

Weiler, Paul C. 'Promises to Keep: Securing Workers' Rights to Self Organization Under the NLRA', *Harvard Law Review*, vol. 96, no. 8.

Weiss, Manfred (1987) *Labour Law and Industrial Relations in the Federal Republic of Germany*, Kluwer, Deventer.

Weitzman, M. L. (1984) *The Share Economy*, Harvard University Press, Cambridge, Massachusetts.

Wever, Kirsten R. (1986) 'Power, Weakness and Membership Support in Four United States Airline Unions', PhD thesis, Department of Political Science and Industrial Relations Section, Sloan School of Management, Massachusetts Institute of Technology, September.

Willman, Paul (1986) 'New Technology and Industrial Relations: A Review of the Literature', *Department of Employment Discussion Paper*, 56.

Windmuller, John P. and Alan Gladstone (eds) (1984) *Employers Associations and Industrial Relations: A Comparative Study*, Oxford University Press, New York.

WSI (1984) 'Tarifvertragliche Bestimmungen zur Teilzeitarbeit', Wirtschaffts und Sozialwissenschaftliches Institut des Deutschen Gewerkschaftsbundes-Tarifarchiv, Düsseldorf.

# Index

Accord (Australia), 9–10, 151–2, 158, 168, 171–2, 175
Act of 13 November 1982 (France), 96, 98, 104
Act of 5 August 1985 (France), 101
Act of 18 February 1986 (France), 105
Act of 30 December 1986 (France), 105
Act of 28 June 1987 (France), 103–5
ACTU, 10, 151, 153, 157–8
Adam Report 1981 (France), 177
Advisory, Conciliation and Arbitration Service (U.K.), 131, 136, 166, 176
Affirmative Action and Equal Opportunity Employment (U.S.), 26
AFL-CIO, 21–2, 46, 49
agreements, see labour agreements
agriculture, in Germany, 87
AIDC, 159
Air Line Pilots Association (U.S.), 40, 50
airline industry, in the United States, 39
alienation, in the United States, 176
ALP, 151
Amalgamated Clothing and Textile Workers Union (U.S.), 42
Amalgamated Engineering Union (U.K.), 144
amalgamation, of trade unions, see under trade unions
American Airlines, 37

American Federation of Labor, 21
American Federation of Labor and Congress of Industrial Organisations, 21–2, 46, 49
American labour, philosophy of, 20
anti-unionism
in Germany, 87, in the United States, 8, 51
Arbeitsgemeinschaft Selbständiger Unternehmer, 74
Arbitration Commission (Australia), see Industrial Relations Commission (Australia)
arbitration procedures, see dispute resolution
ASU, 74
Aubry Report 1988 (France), 177
Auroux laws, France 1982, 15, 165, 171, 177
Australia, industrial relations in, 147–63, 167, 174
Australia Post, 154
Australia reconstructed, 158–60
Australian Conciliation and Arbitration Commission, see Industrial Relations Commission (Australia)
Australian Constitution, 174, 177
Australian Council of Trade Unions, 10, 151, 153, 157 visit to Europe 1986, 158
Australian Government Publishing Service, 158
Australian Industry Development Corporation, 159

Australian Labor Party, 151
Austria
  industrial relations in, 170,
  post-war reconstruction in, 165
Austro-Keynesianism, 158
automobile industry
  in France, 99, in Germany, 65,
  77–8, in the United States, 24, 30,
  32, 39

ballots, secret, see secret ballots,
  compulsory
banking system, in Germany, 66
bankruptcy law, in the United States,
  173
Banque de France, 103
bargaining, see collective bargaining
barriers, to change in industrial
  relations, 177–9
BCA, 157
BDA, 53–4, 60, 73–4
BDI, 54
Belgium, industrial relations in, 170
Biedenkopf Committee 1971
  (Germany), 177
blue-collar workers
  in France, 99, in Germany, 53,
  64, 71, in Sweden, 167, in the
  United Kingdom, 123, 128–9
Board Representation Act 1972
  (Sweden), 167
Boeing, 43
bonuses, in France, 103
Boussac (Textile), 101
boycotts, restrictions on, 23
Britain, see United Kingdom
British Steel, 120
Bullock Committee of Inquiry on
  Industrial Democracy 1975 (U.K.),
  176
Bundesvereinigung der Deutschen
  Industrie, 54
Bundesvereinigung Deutsche
  Arbeitgeberverbände, 53–4, 60,
  73–4
Bureau of Labor-Management
  Relations and Cooperative
  Programs (U.S.), 48
Bush, George, 48
Business Council of Australia, 157

Business Roundtable (U.S.), 23, 26

Canada, industrial relations in, 169,
  178
CDU, 61, 87
centralisation, of collective
  bargaining, see under collective
  bargaining
CFDT, 90–2, 97, 107–9
CFTC, 90–2
CGC, 91–2, 110
CGPME, 91
CGT, 90–2, 97–9, 102
CGT-FO, 90–2, 97
CGTU, 90
Chamber of Commerce (U.S.), 23
charter of workers' rights (U.K.), 139
chemical industry, in Germany, 57,
  64–5
Chirac, Jacques, 104, 106
Christian Democratic Party
  (Germany), 61, 87
Christian trade unionism (France),
  90
Chrysler Corporation, 32, 37, 45
Churchill, Winston, 173
Citrine, Walter, 175
Citroen, 101
civil law, use of in industrial
  disputes
  in Australia, 152, in the United
  Kingdom, 125
civil rights, and the American labour
  movement, 22
civil service, see public employees
Civil Service Pay Research Unit,
  abolition of, 166
Clarke, Kenneth, 139, 140
closed shops
  in Germany, 75, in the United
  Kingdom, 15, 119–20, 135, in the
  United States, 23
CNPF, 91, 94–5, 102–5, 110–11
coal industry
  global decline of, 5, in the United
  Kingdom, 120, 125, 130, 136–7
codetermination
  in Germany, 54–5, 60, 70, 72,
  75–6, 78, 85–6, 172, in Sweden,
  167

Codetermination Act 1976
  (Germany), 169
Codetermination at Work Act 1976
  (Sweden), 13, 167
collective bargaining, 9–11
  centralisation of, 24
    in Australia, 150–2, 161, in
    France, 92, 94, 111–12, in
    Germany, 56, 74, 79, in
    Ireland, 9, in Portugal, 9, in
    Spain, 9, in Sweden, 167, in
    the United Kingdom, 116,
    126–7, 130, 141, in the United
    States, 164
  changes in, 171
    in Germany, 169, in the United
    States, 33–42
  concessions from unions, in the
    United States, 8, decentralisation
  of
    in Australia, 156–7, 163, in
    France, 93, 111–12, in
    Germany, 9, 60, 74–6, 84, 87,
    in New Zealand, 9, in Sweden,
    9, in the United Kingdom, 9,
    116, 121, 127, 141, 143, in the
    United States, 9, 23–4, 39,
    50–1
  and economic policy, in Spain,
    170, effect of decline in trade
    union membership on, 8, 98,
    effect of labour law on, in the
    United Kingdom, 166, effect of
    strike legislation on, in Germany,
    81, on a firm-by-firm basis, see
  collective bargaining,
    decentralisation of, history of, in
    the United States, 20–1, on an
    industry-wide basis, see collective
    bargaining, centralisation of
    and labour–management
  co-operation
    in Australia, 162, in the United
    Kingdom, 132, in the United
    States, 44
  legislation,
    in France, 9, 15, 91–3, 96, 106,
    in Germany, 61, 81, in the
    United Kingdom, 135, 145n,
    166

management strategy in, 121, 170,
    and new technology, in the
    United Kingdom, 129, in postwar
    Europe, 3, and price stability, 10,
    and productivity increases
    in Australia, 9, 153–4, in the
    United Kingdom, 132–3
  role of the Advisory, Conciliation
    and Arbitration Service (U.K.),
    136
  structure of
    in France, 110–11, in Germany,
    54–5, in the United Kingdom,
    116, 126–7, 137,
    and voluntarism, in the United
    Kingdom, 115, see also two-tier
    wage scales
commercialisation, of public
    enterprises, in Australia, 148
Committee on the Future of Work
    1985 (U.S.), 46
common law, see civil law
Common Situs Picketing Bill (U.S.),
    168
Communications Headquarters
    (GCHC), (U.K.), ban on trade
    union membership, 136
Communications Workers (U.S.),
    50
company bargaining, see collective
    bargaining, decentralisation of
company takeovers, in Australia,
    149, 157
competition, domestic, in Germany,
    78
competition, international, 19
    effect on Australia, 147–9, 154,
    157, 167, effect on France, 99,
    effect on Germany, 56, 65–6, 72,
    77–8, effect on the United
    Kingdom, 115, 129, 146n, effect
    on the United States, 25, 27, 34,
    49
concessions, in bargaining, 8, 10, 40,
    161
conciliation, see dispute resolution
Confédération Française de
    l'Encadrement, 91–2, 110
Confédération Française
    Démocratique du Travail, 90–2,

97, 107–9
Confédération Française des
    Travailleurs Chrétiens, 90–2
Confédération Générale de la
    Production Française, 91
Confédération Générale des Cadres,
    91–2, 110
Confédération Générale des Petites
    et Moyennes Entreprises, 91
Confédération Générale du Travail,
    90–2, 97–9, 102
Confédération Générale du
    Travail/Force Ouvrière, 90–2, 97
Confédération Générale du Travail
    Unitaire, 90
Confederation of Australian Industry,
    153
Confederation of British Industry,
    121, 124, 128, 136, 138, 144
conflict resolution, see dispute
    resolution
Congress of Industrial Organisations
    (U.S.), 21
Conseil National du Patronat
    Français, 91, 94–5, 102–5,
    110–11
consensus
    in Australia, 159, 168,
    Conservatives' rejection of, in the
    United Kingdom, 124, 166, and
    the facilitation of change, 175
conservatism, in politics, 6
Conservative government (U.K.)
    1979–
counter-inflationary policy, 119,
    election 1979, 175, industrial
    relations policy, 117, 135, 140–1,
    144, labour legislation, 120–1,
    125, 135, 166, 178, re-election
    1987, 138
Conservatives (France), 104
construction industry, in the United
    States, wage increases in, 31
consultative bodies, 175–6
consumer demand, in France, 93
Continental Airlines, 40
copper industry, in the United
    States, 40
corporate leadeship, in Australia,
    156–8

corporate shareholding, in Australia,
    149
Court of Conciliation and
    Arbitration (Australia), 174
courts, see civil law; labour courts;
    labour courts, labour law; judiciary

DAG, 53, 55
Dahrendorf, Ralf, 63
Dawkins, John, 159
DBB, 53, 55
decentralisation, of collective
    bargaining, see under collective
    bargaining
decentralised business units, and the
    determination of wages, 39
decentralism, 170
    in Australia, 161, in the United
    States, 169, see also collective
    bargaining, decentralisation of;
    deregulation
de-certification, of trade unions, see
    under trade unions
deficits, see trade deficit
de-indexation, of wages, see wages,
    indexation of
Delta Airlines, 40, 45
demarcation lines, in Australia, 154,
    163
Democratic Party (U.S.), 48
demography, of the workforce, in the
    United States, 30–1
Department of Employment and
    Industrial Relations (Australia),
    151
de-registration, of trade unions, see
    trade unions, de-certification of
deregulation
    in Australia, 147, 149, 151–2,
    154–60, 163, in Germany, 60, 73,
    in Spain, 170, in the United
    Kingdom, 117, 120, 123, 128–9,
    134–8, 141, in the United States,
    26, 39, see also collective
    bargaining, decentralisation of;
    labour market
determination, of wages, see wages,
    negotiation of
Deutsche Angestellten-Gewerkschaft,
    53, 55

Deutsche Beamtenbund, 53, 55
Deutsche Gewerkschaftsbund, see DGB
devolution, 161
DGB, 55, 71, 73, 78, 80, 87
  role in collective bargaining, 54, structure of, 53
discrimination, and labour law, 24
dismissal, of workers, 16
  in France, 100-01, 105-6, 110, in Germany, 59, 76, in the United Kingdom, 120, 123-4, 131, in the United States, 48
dispute resolution
  in Australia, 150-1, 154, 159, 163, 167, 174, in Germany, 55, 75, 169, management techniques, 8, in postwar Europe, 3, in the United Kingdom, 125, 131-2, 137, in the United States, 20, 24
disputes, see dispute resolution; industrial conflict
diversification of industry, in Germany, 66
diversification of work, in France, 107
divisions of labour, 50,
  in the United Kingdom, 142, see also labour-management co-operation
dollar, American, 27
Donovan Commission on Trade Unions and Employers Associations 1968 (U.K.), 115, 117, 165, 176
Dunlop's Industrial Relations System Framework, 147
duty statements, in Australia, 154

early retirement programmes
  in France, 99, 101, 105, state assistance for, 100, in Germany, 57-8, 67
Eastern Airlines, 42
economic growth
  1960s and 1970s, 4, in Australia, 151-2, 158, and the environment, 62, and industrial relations, in the United States, 20, 26-9, post-World War II, 3, see also productivity, growth of
economic planning, in consultation with unions, in Australia, 151
economy, West German, overview of, 65-7
education,
  in Australia, 159, in Germany, 67, in the United Kingdom, 142
EEC, 17, 111, 170, 175, 177
efficiency in work practices, in Australia, 148-9, 153-5, 157, 159, 161, 168
electrical and electronic industries, in the United States, 30
Electricians' Union (U.K.), 125, 144
Electricité-Gaz de France, 103, 108
electricity industry, industrial conflict within (U.K.), 121
employee participation, see industrial democracy; labour-management co-operation; worker participation
Employee Retirement and Income Security Act (U.S.), 26
employee share ownership,
  in the United Kingdom, 134-5, in the United States, 39-40
employer associations
  as agents of change, 172, 177, in Australia, 9, 150, 159, in Europe, 8-9, in France, 91, 103, in Germany, 53-4, 79-82, in the United Kingdom, 124-6, 138, 144, in the United States, 8, 23
employers
  as agents of change, 172, easing of restrictions on, in France, 104, in Sweden, 172, unfair labour practices of, 33, wages policy of, in France, 94-5
employment
  in Australia, growth in, 152, in Germany, 60, post-World War II, 3, in the United Kingdom, structure of, 122-4, in the United States, 30-1, 51
  see also unemployment
Employment Act 1980 (U.K.), 120
Employment Act 1982 (U.K.), 133
Employment Act 1988 (U.K.), 120, 139

Employment Promotion Act 1985 (Germany), 60–1, 73, 87
Employment Protection Act 1975 (U.K.), abolition 1980, 120,
employment security, *see* job security
engineering industry in Sweden, 172, in the United Kingdom, 122, 127, 134
enterprise bargaining, *see* collective bargaining, decentralisation of
environment, and economic growth, 62
equipment, maximising utilisation of, 110
European Economic Community, 17, 111, 170, 175, 177
exchange rates, in the United Kingdom, 138
Executive Order 10988, 1962 (U.S.), 16
exports and imports, *see* competition, international; trade deficit.

Factories Act (U.K.), 115
Fair Wages Resolution 1946 (U.K.), revocation of, 136, 145n
Federal Association of German Employer Associations, 53–4, 60, 73–4
Federal Association of German Industry, 54
Federal Unions Conference 1986 (Australia), 152
Federation de L'Education Nationale, 90
financial services industry, in the United Kingdom, 134, 138
Finland, industrial relations in, 170
fixed-term employment, 6, 123
Fleet Street (U.K.), 121, 129
flexibility in the labour market, *see* deregulation; labour market in organisational structure, *see* organisational structure
FNE, 100–01, 105
FO, 90–2, 97

Fonds National Pour L'Emploi, 100–01, 105
Ford, 32, 45
Ford, Gerald, 169
foreign debt, of Australia, 149
foreign-owned companies, in the United Kingdom, plant bargaining within, 127
foreign workers in France, 101, 108, in Germany, 67, 69
four tiers, in Australian industrial relations, 147
France consultative bodies in, 175, industrial relations in, 90–114, 165, public inquiries in, 176–7, student revolt 1968, 4
French Confederation of Christian Workers, 90–2
French Democratic Confederation of Labour, 90–2, 97, 107–9
French Management Confederation, 91–2, 110
French Rail, 108–9
French Railways, 103
functional flexibility, in Australia, 154
*Future Strategies for the Trade Union Movement*, 160

General Confederation of Labour (France), 90–2, 97–9, 102
General Electric, 46
General Motors, 32, 42, 44–5, 47, 50–1
German Association of Civil Servants, 53, 55
German Staff Union, 53, 55
German Trade Union Federation, *see* DGB
Germany industrial relations in, 53–89, 169, post-war reconstruction in, 165, public inquiries in, 176–7
Gesamtmetall, 59, 74, 80
Gewerkschaft Offentliche Dienste, 55
global rationalisation of production, 5

government
  role in industrial relations, 15–17,
    172–3
    in Australia, 15, 151, 157–9,
    in Belgium, 16, as employer,
    16–17, in France, 15–17, 91–2,
    93–4, 111, in Germany, 16–17,
    53, 60, 86–7, in Iceland, 16, in
    Japan, 17, in the Netherlands,
    16, in New Zealand, 15, in
    Sweden, 17, 167, in
    Switzerland, 16, in the United
    Kingdom, 15, 17, 117, 119–21,
    131, 134, 136, 138, in the
    United States, 15–17, 20–1,
    25–6, 48–50
Great Depression, 153, 164
Greece, industrial relations in,
  165
Green Party (Germany), 62
grievance procedures, see dispute
  resolution
gross domestic product, in the
  United Kingdom, 118

Hancock Committee 1983–5
  (Australia), 176
Handel, Banken und
  Versicherungen, 73
Hawke, Bob, 175
Hawke Labor government
  (Australia), 157, 168
HBV, 73
health insurance, 48
  in Australia, 168, see also
  occupational health and safety
Heath government (U.K.), 120
high-technology industry, in the
  United Kingdom, 122
Holding, Clyde, 159
home-working, in the United
  Kingdom, 123
Hong Kong, 5
hours, see working hours
housing, investment in, in Australia,
  159
human resources, utilisation of, 8
  in Australia, 149, in France, 97,
  in Germany, 64–5, 76, 79, in the
  United Kingdom, 124, 146n

IBM, 45
IG Chemie, 64
IG CPK, 57
IG Metall, 56–7, 59, 61, 64, 80–1,
  83
immigration, in Australia, 151
imports and exports see competition,
  international; trade deficit
income inequality
  in Australia, 153, in Germany,
    85, in the United Kingdom,
    140, in the United States, 31, 33,
    169
incomes policy
  in Australia, 168, in Germany,
    55–6, in the United Kingdom,
    119
indexation, of wages, see wages,
  indexation of
individuals, as agents of change, 172,
  174
induction, in Australia, 151
industrial conflict, 10–11,
  in France, 92, 106, 113, in
    Germany, 79–88, in the United
    Kingdom, 120–1, 125, 130–2,
    137, in the United States, 20, 40,
    see also dispute resolution;
    lock-outs; strikes
industrial democracy, 3, 13–15,
  in Australia, 158, in Europe,
    13–15, in Japan, 13–14, in
    Sweden, 172, in the United
    Kingdom, 13–14, 133, 176,
    in the United States, 13–14, see
    also labour–management
    co-operation; worker participation
industrial disputes, see industrial
  conflict
industrial modernisation, in
  Germany, 66, 84–5, 88
industrial relations
  change in, 164–79
  characteristics of, 1, 179
    in Germany, 53–6, 82–8, in the
    United Kingdom, 115–17
    international aspects of, 17–18,
    159, see also specific countries
Industrial Relations Act 1971 (U.K.),
  120, 166

Industrial Relations Act 1988
(Australia), 174
Industrial Relations Commission
(Australia), (formerly the
Australian Conciliation and
Arbitration Commission), 9, 151,
168, 174
Industrial Relations System
Framework, 147
Industrial Training Boards (U.K.),
136
industrial tribunals
as agents of change, 172, in
Australia, 150, 174, in the United
Kingdom, 132
industrialisation, see industrial
modernisation; organisational
structure; technological change
Industrie Gewerkschaft
Chemie-Papier-Keramik, see IG
CPK
inefficiency, in the labour market, in
the United Kingdom, 117
inertia, as a barrier to change, 177
inflation, 4, 170
in Australia, 148, 151, 168,
defending wages against, in
Germany, 74, in France, 93–4,
106, in the United Kingdom, 117,
139
information agreements, 125, 133
information technology, unions slow
to adopt, in the United Kingdom,
129
Institute of Directors (U.K.), 138
interest rates
in Australia, 148, in the United
Kingdom, 121, 138
International Association of
Machinists and Aerospace
Workers (U.S.), 40, 43, 50
International Brotherhood of
Teamsters (U.S.), 22
International Business Machines, 45
international competition, see
competition, international
international industrial relations, see
industrial relations, international
aspects of
International Labour Organisation

Convention No. 89, (1948), 16
International Masonry Institute
(U.S.), 47
investigative bodies, 176–7
Ireland
consultative bodies in, 176,
industrial relations in, 170
Irish Employer–Labour Conference,
176
iron industry, in France, 99, 101
Italy
consultative bodies in, 175,
industrial relations in, 170

Japan
consultative bodies in, 176,
industrial relations in, 169, 177,
planning for change in, 169,
post-war reconstruction in, 165
JIT, 161
job allocation, in Germany, 78
job classifications, in France, 95,
111
job conversion leave, in France, 99,
101, 105
job creation, in Australia, 158
job protection, 11–12,
in France, 11, 105, in Germany,
80, in Italy, 11, in the
Netherlands, 11, in Spain, 11, in
the United Kingdom, 123
job satisfaction, 107
job security
in Australia, 156, in France, 97,
107, 110, in Germany, 77, 84, in
the United Kingdom, 128, in the
United States, 40, 45
Job Security Act 1974 (Sweden),
167
Job Training Partnership Act 1981
(U.S.), 49
job transfers
in France, negotiations on,
100–01, in the United Kingdom,
128
joint consultative committees (U.K.),
132, 133
judiciary, as an agent of change, 172
Junta (U.K.), 175
just in time, 161

Kennedy, John F., 16, 25
Kohl, Helmut, 56, 60
Korea, low labour costs in, 148
Labor Law Reform Bill (U.S.), 169
Labor–Management Advisory Panel
    (U.S), 25
Labor–Management Relations Act
    1947, 178, see Taft-Hartley Act
    1947 (U.S.)
Labor–Management Reporting and
    Disclosures Act 1959, 178, see
    Landrum-Griffin Act 1959 (U.S.)
labour, political influence of, in the
    United States, 22
labour agreements, 178
    in Australia, 152, 174, in France,
    statistics, 112, in the United
    Kingdom, 125, 128, see also
    collective bargaining; information
    agreements; labour-management
    co-operation
labour concessions, 37–42
labour courts
    as agents of change, 173, in
    Australia, 174, in France, 91, in
    Germany, 54, 75, 169, 173
labour disputes, see industrial
    conflict
Labour Inspectorate (France), 92,
    97
labour law, 15
    as an agent of change, 172–3,
    177, in Australia, 15, 150, in
    France, 91–3, 97–8, 101, 104,
    109, 111, in Germany, 53–4, 58,
    60–1, 80–1, 85, 169, 173, 177–8,
    in Ireland, 170, in Japan, 169,
    177, in the United Kingdom, 115,
    120–1, 125–6, 134–6, 139, 141,
    144, 165–6, 172, 175, 178, in the
    United States, 24, 29, 48, 173,
    177–8
labour–management co-operation,
    13–15, 172–3,
    in Australia, 151, 162, in France,
    106–7, in Germany, 56, 76, 79,
    82–8, and the introduction of
    technology, 12, in the United
    Kingdom, 121, 124–6, 131–3,
    143–4, 165, in the United States,

    25, 42–8, 50–1, see also industrial
    democracy; worker participation
labour market
    in Australia, 147, 149, 151–2,
    154—60, 163, in Germany, 60,
    73, in Spain, 170, in the United
    Kingdom, 117–19, 121–3, 128–9,
    134–5, 137, 140–3, in the United
    States, 39
labour movement, in the United
    States, compared with OECD
    countries, 22–3
Landrum-Griffin Act 1959 (U.S.), 3
law, see civil law; labour law
law courts, see judiciary; labour
    courts; labour law
lay-offs, see dismissal, of workers; job
    conversion leave; redundancy;
    strikes; unemployment
legislation, see bankruptcy law; civil
    law; labour law
Liberal–National government
    1975–83 (Australia), 168
line managers, in Australia, 162
local government, industrial conflict
    within (U.K.), 121, 125
lockouts, in Germany, 79–80
    see also strikes
lump sum payments, for voluntary
    resignation, in France, 101

machine tool industry, in Germany,
    65
macroeconomic policy, in Australia,
    158
management award, determination of
    pay by, in the United Kingdom,
    141
management–labour co-operation,
    see labour–management
    co-operation
management strategy, 8, 20, 170
    in Australia, 157, 160–1, in
    France, 97–8, in Germany, 78, in
    Sweden, 148, in the United States,
    44–6, see also labour–management
    co-operation
manning levels, determination of
    in Australia, 163, in Germany, 78,
    in the United Kingdom, 127–9

Manpower Services Commission
(U.K.), 136
manufactured goods
Germany as a producer of, 65–6,
output of, in the U.K., 118
manufacturing industries
in Australia, 148, 150, in
Germany, 65–6, 77,
in the United States, 30–1, 33, in
the United Kingdom, 116, 122,
124, 126, 128, 130–1, 142
mass picketing, see picketing
meatpacking industry
in France, 104, in the United
States, 29, 39
media, 175
mergers
of job classifications, in Australia,
156, of trade unions, in the
United Kingdom, 124
metal industry
in Australia, 154, in France, 103,
109, in Germany, 58–9, 64, 80,
174, in the United States, 30
militancy, of unions, in France,
107–9, minimum wage, in the
United Kingdom, 137
mining industry, in the United
States, wages increases in, 31
Mitterand, François, 92, 104, 111
modernisation, see industrial
modernisation
monetary policy
in Germany, 56, 74, in the
United Kingdom, 118, 120–1
multinational enterprises, 170
multi-skill craftsmen
in Australia, 154, 156, in the
United Kingdom, 123, 129

National Association of
Manufacturers (U.S.), 23, 26
national bargaining, see collective
bargaining, centralisation of
National Development Fund
(Australia), 159
National Dock Labour Scheme
(U.K.), 117
National Economic Development
Council (U.K.), 136

National Employment and Training
Fund (Australia), 159
National Employment Fund
(France), 100–01, 105
National Enterprise Board (U.K.),
136
National Labor Relations Act 1935
(U.S.), 20, 24, 178
National Labor Relations Board
(U.S.), 24, 33, 48, 169
National Labour Consultative
Council (Australia), 176
National Mediation Board (U.S.), 24
national press (U.K.), 121, 129, 137
National Union of Mineworkers
(U.K.), 144
nationalisation, in France, 93
Netherlands
consultative bodies in, 175
industrial relations in, 170
Neue Heimat, 61–2, 72
New Deal system (U.S.)
collapse of, 34–49, and
decentralisation, 26, 33, history,
20, 164, 171, in Japan, 2,
legislation, 24, post-World War II,
3, and trade unions, 43, 45, 52,
vain attempts to strengthen, 168
new industry, investment in,
in Australia, 159
New Right, in Australia, 152
New South Wales Labor Council,
152
new technology, see technological
change
New United Motors Manufacturing
Incorporated (NUMMI), 45
New Zealand Labour Relations Act
1987, 9, 15
newspaper industry, in the United
Kingdom, 121, 129, 137
Nolan, David, 153
Normed shipyards, France, 101
Norway
consultative bodies in, 176,
industrial relations in, 170
Norwegian Contact Committee, 176
Norwegian Worker Protection and
Working Environment Act 1977,
12

occupational safety and health, 15
  and the American labour
  movement, 22, in France, 93, and
  labour law, 24
Occupational Safety and Health Act
  1970 (U.S.), 16
Occupational Safety and Health
  Administration (U.S.), 26
OECD, 2, 17, 105
offshore, movement of business, in
  Australia, 157
oil prices, increases in, 4, 66, 118
OPEC, 4, 66
Ordinance of 16 January 1982
  (France), 96, 103–4
Ordinance of 11 August 1986
  (France), 105
Organisation for Economic
  Co-operation and Development, 2,
  17, 105
Organisation of Petroleum Exporting
  Countries, 4, 66
organisation of production
  in Australia, 154, 161–2, in
  France, 93, 98, in Sweden, 148,
  in the United Kingdom,
  129, 133
organisation of work, see
  organisation of production;
  organisational structure
organisational structure
  in Australia, 147–8, 154–5,
  157–9, 161
  in France, 95, 99–102, 106–7
    concept of flexibility, 96–7,
    104
  in Germany, 75–9, 82–8, in
  industrial relations, lack of change
  of, 171, in Sweden, 167
  in the United Kingdom, 115, 129
    changes by management, 121,
    124, 144, and collective
    bargaining, 126–7, effects of
    recession on, 141, informing
    employees about, 133, and
    work stoppages, 131
OTV, 55
overtime
  in Australia, 155, 163, in the
  United Kingdom, 123

part-time employment, 6, 16
  in France, 98–9, in Germany,
  68–9, 84, in the United Kingdom,
  122–3, 141, in the United States,
  31–3
pay scales, integration of, for blue-
  and white-collar workers, 64
pensions
  growth of, in Australia, 149
  reform of, and the American labor
  movement, 22
performance appraisal, 8
  in France, 97, in the United
  Kingdom, 139
personnel management see human
  resources, utilisation of
Phelps Dodge, 40
picketing, in the United Kingdom,
  119, 120, 125, 139
plant bargaining, see collective
  bargaining, decentralisation of
politics
  in Australia, 151, 157, 168, in
  France, 111, 165, in Germany,
  56, 61, 83, 86–7, in the United
  Kingdom, 117, 119–20, 134–6,
  138, 140, 166, 175, in the United
  States, 22
Portugal
  industrial relations in, 165, 170,
  political upheaval in, 171
postwar industrial relations, 2–3
price stability
  in France, 113–14, in the United
  Kingdom, 118, 141, in the United
  States, 24
prices and wages freeze
  in Australia, 168, in France, 93,
  98
primary exports, decline of, in
  Australia, 148–9, 167
printing industry, in Germany, 77,
  80
private sector, unions in, in Japan,
  169
privatisation
  in Australia, 149, in the United
  Kingdom, 134–5, 137
product quality
  in Germany, 66, in Japan, 169

production bonuses, in France, 103
productivity
and employee consultation, in the
United Kingdom, 132-3
growth of
in the United Kingdom,
118-19, 122, in the United
States, 19, 21, 27
in Japanese culture, 169
and trade unions
in Germany, 86, in the United
States, 47
and wage claims, 10
in Australia, 153-4, 159, 168,
in Germany, 56, 59, 62-3, 74,
in the United Kingdom, 134,
141, 145, 146n, 166
Productivity Council (Japan), 176
profit-related pay, see profits, and
wages
profit-sharing
in France, 103, in the United
Kingdom, 134—5, in the United
States, 39, 40
profits
squeeze on
in Australia, 148, in the United
Kingdom, 121
and wages, 10
in Australia, 154, in the
United Kingdom, 134-5, 145n
protectionist policies, in Australia,
148
public employees, 16-17
in France, 100, 103, 107-8, 110,
in the United Kingdom, 120,
125-6, 139
public expenditure, in the United
Kingdom, 119-20, 131
public inquiries, 176-7
public sector
in Australia, 148, 155, in Japan,
169, in Sweden, 167, in the
United Kingdom, 125, 130-1,
136, 140, 142, 145, 166
public sector borrowing, in the
United Kingdom, 119
Public Services and Transport
Workers Union (Germany), see
OTV

public utilities sector, in the United
States, wage increases in, 31

quality circles
in France, 98, in the United
Kingdom, 132
quality control, in Japan, 169
quality of worklife programmes,
43-4, 62
in France, 110, in Germany, 75

Railway Labor Act 1926 (U.S.),
24
rationalisation of production, global,
5
Reagan administration (U.S.), 16, 48,
169
real wages, see under wages
recession, world, 118, 124, 128, 138,
141, 144
reconstruction, post-war, see under
specific countries
records, keeping of, in Australia,
151
recruitment
in Australia, 151, 155, in
Germany, 76
redeployment
in Germany, 76, in the United
Kingdom, 127-9
redundancy
after the 1980-82 recession, 11,
in Australia, 149, in France, 97,
in the United Kingdom, 122,
127-8, 131, see also dismissal, of
workers
regionalisation, of government
departments, in France, 93
Renault, 101
Rengo, 169
Republican Party (U.S.), 22
research and development, in
Australia, 148
restrictive practices
in Australia, 149-51, 153, 159,
163, in Germany, 86
restructuring, of industry, see
organisation of production;
organisational structure,
technological change

retail distribution, in the United
    Kingdom, 134, 138
retirement pensions
    in France, 97, 110, in the United
    States, 22
retirement programmes, see early
    retirement programmes
retraining
    in France, negotiations on,
    100–01, in Germany, 76–7, 83,
    86, in the United Kingdom, 128,
    in the United States, 49
retrenchment, 11
    in the United Kingdom, 119, see
    also dismissal, of workers;
    redundancy
Rocard, Michel, 111
Royal Commission on Trade Unions
    (U.K.), 175
rubber industry, in the United States
    collective bargaining in, 39, and
    unemployment, 29
Saltsjobaden agreement, Sweden
    1938, 164, 171
Schmidt, Helmut, 56
schoolteachers, see education;
    teaching profession
SCNF, 108–9
SDP, 61, 63
secret ballots, compulsory
    in Germany, 174, in the United
    Kingdom, 120, 131, 137, 139,
    143
segmentation, of the labour market,
    8, 70, 159
self-employment, in the United
    Kingdom, 123
service sector
    attempts to unionise, in the
    United Kingdom, 124, growth of,
    5, in Germany, 66, in the United
    Kingdom, 122, 128, in the United
    States, 30–1, 33, 49
share ownership, see employee share
    ownership
shift work
    in Australia, 155, in France,
    103–4
shipbuilding
    in France, 99–101, in Germany,

79, global decline of, 5, in
    Sweden, 167
shop steward system (U.K.), 14,
    125
Shop Stewards Act 1974 (Sweden),
    167
shopfloor organisation, see
    organisation of production
short-term contracts, in France,
    93
Singapore, 5
skilled workers
    in Australia, 150, 159, in
    Germany, 77, 85, 88, 89n, in the
    United Kingdom, 142
Social and Economic Councils
    (France and Italy), 175
Social Democrat Party (Germany),
    61, 63
social security legislation
    and the American labor
    movement, 22, in France, 110, in
    Germany, 61
social welfare, see social security
    legislation; unemployment
    benefits
South Korea, 5
Spain
    industrial relations in, 165, 170,
    political upheaval in, 171
staff planning, 8
state, role in industrial relations, see
    government, role in industrial
    relations
statutory authorities, in Australia,
    148
statutory discussion groups, in
    France, 98, 106
steel industry
    in France, 99, 101, in Germany,
    79, global decline of, 5, 11,
    in the United Kingdom, 125, in
    the United States, 9, 29, 42
stock market collapse 1987, 135
strikes, 170
    in Australia, 168, in Belgium
    1969–70, 4, in France, 92,
    108–10
    in Germany, 79–82, 174
    1969–70, 4, 1984, 58–9,

insurance for, 81, and works
    councils, 55
in Spain, 170, in Sweden
    1969-70, 4
in the United Kingdom, 15,
    130-1, 136
    effects of declining union
    membership on, 121, in
    essential services, banning of,
    139, insurance for, 121,
    legislation, 165, no-strike
    clauses, 125, and workforce
    opinion, 119
in the United States, 40, 42, see
    also industrial conflict; lock-outs
subcontracting, 8,
    in the United Kingdom, 123, in
    the United States, 31-3, 42
subsidisation, of industry, in
    Germany, 79
Sudreau Committee (France), 177
superannuation, in Australia, 152-3,
    159, 168
supervisor, change in role of, in
    Australia, 162
Sweden
    avoidance of government in
    industrial relations, 171, industrial
    relations in, 148, 164-5, 167,
    171-2, Third Way, 158
Switzerland
    avoidance of government in
    industrial relations, 171, industrial
    relations in, 164

Taddei Report 1986 (France), 177
Taff Vale judgment 1901, 173
Taft-Hartley Act 1947 (U.S.), 3,
    23
Taiwan, 5
takeovers, see company takeovers
tariffs, in Australia, 148
Tavistock Institute (U.K.), 14
tax benefits
    in Australia, 168, and employee
    share ownership, in the United
    Kingdom, 135
taxation, in Australia, 152, 158
TDC, 158
teaching profession, industrial

conflict within (U.K.), 120, 125,
    166
technological change, 6, 12
    in Australia, 148, 157, in France,
    negotiations on, 97, 102, in
    Germany, 59, 62, 67, 73, 75-9,
    86, 88, in Scandinavia, 12, in the
    United Kingdom, 121, 128-9,
    131, 144, in the United States,
    42-3, 49
technological unemployment,
    theory of, 78, 83
technology transfer, in Germany, 79
telecommunications, in Germany, 66
temporary employment, 6, 16
    in France, 93, in the United
    Kingdom, 123, 141, in the United
    States, 32-3
textile industry, global decline of, 5,
    11
Thatcher government (U.K.), see
    Conservative government (U.K.)
    1979-
total quality control, 161
TQC, 161
trade, global, see competition,
    international
trade deficit
    in Australia, 149, 152, in the
    United States, 19, 27
Trade Development Council
    (Australia), visit to Europe 1986,
    158
Trade Disputes Act 1906 (U.K.),
    173
trade-offs, 8, 10, 40, 161
Trade Union Act 1913 (U.K.). 173
Trade Union Act 1984 (U.K.), 120,
    131
trade unions
    accountability of officials, in the
    United Kingdom, 126, 135, 167,
    as agents of change, 172, 177,
    amalgamation of, 160, 170,
    associate membership of, 47
    changes in,
        in Australia, 162-3, in France,
        107-10, in Germany, 82-6, in
        the United Kingdom, 137, in
        the United States, 46-8,

de-certification of, in the United
States, 42
decline of
   in the United Kingdom, 124,
   139, 141, in the United States,
   31-2, 37, 46
democracy within, in the United
Kingdom, 15, 119, dispute
resolution outside, 3, election of
officials, in the United Kingdom,
120, 143, employer resistance to,
in the United States, 32-3,
history, in France, 90-1, hostility
from membership, in Australia,
161, immunity of officials, in the
United Kingdom, 120, 125,
income of, in Germany, 72
internal conflicts
   in France, 109, in the United
   Kingdom, 135, in the United
   States, 40, 49-50
in Japan, 169, leadership of, in
Australia, 156, 158-60
levels of unionisation
   in Australia, 150, in France,
   165, in the United Kingdom,
   124, in the United States, 23,
   26-7, 30-1, 169, see also
   membership under trade unions
membership of, 6-7, 170,
   in France, 98, 107, 110, 112, in
   Germany, 70-2, in the United
   Kingdom, 121, 124-5, 131,
   143, 146n, in the United States,
   49,
participation in management, see
labour-management co-operation,
political strategies, need for, in
the United States, 52
problems of
   in France, 107-10, in the
   United Kingdom, 124-6
public opinion of, in the United
Kingdom, 175
role in industrial relations
   in Australia, 158, 160, in
   France, 90, 107-10, in
   Germany, 53-4, 70-3, 79-82,
   in the United Kingdom, 119,
   124-6, 136-8, in the United

States, 20-3, 31-3, 42-4, 46-8,
   51-2, see also collective
   bargaining; specific issues such
   as wages, working hours, etc.
structure of
   in Australia, 150, 160, in
   Germany, 53
   see also anti-unionism; union
   avoidance
Trades Union Congress (U.K.), 121,
   125, 128, 136-7, 139, 144, 175
training, see retraining; vocational
training
Transport and General Workers
   Union (U.K.), 144
transportation industry, in the
   United States, wage increases in,
   31
Truck Acts (U.K.), 120
trucking industry, in the United
   States, 39
TUC, 121, 125, 128, 136-7, 139,
   144, 175
Turkey, industrial relations in, 165
two-tier bargaining, see two-tier wage
   scales
two-tier wage scales
   in Australia, 152-6, 160-1,
   168-9, in Canada, 170, in the
   United States, 8, 37-9, 169

UIMM, 91
unemployment, 6
   in Australia, 148-9, 151-2, 168,
   effect on industrial conflict,
   10-11, 135
   in France, compensation for,
   107-8, as a government
   priority, 111, legislation, 92-3,
   structure of, 98-9, 106, and
   wages policy, 93
   in Germany, 56, 60, 62-3, 66-7,
   73, 77-8, 83, 85-8
   structure of, 69-70
   in Spain, 170, in the United
   Kingdom, 117-18, 124, 134-6,
   139, 145, in the United States, 29,
   33, see also employment
unemployment benefits, paid during
   strikes, in Germany, 58-9, 61, 81

unemployment insurance, in France, 97, 99, 110
union avoidance
in Germany, 87–8, in the United Kingdom, 125, 129, 133, in the United States, 45–6, 51, *see also* anti-unionism
Union des Industries Métallurgiques et Minières, 91, 103
unionisation, *see* levels of unionisation *under* trade unions
unionism, *see* trade unions
unions, *see* trade unions
United Airlines, 37
United Auto Workers (U.S.), 32, 40, 42, 44–5, 47, 50–1
United Food and Commercial Workers (U.S.), 40, 50
United Kingdom, industrial relations in, 115–46, 165
United Rubber Workers (U.S.), 40
United States
industrial relations in, 19–52, 164–5, 168–9, 172–3, 177, public inquiries in, 176
unskilled workers
in France, 95, in Germany, 69–70, 85
USX Corporation, 42

Val Duchesse talks, 18
vocational training
in Australia, 148, 150–1, 154, 156, 158–9, in France, 97, 104, 111, in Germany, 54, 56, 59, 64–5, 69–70, 77, 79, 86, in the United Kingdom, 137, 142–3, 145n
voluntarism, in British industrial relations, 115, 144, 165
wage differentials, *see* income inequality
Wage Earner Funds Act 1983 (Sweden), 167
wages
electronic funds transfer of, in Australia, 163, employers' policy on, in France, 94–5 flexibility, *see* deregulation; labour market government policy on, in France,

93–4
indexation of,
in Australia, 151–2, in France, 94, 97
inflation of, in the United Kingdom, 117–18, 141, 166 and management techniques, 8
negotiation of, 170
1960s and 1970s, 4, in Australia, 10, 150, 153, 155–6, 158–9, 161, in France, 93–6, 102–3, 107–8, 111, in Germany, 59, 74–5, 78, 80, 84, in Japan, 169, pre-World War II, 3, in the United Kingdom, 10, 15, 116, 119, 129, 166, in the United States, 20–2, 34–42, 48
of part-time workers, in the United States, 31
payment of, in France, 97
policy, in Sweden, 172
post-dating of increases, in Australia, 168
in the public sector, in the United Kingdom, 140, 142
real, increases in
in France, 95, 103, in the United Kingdom, 118, 146n
restraint
in Australia, 149, 151–2, 158, 161, in France, 111, in Germany, 56
and vocational training, 65 *see also* minimum wage; two-tier wage scales; wage claims *under* productivity
wages and prices freeze, *see* prices and wages freeze
wages councils, in the United Kingdom, 15, 16, 115, 120, 136, 140
Wagner Act (U.S.), 14, 33
war, 165, 171
War Labor Board (U.S.), 24
waste, elimination of, in production, in Australia, 163
water supply industry, industrial conflict within (U.K.), 120
Weitzman analysis, 134

Western Airlines, 40
white-collar workers
  in France, 90, 99, in Germany,
  53, 64, 73, 85, 88, in Sweden,
  167, in the United Kingdom, 123,
  128-9
Whitley Committee (U.K.), 132
women, in the workforce, 6, 16
  in Australia, 155, in France, 98,
  in Germany, 61, 67-9, 73, in the
  United Kingdom, 122-4, in the
  United States, 30-1
Woods Task Force 1968 (Canada),
  176
Work Environment Act 1978
  (Sweden), 167
work organisation, see organisation
  of production; organisational
  structure
work practices, see organisation of
  production; restrictive work
  practices; working conditions
work stoppages, see industrial
  conflict; strikes
worker alienation, in the United
  States, 176
worker dislocation, in the United
  States, 30-1
worker participation
  in France, 106, and management
  techniques, 8, in postwar Europe,
  3, in the United Kingdom, 125,
  132-3, 176, in the United States,
  42-4, see also industrial
  democracy; labour–management
  co-operation
workers' expression, in France, 98,
  106
Workers' Strength (France), 90-2,
  97
workforce, structure of
  in Germany, 66, 71-2, in the
  United Kingdom, 122-4, see also
  employment; labour market;

organisational structure;
  unemployment
working conditions, 8, 20, 170
  in Australia, 150, 161, in France,
  93, in Germany, 75-6, 80,
  pre-World War II, 3, in the
  United Kingdom, 116, see also
  occupational health and safety;
  wages; working hours
Working Group of Independent
  Entrepreneurs, see ASU
working hours, 12-13, 16
  in Australia, 163, in France, 93,
  95-7, 103-8, 110-11, 165, in
  Germany, 57-60, 62, 67-8, 73,
  78, 80, 83, 86, in the United
  States, 20
working methods, see organisation of
  production; organisational
  structure; technological change
workplace
  changes in, 11-13, decline in size
  of, 6
Workplace Industrial Relations
  Survey 1984, 126
Works Constitution Act 1972
  (Germany), 55
works councils
  in France, 92-3, 97, in Germany,
  3, 55, 60, 65, 74-6, 78, 84, 87-8,
  and industrial democracy, 13-15
Works Councils Act 1972
  (Germany), 169
World War II, 165, 171

Xerox, 42

yen, Japanese, 27
youth, in the workforce, 16
  in France, 99, in Germany, 69,
  73, in the United Kingdom, 118,
  120, 142
Youth Training Scheme (U.K.), 137,
  142

For Product Safety Concerns and Information please contact our
EU representative GPSR@taylorandfrancis.com Taylor & Francis
Verlag GmbH, Kaufingerstraße 24, 80331 München, Germany